Trapped by Worldliness

A practical and concise guide to help believers to orientate to a new life in Christ.

Trapped by Worldliness

Copyright © 2025 by Walter B. Pennington. All rights reserved. This book is protected by the copyright laws of the United States of America. No part of this publication may be reproduced, stored in a retrieval system, or transmitted in any form by any means- electronic, mechanical, digital, photocopy, recording, or any other, for commercial gain or profit. The use of short quotations or occasional page copying for personal or group study is permitted and encouraged. Permission will be granted upon request.

Walter B. Pennington
penningtonwalter@bellsouth.net

Scriptural text utilized in this writing are primarily taken from The New King James Bible and are printed in bold *italics*.

Acknowledgments

First and foremost, I give all glory and honor to my Lord and Savior Jesus Christ, whose truth continues to expose the lies of this world and whose grace empowers us to live set apart. Without His Spirit's leading, this book would never have been conceived or completed.

To my wife, thank you for your unwavering support, patience, and encouragement during the long hours spent writing and praying over these pages. Your love and understanding were a constant source of strength.

To Dr. June Paul, Pastor Leonard Butler, and my spiritual Brother Felipe Coronada, my fellow warriors for Christ, you poured into my life with truth, and wisdom. Your timely words of encouragement and hope helped shape my convictions and inspired my deeper walk with God.

To the friends and fellow believers who engaged in heartfelt conversations about worldliness in the Church—your honesty and spiritual hunger confirmed the need for this message and fueled my passion to write it.

To the readers, thank you for joining me on this journey. My prayer is that these words stir your heart, challenge your walk, and draw you closer to the holiness and purpose that God has called you into.

Lastly, I would like to thank everyone, especially the A.C.R.O.P.S. Ministry in Mandeville, Louisiana and my immediate family, who prayed for me throughout this process. Your intercession carried me through the moments of doubt and reminded me that this work is not about me, but about glorifying Christ.

Soli Deo Gloria, Gloria solo a Dios, to God alone be the glory.

"Do not love the world or the things in the world. If anyone loves the world, the love of the Father is not in him. For all that is in the world, the lust of the flesh, the lust of the eyes, and the pride of life, is not of the Father but is of the world."

1st John 2:15-16

"Do not conform to the pattern of this world, but be transformed by the renewing of your mind."

Romans 12:2

"Set your minds on things above, not on earthly things."

Colossians 3:2

"You adulterous people, don't you know that friendship with the world is hatred toward God? Anyone who chooses to be a friend of the world becomes an enemy of God."

James 4:4

"No one can serve two masters. Either you will hate the one and love the other, or you will be devoted to the one and despise the other."

Mathew 6:24

"Christians should live in the world, but not be filled with it. A ship lives in the water, but if the water gets into the ship, she goes to the bottom. So Christians may live in the world; but if the world gets into them, they sink."

Dwight L. Moody

"I find nothing in the Bible but holiness, and nothing in the world but worldliness. Therefore, if I live in the world, I will become worldly; on the other hand, if I live in the Bible, I will become holy."

Smith Wigglesworth

"When the devil is called the god of this world, it is not because he made it, but because we serve him with our worldliness."

Thomas Aquinas

"The sin of worldliness is a preoccupation with the things of this temporal life. It's accepting and going along with the views and practices of society around us without discerning if they are biblical. I believe that the key to our tendencies toward worldliness lies primarily in the two words "going along." We simply go along with the values and practices of society."

Jerry Bridges

Message of Hope to the Body of Christ

To my brothers and sisters in Christ,

Grace and peace be multiplied to you in the name of our Lord and Savior Jesus Christ. As a fellow servant of the cross, I write to you not as one who has arrived, but as one who has wrestled, and walked through the snares that this world so craftily sets before us. This message is birthed from a heart deeply burdened by what I have seen, heard, and experienced, believers who are flickering under the weight of worldliness.

We live in an age where compromise is often cloaked in culture, and distractions come disguised as blessings. The enemy has not changed his tactics. He still offers kingdoms, applause, wealth, and relevance in exchange for our worship, our focus, and our purity. Far too many in the Church have settled for the fleeting pleasures of this life. But I believe with all my heart that the Spirit of God is still calling us out of the shadows and into the marvelous light in this end-time season.

This book is not written to condemn, but to awaken. It is a cry to the Church for holiness, to develop a passion for Christ, and to lay aside every weight that hinders our walk. We cannot be the salt of the earth if we have no flavor. We cannot shine as lights in the world if we remain dimmed by compromise.

My prayer is that this message stirs your spirit, convicts your heart, and compels you to examine your walk. May it cause pastors to reevaluate their pulpits, worshipers to purify their praise, and every believer to fall in love with Jesus as never before. Let us reject a form of godliness that lacks power and embrace the fullness of a fully surrendered life to Christ.

Let us rise from the traps of worldliness and run the race with endurance, fixing our eyes on Jesus, the Author and Finisher of our faith.

With humility and hope,
Walter B. Pennington
Servant of Christ and watchman for the Body

Table of Contents

Introduction _____ 9
1. The Spiritual Challenge as a New Believe _____ 11
2. A New Life in Christ _____ 15
3. What is Worldliness? _____ 23
4. Satan's Subtle Traps _____ 27
5. The Crisis of Churches Being Conformed to Worldly Cultures _____ 35
6. The Spiritual Dilemma of Trusting in Man vs. Trusting in God _____ 59
7. Double-Minded Christians: Trapped between Worldliness and Holiness _____ 67
8. Trapped by the Hunger for Entertainment _____ 79
9. Trapped by the Deception of Secret Societies ___ 103
10. Trapped by the Evilness of Racism _____ 115
11. Honoring and Celebrating Pagan Holidays and Events _____ 135
12. False Teachers and Celebrity Preachers _____ 153
13. The Deception of the Prosperity Gospel _____ 169
14. The Spirit of Covetousness _____ 183
15. Living a Lukewarm and Comfortable Life _____ 197
16. Worldly Success vs. Biblical Success _____ 209

17. Christians Trapped in Idolatry _____ 221

18. The Narrow Road to Spiritual Wholeness_____ 233

Appendix 1: Christian Consecration_____ 242

Appendix 2: Consecration Considerations _____ 246

Appendix 3: Prayers for Freedom and Restoration ____ 249

Bibliography _____ 254

Notes_____ 258

Introduction

There is a war raging within the hearts of Christians today, a quiet, unseen conflict that is choking the spiritual life out of believers. It is not a war waged with bullets or blood, but with distraction, deception, and seduction. It is the war of worldliness.

Many Christians today find themselves unknowingly entangled in the values, pleasures, and pursuits of the world. While professing faith in Christ, they live lives that mirror the culture of this world more than the cross. This writing exposes the subtle and dangerous ways the world influences believers, through entertainment-driven churches, secret societies, materialism, racism, social media, and more.

This book shines a biblical light on these snares, offering spiritual insight, scriptural guidance, and practical steps toward repentance and renewal. Through real-life examples, heartfelt exhortations, and probing questions for personal reflection and group study, readers are invited to examine their lives and break free from worldly entrapments.

Worldliness is not merely about participating in obviously sinful behaviors. In fact, its greatest danger lies in how subtle it is. Like a deadly gas, it seeps in unnoticed, dulling our spiritual senses, normalizing compromise, and slowly replacing our hunger for holiness with an appetite for comfort, acceptance, and self-fulfillment.

Many professing Christians do not realize they have been ensnared. They still attend church. They still sing songs of praise to God. They may even read their Bibles occasionally. But God is not the center. He is overshadowed by self, success, or society's approval. They have a form of godliness, but they lack the power of the Holy Spirit (2nd Timothy 3:5). They are present in body but absent in spirit.

This book is not written to condemn but to awaken. It is written with urgency and love, offering both diagnosis and direction. Through biblical insight, real-life examples, and honest reflection, *"Christians Trapped by Worldliness"* will help you identify the ways the world may have crept into your walk with Christ, and how to break free.

If you sense that the fire you need for God is not within you, if you find yourself compromising where you should stand firm, or if you feel more at home in the world than in the presence of God, then this message is for you.

We are living in the last days. Scripture warns us that in these times, many will be lovers of pleasure more than lovers of God, having itching ears and turning away from truth to follow fables (2nd Timothy 3:4, 4:3-4). The greatest threat to your walk with Christ may not be persecution, but something much worse, a life consumed with spiritual apathy through the comforts and distractions of the world.

This book exposes many of the traps the enemy has set for modern believers. It shines a light on how culture, media, materialism, and even certain church trends are luring professing Christians away from the narrow path that leads to eternal life. But more importantly, it will offer hope, a way to freedom, to truth, and to a life fully surrendered to Jesus.

The good news of the Gospels is that you don't have to stay trapped. The same God who calls you to come out from among them (2nd Corinthians 6:17) is ready to receive you, cleanse you, and empower you to walk in purity and purpose.

The war is real. The enemy is deceptive and religious deception remains his greatest tool of spiritual warfare. But deliverance is available and victory is possible.

Whether you are a church leader, a new believer, or someone simply seeking truth in a confused church, world, and society, this book is for you. Let it challenge you. Let it convict you. But most of all, let it lead you to the purity, power, and purpose found only in a wholehearted pursuit of God.

The time has come for the professing body of Christ to stop blending in with the world, but to stand apart.

Let us begin the challenging journey that leads to spiritual wholeness.

(The term "professing" is used throughout this writing when referencing twenty-first-century Christians because their claim may be proven to be invalid.)

(Numerous slightly altered versions of actual stories of worldliness are utilized in this writing. The actual names were changed to protect their identity. However, some are fictional and represent a salvation-destroying mindset.)

Chapter 1

The Spiritual Challenge as a New Believer

If you are a new believer in Christ, let me welcome you into the body of Christ. Indeed, you have made the most important decision of your lifetime on earth and throughout eternity.

Now that you have received Jesus as your Lord and Savior, you are considered to be a believer in Christ. As a believer in Christ, the Bible promises us the Holy Spirit as our guide. He is present to guide you in all matters of life.

We Face a Real Enemy

However, we face an enemy who is determined to prevent your spiritual growth. Satan is his title or description derived from the Hebrew word *"ha-satan,"* meaning "the adversary" or "the accuser." It signifies his role as an adversary of God and humanity. He is also called the "Devil" which comes from the Greek word meaning "slanderer" or "false accuser." He is fully aware of your decision to separate from his kingdom and the spiritual implication of your new status with God. He will do everything within his power to confuse you by reminding you of the enticements of this evil world that previously occupied your time, resources, and energy, his evil enticements that brought you a false sense of joy and satisfaction.

His goal is to keep you within his kingdom and prevent you from growing and developing a relationship with God, his eternal enemy. He realizes that with your new commitment and the associated leadership and guidance of the Holy Spirit, you will become an opposing empowered soldier against his army and kingdom.

Satan's strategy is to maintain his relationship with you and his influence through you that has benefited his kingdom by continually tempting you with the enticements of this evil world that he controls (John 14:30). This was the strategy that he used against Jesus after Jesus was baptized by John the Baptist.

So, What is Next?

You are probably wondering what is next. To help with this beginning phase of your new journey, I must use a few terms and expressions that can be confusing and are considered to be theological, so bear with me. I will make this as painless as possible.

You now must consecrate yourself to God. **Consecration** is simply setting yourself apart from worldliness and dedicating yourself to the service and worship of God. Consecration begins with laying the required foundation for Godliness by removing ourselves from our past worldly attachments. To maintain them will be a stumbling block in developing a prosperous, fruitful, and Biblically-required relationship with God (In describing worldliness, the Bible also uses the word "**carnal**" in referencing fleshly human nature or desiring Biblically prohibited pleasures). This process of purging all ungodliness from our lives includes all ungodly contents of our homes, vehicles, workspaces, sources of entertainment, hobbies, organizational affiliations, etc. This process of purging ourselves from all ungodliness does not include an ungodly spouse (ref. 1st Corinthians 7:12-14), but all else.

This beginning process may be viewed as "cleaning our house" and getting our lives in order so that Jesus can enter and live in and through us as He desires. This is the beginning process for the hopeful and desired result being **"sanctification"** or being set apart by God from our previous attachments of worldliness for His use. Sanctification is becoming holy and developing the likeness and character of Jesus. At first glance, consecration and sanctification seem to have the same meaning. Though they are similar and sometimes used interchangeably, there is a difference. Sanctification begins with consecration and consecration may be viewed as laying the foundation for sanctification. I realize that this is confusing, just bear with me. I am almost finished.

The Goal of Holiness

John Wesley, a noted 18th century evangelist, stated, "The goal of the Christian life is holiness, 'the fullness of faith.' This means the consecration of the whole self to God and to thy neighbor in love. This, in turn, involves a process of corporate discipline and effort, guided by the motives of 'devotion,'" by which he meant the delivering up of one's whole life to God.

I realize that the last thing that a new convert desires to hear is a theological presentation with confusing terminology. However, I must use a few more terms to help lay the foundation for your understanding of your new beginning. I promise that I will not consciously use any more throughout the remainder of this writing.

Conversion and Consecration

Conversion is simply a spiritual turning away from **sin** (transgressing God's Divine laws) in repentance and turning to Christ in **faith** (trusting Him completely). It is a purposeful turning away from our old life of worldliness in order to pursue an entirely new life in Christ. From this point forward, we live to **magnify** (to praise enthusiastically; to glorify) God.

Regretfully, many new converts do not make this required transition and spend a life-long existence of spiritual mediocracy in the practice of man-designed religion. Most new converts develop a non-spiritual church life centered in church activity-related involvement, but never develop a personal relationship with Christ in whom they profess as their Lord and Savior. Sadly, because of worldly attachments, many professing believers live their entire lives spiritually trapped without ever experiencing the fullness of God.

After conversion and the repentance of our past sins, we must consecrate ourselves to God by willfully dedicating our total being to Him for His glory. Our total being includes our body, our heart, our soul, our thoughts, all that we are, and all that we possess (ref. Appendixes no. 1 and 2).

Also, as a new convert, you must understand that your lifeline with God is your Bible and developing a ceaseless prayer life (ref. 1st Thessalonians 5:17) where you truly learn to not just understand God and His expectations for the remainder of your life, but also how to effectively communicate with Him.

This writing addresses spiritual entrapments that Satan successfully utilizes against twenty-first-century professing believers. Many seasoned believers are spiritually trapped by the enticements of worldliness. They have yet to heed God's instructions and turn from all worldliness. Because of this resistance, perhaps surprising to many, they are yet to be received by God (ref. 2nd Corinthians 6:14-18).

Many are practicing a worldly form of religion void of the Holy Spirit's presence, power, and oversight. This writing may be viewed as a guide for not just new believers, but seasoned believers who desire a new life in Christ, void of all evil-inspired worldly attachments.

Is Satan Real?

As earlier noted, God has a real enemy in Satan who desires to stunt all spiritual growth in the likeness of Christ. He is the architect and strategist behind all worldliness. Ironically, in opposition to the revelation of the holy Bible, he has convinced most believers that he is not a real living spiritual being.

Not only is he a real living spiritual being, but he will do anything within his limited power to stunt your spiritual growth. One of his primary weapons is to keep you trapped by the enticements of worldliness through deception, lies, and confusion resulting from false teachings and worldly lifestyle allowances. He realizes that if he can successfully accomplish this goal, he can negate your conversion and the benefits of eternal life in Christ here on Earth.

Therefore, you must view the Bible as your one offensive weapon in the many battles of spiritual warfare with Satan and his forces of evil (ref. Ephesians 6:17).

Again, if you are a new believer, welcome to the body of Christ. If you are a seasoned believer I applaud your desire for a spiritual reset and new direction for spiritual oneness and wholeness. May the Spirit of God give you guidance.

Chapter 2

A New Life in Christ

After Jesus was baptized by John the Baptist, Matthew 4:1-11 states, *"Then Jesus was led by the Spirit into the desert to be tempted by the devil. After fasting forty days and forty nights, he was hungry. The tempter* (**Satan**) *came to him and said, "If you are the Son of God, tell these stones to become bread." Jesus answered, "It is written: 'Man does not live on bread alone, but on every word that comes from the mouth of God."*

Then the devil took him to the holy city and had him stand on the highest point of the temple. "If you are the Son of God," he said, "throw yourself down. For it is written: "'He will command his angels concerning you, and they will lift you up in their hands, so that you will not strike your foot against a stone.'"

Jesus answered him, "It is also written: 'Do not put the Lord your God to the test.'"

Again, the devil took him to a very high mountain and showed him all the kingdoms of the world and their splendor. "All this I will give you," he said, "if you will bow down and worship me." Jesus said to him, "Away from me, Satan! For it is written: 'Worship the Lord your God, and serve him only.'"

Then the devil left him, and angels came and attended him."

Points to be Noted from Jesus's Confrontation With Satan Immediately After His Baptism

There are some important points that we should note regarding the temptation of Jesus by Satan after Jesus' baptism. We will highlight four important points for the edification of all believers.

First, it is important to note that if Satan tempted Jesus, the only begotten Son of God (not fathered by man but by the Holy Spirit), it would be naïve for anyone to think that he would not tempt all believers. Spiritual warfare is a reality for all believers in Christ. As a new believer in Christ, you must prepare for spiritual encounters with Satan and his legion of demons that will attempt to derail your spiritual growth and ultimately remove you from the body of Christ. Satan's eternal goal is the eternal damnation of all humanity.

Second, we should note the nature of Satan's temptations. His three temptations involved the lust of the flesh, the pride of life, and the lust of the eye.

Lust is an intense desire for an object or circumstance to indulge or content oneself. At the heart of lust is a desire to take, in contrast to love, which desires to give. In the Bible, 'flesh" often has a negative meaning. It often references actions and decisions that are made with a focus of self-gratification and often highlights the lack of faith in God, our eternal provider. Romans 8:13 states, ***"For if you live according to the flesh you will die; but if by the Spirit you put to death the deeds of the body, you will live."***

Satan's temptations have proven to be consistent since God's Creation in the Garden of Eden as these remain his primary focuses for the temptations of all new and seasoned believers in Christ today.

Satan's first temptation against Jesus (Matt. 4:3-4) was for Jesus to relieve His physical hunger after fasting for forty days. This temptation reflected the lust of the flesh. The lust of the flesh is simply any evil desire resulting from our emotional or physical needs. In other words, a hungering desire to please ourselves.

The second temptation (Matt. 4:6-7) reflected the pride of life. This temptation also is seen in Satan's temptation of Eve in the Garden of Eden in the Book of Genesis when she was tempted to eat the fruit that God had forbidden. The pride of life stems from a love of the world and advancing oneself within its means. This is anything that can lead to pride, arrogance, or boasting. It is simply anything that exalts us above God's required humility for humanity.

The third temptation (Matt. 4:8-10) reflected the lust of the eye. The lust of the eye is any evil desire for things that we see and covet. This is more commonly revealed in a hungering desire for material things or sensual pleasures. These worldly desires are not from God but result from our sin nature. This nature results from our desire to provide for our own interests which results in rebellion against God.

The Bible gives its clearly understood perspective on these three commonly-used sin entrapments of Satan. 1st John 2:16 states, ***"For everything in the world, the lust of the flesh, the lust of the eyes, and the pride of life comes not from the Father but from the world."***

Third, we should note the weapon that Jesus used in repelling Satan's attacks. Jesus used the Word of God which has proven to stand the test of time. Jesus effectively used the Word of God from the book of Deuteronomy to deflect each of Satan's temptations and ultimately defeat him.

Jesus revealed the necessity and effectiveness of God's Holy Word in our confrontations with evilness. It is important to note that Jesus quoted relevant scriptures from memory. He did not have the time or the need to research the written Word of God during his spiritual battle. This confrontation highlighted the necessity of knowing the Word of God and living the Word of God. His knowledge of God's Word was crucial and resulted from a committed life that had remained in God's Word. In His communion with the Father, Jesus was unyielding to the principles to which His life was committed.

Jesus demonstrated to every believer the need for studying and memorizing God's Holy Word. As believers in Christ we must always be mindful that our lives on earth will be challenged by spiritual confrontations, and victory will only be achieved through faith and knowing the Word of God and living the Word of God. His Holy Word is our one and only life-long offensive weapon for spiritual warfare. The Bible calls this weapon of warfare the 'sword of the spirit' (Ephesians 6:17).

All believers in Christ could experience victory over the enemy through a disciplined life of obedience to the Word of God, constant communion with God, a commitment to abiding in the Word of God, and total faith in God.

Fourth, one other point should be noted in Jesus' confrontation with Satan. After hearing Jesus' scriptural response to his first temptation, Satan observed that Jesus' strategy was to effectively use the Word of God against him. At this point, Satan altered his strategy. He reinforced his second temptation by the perverted use of Jesus' strategy, using God's Holy Word (vs. 6). Satan revealed his knowledge of Scripture (Every believer in Christ must be mindful that Satan has lived with God before the creation of this world and also studied the Word of God since the creation of humanity).

Christ had quoted scripture against him, so he would show that he could quote scriptures as well as He. It has been usual with heretics and seducers to pervert scripture and to press the sacred writings into the service of the worst of wickedness. This reinforces the need for every believer in Christ to abide in the Word of God. True knowledge of scripture will enable disciples to discern what is scriptural truth and what is a scriptural perversion. All believers must be mindful that if Satan was bold enough to attack Jesus, the only begotten Son of God, it would be naïve of believers in Christ to not expect some form of demonic encounters and intrusions in their lives.

As Jesus modeled for all of humanity, we must resist Satan's worldly enticements and the distractions of his kingdom. In so doing, your journey will be fruitful, prosperous, and successful because of the guidance of the Holy Spirit. We are commanded to *"Submit to God. Resist the devil and he will flee from you"* (James 4:7). We must resist all temptations of Satan. Then he will have no choice but to flee. Our successful resistance is proof to him that we are now separated from him and the allures of worldliness. He will truly see that we are now in the Kingdom of God with freedom to pursue our new goal. The goal of every believer is to develop a Christian life (one of holiness), a life that reflects the empowerment of God and our bond with Christ.

What is a Christian?

So, what is a Christian? Contrary to popular belief within the body of Christ, a believer is not necessarily a Christian. However, all Christians are believers. When we repent of our sins and receive Jesus as our Lord and Savior, we become a believer and thereby receive the free gift of salvation. Christianity results from a life-altering commitment to Christian discipleship. The character-revealing definition of a **"Christian"** is a person who manifests the quality and Spirit of Jesus, or someone who is "Christlike." Another way that this may be stated is "a person whose life is an image of the character of Christ." The character of Christ is the aggregate of His beliefs, attributes, and traits that form His nature based on the sacrificial love of God the Father. Because of the unbiblical understanding and teaching of the twenty-first-century institutional Church, many professing believers erroneously identify themselves as "Christian" or "Christlike" without His character existing within them.

Beginning a Life of "Christlikeness"

To develop a life of "Christlikeness" we must begin the difficult task of turning from the worldliness of our past life and no longer walk according to the carnal flesh (entertaining carnal, fleshly desires). This transition involves a process of corporate discipline and effort, guided by the motives of devotion.

The goal of professing believers is to be conformed into the image of Christ, or as Biblically stated, Christian perfection (Hebrews 6:1). In so doing, we will share in God's rule on the earth as His empowered sons and daughters and thereby give Him glory and honor (ref. *"The Fanaticism of Christian Discipleship"* by this same writer for more detail).

Our mission as new converts is to become disciples of Christ. Through spiritual growth and God's empowerment, eventually we are to teach and develop other new disciples. This has remained the desire of Jesus since His physical existence on Earth (Matthew 28:19). With the empowerment of the Holy Spirit they will live as Christ just as all of the subsequent Christians lived after Christ while here on earth. The sacrificial, committed life that they modeled must become our desire and goal. Their only focus was glorifying God through all of their being which required living a life void of all worldliness. Christian discipleship is simply the process of developing into the image of Christ.

The Apostle Paul wrote in a letter to the Roman believers, ***"There is therefore now no condemnation to those who are in Christ Jesus, who do not walk according to the flesh, but according to the Spirit. For the law of the Spirit of life in***

Christ Jesus has made me free from the law of sin and death. For what the law could not do in that it was weak through the flesh, God did by sending His own Son in the likeness of sinful flesh, on account of sin: He condemned sin in the flesh, that the righteous requirement of the law might be fulfilled in us who do not walk according to the flesh but according to the Spirit. For those who live according to the flesh set their minds on the things of the flesh, but those who live according to the Spirit, the things of the Spirit. For to be carnally minded is death, but to be spiritually minded is life and peace. Because the carnal mind is enmity against God; for it is not subject to the law of God, nor indeed can be. So then, those who are in the flesh cannot please God" (Romans 8:1-8).

According to this writing by Paul, we can now be empowered by the Holy Spirit to live for Christ. To live for Christ implies that we are moving from fleshly desires and developing the character of Christ.

As a believer, we are in right standing before God, not by following a list of laws and regulations or performing various works to please God, but by being in Christ and walking according to the Holy Spirit. As we remove the entrapments of worldliness from our lives, we can better hear and follow the leading of the Holy Spirit. He always desires to communicate with us, thereby assisting the spiritual growth process and our walk through the spiritual-confusing maze of this evil world.

"The Greek word rendered in Paul's writing for "set their minds" includes a person's will, thoughts, and emotions. It also includes assumptions, values, desires, and purposes. Setting the mind "on the things of the flesh" or on the "things of the Spirit" means being oriented to or governed by those things on which we focus.

A believer can live according to the flesh with the result of spiritual death, or else by the renewed spirit, so as to experience life in Christ. Paul elaborates on these two possibilities, showing the possibility and the benefit of living according to the Spirit.

The reason that being carnally minded results in death (verse 6) is that the carnal mind is an enemy of God. The mind of the flesh is hostile to God and can never submit itself to the law of God. Being in the flesh is different from walking according to the flesh. Being in the flesh means being unregenerate (refusing to believe in the existence of God) or sinful. People in that state cannot please God.

The Detriment of Worldliness

The detrimental impact of worldliness in a believer's life is generally not elevated to the level of importance in the twenty-first-century Church as the Bible demands. One can never become a Christian or "Christlike" with the attachments of worldliness.

As believers in Christ, we are cautioned in James 4:4, ***"Adulterers and adulteresses! Do you not know that friendship with the world is enmity with God? Whoever therefore wants to be a friend of the world makes himself an enemy of God."***

James uses the terms "adulterer" and "adulteress" in describing the relationship of a believer who entertains the things, ways, and values of this evil world. Adultery is voluntary sexual intercourse between a married person and someone other than his or her spouse. The relationship between a believer and God is considered a sacred marriage with an unalterable commitment of fidelity. Infidelity, or entertaining the things, ways, and values of the world severs the marriage bond. Our required union with God never materializes if we maintain our worldly attachments and our friendship with the world.

A friend is often someone that we share a loving bond with, someone in whom we will trust and whose company we enjoy. Often, we will share common beliefs, interests, and values with our friends.

The world reflects the kingdom of Satan, the enemy of God. The friend of God's enemy also becomes His enemy. God then views us as someone who opposes Him and does not share His values and beliefs. As God's enemy, all hopes for eternity within His Heavenly Kingdom are for naught.

It is vitally important that all believers prioritize a life existence free of all forms of worldliness to remain in God's will and receive the benefits of sonship.

Regretfully, as noted in Chapter 1, most twenty-first-century professing believers are anticipating an eternity in the presence of God, but are trapped by worldliness. In spiritual reality, the

Bible informs us that they are enemies of the One true living God that they openly profess and serve.

Conclusion

Though God created all things for Himself and for His glory, Satan invariably perverts God's creations and deceptively orchestrates their use for his glory through his sinful entrapments of undiscerning humanity.

Colossians 1:16 states, *"For by him all things were created: things in heaven and on earth, visible and invisible, whether thrones or powers or rulers or authorities; <u>all things were created by him and for him.</u>"*

For the edification of the body of Christ, the remainder of this writing will address worldliness and what we consider the more prevalent worldly entrapments of Satan within the Body of Christ.

Reflection Questions

1. If Satan tempted Jesus, as his followers, what should we anticipate?
2. What was the nature of the three temptations against Jesus? Can you recall in your personal life instances of those temptations? If so, how did you respond?
3. What was the weapon that Jesus used to defeat Satan? What does that reveal about what your priority in life should be?
4. In your own words, how would you define a "believer?" a "Christian?" Have you ever confused the two?
5. What is the goal of professing believers in Christ?
6. Why do you think that God considers those who are worldly his enemies? What are the spiritual implications of this understanding for the body of Christ?
7. What are the emotions that arise in you in knowing that God is a jealous God, and will not tolerate a divided allegiance or share His creation?

Chapter 3

What Is Worldliness?

Before we can be free from worldliness, we must first understand what it truly is. Many believers have a shallow or incomplete view of worldliness. Some think it's limited to watching certain movies, listening to secular music, or wearing trendy clothes. Others define it as anything fun or pleasurable. But worldliness is far deeper than surface behavior. It is a condition of the heart—a mindset, a value system, a spiritual disease that infects the soul.

Worldliness is a passion for or concern with material values or simply anything that excludes God or anything that draws our heart away from God.

The apostle John clearly identifies the three critical elements of worldliness in 1 John 2:15-17:

"Do not love the world or the things in the world. If anyone loves the world, the love of the Father is not in him. For all that is in the world—the lust of the flesh, the lust of the eyes, and the pride of life—is not of the Father but is of the world. And the world is passing away, and the lust of it; but he who does the will of God abides forever."

As noted in Chapter 1, these verses highlight three critical elements of worldliness as was highlighted in Chapter 1:

1. **The Lust of the Flesh**: This is the craving for physical pleasure and indulgence. It drives people to prioritize feelings and fleshly desires over obedience and self-control. It says, "If it feels good, do it."

2. **The Lust of the Eyes**: This is the desire for more: more possessions, more beauty, more recognition. It feeds discontentment and covetousness, constantly chasing what is seen but never satisfied.

3. **The Pride of Life**: This is the obsession with status, image, and self-glorification. It exalts man above God. It

is self-promotion, self-importance, and the illusion of self-sufficiency.

These three forces are not just out in the world, they seek to take residence in our hearts. They form the foundation of worldly thinking, which is the opposite of kingdom thinking.

The Enemy's Blueprint

In the Garden of Eden, Satan used these very same temptations on Eve:

"So when the woman saw that the tree was good for food (lust of the flesh), that it was pleasant to the eyes (lust of the eyes), and a tree desirable to make one wise (pride of life), she took of its fruit and ate." (Genesis 3:6)

He has no new tricks. He still tempts us in the same way today, using culture, media, relationships, and even religious language to package sin as wisdom, beauty, or fulfillment.

Worldliness Is a Way of Thinking

Romans 12:2 tells us, *"Do not be conformed to this world, but be transformed by the renewing of your mind."* Conformity to the world begins in the mind. Before a Christian dresses like the world, talks like the world, or lives like the world, they first begin to *think* like the world.

- The world says, "Follow your heart." Scripture says, *"The heart is deceitful above all things"* (Jeremiah 17:9).
- The world says, "Live your truth." Scripture says, *"God's Word is truth"* (John 17:17).
- The world says, "You deserve to be happy." Scripture says, *"You were bought at a price. Therefore glorify God in your body"* (1 Corinthians 6:20).

Worldliness teaches self-centeredness. The gospel teaches Christ-centeredness.

Not of the World

Jesus prayed for His disciples in John 17:14-16:

"They are not of the world, just as I am not of the world."

We are called to live *in* the world, but not be *of* it. This is a call to holy distinction, to be different in our desires, our decisions, and our disciplines. Being worldly is not about where you live, but how you live. You can live in a godless culture and remain pure, or live in a religious one and still be worldly.

The Fruit of Worldliness

Worldliness bears specific fruit in the life of a believer:
- **Compromise**: Slowly relaxing biblical standards to fit personal comfort or cultural norms.
- **Spiritual Apathy**: Losing the hunger for prayer, Scripture, and holiness.
- **Double-Mindedness**: Trying to live for both God and the world and finding peace in neither.

Jesus warned in Matthew 6:24, *"No one can serve two masters."* We will either love God or love the world. There is no middle ground.

The Tragedy of Friendship with the World

James 4:4 issues a strong warning. As noted in chapter 2, James stated,

"Do you not know that friendship with the world is enmity with God? Whoever therefore wants to be a friend of the world makes himself an enemy of God."

This doesn't mean we are to hate people. It means we cannot embrace the value system of a world that rejects the authority of God and calls evil good. To love the world is to oppose the very God who redeemed us.

Conclusion: Know the Real Enemy

Worldliness is not just "out there" in society. It's at war within every believer. It's not just about what we do, but why we do it: the desires we entertain, the influences we allow, and the approval we seek.

To be free, we must recognize worldliness for what it is: a seductive, spiritually deadly force that aims to replace our love for God with love for self.

The first step to victory is exposure. When we know the enemy, we can resist it. When we renew our minds with truth, we transform our lives.

Worldliness is a trap. But by God's grace, you can escape.

Understanding Worldliness

1. How would you define worldliness in your own words?
2. What Scriptures help shape your understanding of what worldliness is?
3. What is the difference between enjoying life and being worldly?
4. Do you think worldliness is always outward and visible, or can it be hidden in the heart and mind?
5. How does the Bible's view of worldliness differ from how the world defines a "successful" or "good" life?
6. How has modern culture influenced the way Christians think about worldliness?
7. Is it possible for churches to unintentionally promote worldliness? If so, how?
8. What are some common signs that a Christian might be slipping into worldliness?
9. Can entertainment, fashion, money, or ambition become forms of worldliness? Where is the line drawn?
10. Have you ever justified something worldly in your own life because it seemed "harmless"? What was the result?
11. What does 1 John 2:15-17 teach us about the dangers of loving the world?
12. Why do you think Jesus warned so strongly about the pull of the world in John 17 and Matthew 6?
13. Have you ever felt convicted by the Holy Spirit about something worldly in your life? What did you do about it?
14. How can Christians guard their hearts and minds against worldliness?
15. What role does fellowship, accountability, and daily devotion play in resisting worldly influence?
16. How can we encourage one another in the group to live more set-apart lives for Christ?

Chapter 4

Satan's Subtle Traps

His entrapments do not happen instantly.

When we think of spiritual warfare, we often imagine dramatic confrontations: demons cast out, miracles performed, darkness driven out by light. But one of Satan's most powerful weapons is not violence or persecution. It is subtlety, not immediately obvious and difficult to detect.

Subtle deception has always been the devil's favorite method. He rarely enters through the front door. Instead, he slips in through cracks, through loopholes in our convictions, blind spots in our character, and unchecked desires in our hearts.

"Now the serpent was more cunning than any beast of the field which the Lord God had made." (Genesis 3:1)

From the very beginning, Satan didn't come to Eve with a pitchfork or a threat. He came with a question. A suggestion. A slight distortion of truth. ***"Did God really say...?"*** (Genesis 3:1).

The Nature of Subtlety

Subtlety doesn't start with full rebellion, it starts with a nudge.

- It sounds like: *"It's not that bad."*
- It looks like: a small compromise justified by a greater good.
- It feels like: an innocent desire that grows until it dominates.

Satan's goal isn't to scare you away from God. It's to *distract* you, *desensitize* you, and *divert* you until you drift so far, you don't even realize you're lost.

No trumpet will sound or alert be given when a Christian becomes worldly. There's no dramatic declaration or public rebellion. More often, the descent is subtle—so subtle, in fact, that many believers don't even realize they've started down the path of spiritual separation from God. It begins with small compromises, justified in the name of balance, relevance, or grace. Before long, the fire that once burned brightly is reduced to flickering embers. The passion for holiness gives way to a preoccupation with comfort, image, and success. The Christian is now trapped—still wearing the name of Christ and doing the things of religion, but not living in the power of His Spirit.

Subtlety Is Satan's Strategy for Spiritual Derailment

Jesus warned us plainly: *"Watch and pray, lest you enter into temptation."* (Matthew 26:41). He knew that temptation would rarely come like a tidal wave. It comes more like a leak in the ceiling—slow, persistent, and easily ignored. And that's what makes worldliness so dangerous.

Worldliness doesn't always look like wickedness. It often wears a smile. It's charming, fashionable, and persuasive. It talks about dreams, goals, and freedom. It may even use religious language. But underneath the surface, it draws the heart away from Christ and toward self.

The enemy of your soul would rather *deceive* you than defeat you. He doesn't need to make you renounce Jesus; he only needs you to replace Him: with your career, your image, your comfort, or your ungodly desires. When that happens, Satan wins without a fight.

The Enemy in Disguise

2 Corinthians 11:14 warns us:

"Satan himself transforms himself into an angel of light."

The most dangerous deception is the kind that looks spiritual. Satan isn't just in the nightclub, he's also in the pulpit. He doesn't only tempt through sin, he tempts through half-truths, legalism, and false doctrine. He whispers just enough Scripture to sound credible but leaves out just enough to strip it of power.

Think of these modern phrases:

- *"God wants you to be happy."*
- *"Follow your truth."*
- *"Love is all that matters."*
- *"Live your best life now."*

They sound good, but they are incomplete. Truth without the whole counsel of God becomes a tool of the enemy.

How to Recognize Subtle Attacks

- **Does it weaken your prayer life?**
- **Does it desensitize your conscience?**
- **Does it justify what God calls sin?**
- **Does it elevate self over Christ?**

If the answer is yes to any of these, you may be under subtle attack. Recognizing it is the first step toward resisting it.

Temptation Dressed as Freedom

One of Satan's favorite tricks is to redefine sin as freedom. He convinces people that boundaries are bondage, and rebellion is liberation.

The prodigal son didn't leave home because he hated his father. He left because he believed life would be better with fewer restrictions.

That's how Satan still works:

- *He calls lust "love."*
- *He calls greed "success."*
- *He calls pride "confidence."*
- *He calls compromise "compassion."*

He speaks to our desire for significance and uses it against us. He tempts us to chase our best life now, at the expense of eternal life later.

Jesus and the Wilderness Test

As highlighted in Chapter 1, Satan tempted Jesus in the wilderness, not with shocking evil but with twisted good. He offered:

- **Bread**: A legitimate need, but through illegitimate means.
- **Rescue**: A spectacle of faith, but driven by pride.
- **Kingdoms**: A shortcut to glory, bypassing the cross. (Matthew 4)

Jesus did not debate with Satan. He stood firmly on God's authority. Jesus quoted the unchangeable Word of God, and that ended the confrontation.

We must do the same.

Christian by Name, Worldly by Nature

We are living in an era where many who claim the name of Christ have embraced the mindset of the world. This is not just about attending church or having a Christian playlist. It's about what dominates our thinking, shapes our priorities, and directs our decisions.

- We say we follow Jesus but spend more time following influencers.
- We say we're citizens of heaven but live like this world is our home and do everything within the power of humanity to remain here.
- We say we love God but remain silent about sin to avoid offending people.

Paul warned about this very danger when he said:
"They will maintain a form of godliness, but deny its power." (2 Timothy 3:5)

Form without power. Ritual without repentance. Attendance without obedience.

That is the trap.

The Culture of Blending In

Modern Christianity, especially in the West, is obsessed with fitting in. Many churches and professing Christians are more concerned with being *liked* than being *light*. We don't want to be seen as "weird" or "judgmental," so we soften our convictions, sanitize our message, and silence our warnings.

But Scripture does not call us to blend in. It calls us to *stand out*. Jesus said,
"You are the light of the world...a city set on a hill cannot be hidden." (Matthew 5:14)

Light doesn't blend. It exposes.

Salt doesn't conform. It preserves.

To be worldly is to hide your light and dilute your salt.

When Culture Becomes a Trap

Satan uses culture as a delivery system for deception. Movies, music, social media, trends: these are not neutral. They either draw you closer to God or subtly pull you away.

The devil doesn't need you to renounce your faith. He just needs you to lose your *sensitivity* to sin.

Little by little, you stop blushing at profanity. You stop grieving over immorality. You laugh at what once broke your heart. The enemy has succeeded, not by attacking your beliefs but by reconditioning your conscience.

When Compromise Feels Like Compassion

One of the most crafty aspects of worldliness is how often it disguises itself as compassion. We now see believers embracing sin in the name of "love," tolerating rebellion in the name of "grace," and affirming what God condemns to avoid "division." But this isn't the compassion of Christ, it's the compromise of culture.

True compassion never affirms what destroys a soul.

True grace doesn't leave us in bondage. It calls us to freedom and transformation.

When Christians are more afraid of offending *man* than offending *God*, they've already been trapped.

Silencing the Warnings

Another subtle strategy is to make conviction seem like condemnation. In today's world, anyone who dares speak the truth is labeled as judgmental, hateful, or intolerant. Even among Christians, there is a growing discomfort with confrontation. The devil loves this because it shuts down the very voice meant to wake us up.

If he can make us fear being labeled more than we fear disobedience, he's won. If we stay quiet to protect our image rather than speak truth to protect souls, we've already been deceived.

The Deception of Delay

Perhaps the most effective strategy of all is the deception of delay. Satan doesn't always say, "Don't obey God." Sometimes, he simply says, "Obey later."

- *Pray tomorrow.*
- *Repent later.*
- *Fast next week.*
- *Forgive when you feel ready.*
- *Give when you can afford it.*

The longer we delay obedience, the weaker our resolve becomes.

What we postpone, we often abandon.

Jesus overcame each subtle trap by quoting **truth in context**. He didn't just know the Word, He lived it. He didn't debate with Satan or give in to his deceptions.

Self at the Center

At the heart of worldliness is self. Worldliness is not just about sinful actions, it's about a sinful orientation. It puts *me* at the center of life instead of Christ. It's the age-old lie of the serpent: ***"You shall be as gods..."*** (Genesis 3:5).

Today, it sounds more like:

- "Follow your heart."
- "Live your truth."
- "You deserve to be happy."
- "Go with your first thought."

But the gospel says:

- ***"Deny yourself."*** (Luke 9:23)
- ***"Take up your cross."***
- ***"Follow Me."***

You can't follow *Jesus* and *yourself* at the same time.

How the Trap Closes

The trap closes slowly, and then suddenly. First, the fire dims. Then, conviction fades. Next comes confusion about truth and about sin, about God Himself. And finally, deception sets in. The professing Christian still talks the talk but has lost their way.

This is not just a theoretical danger, it's a present reality. It's happening right now, in churches, in homes, on platforms, and in hearts.

And it's time to expose it.

Conclusion

1 Peter 5:8 commands us:

"Be sober, be vigilant; because your adversary the devil walks about like a roaring lion, seeking whom he may devour."

Satan may roar like a lion, but more often, he whispers like a friend. His words are smooth. His timing is perfect. And his traps are tailor-made.

The good news of the Bible is that we are not defenseless. We have the Holy Spirit to guide us, the Word of God to anchor us, and the blood of Jesus to cleanse us and to help us up when we fall.

Stay alert. Stay humble. Stay rooted in truth.

The subtle attacks may be unseen, but they are not unbeatable.

Reflection Questions

1. Have you ever experienced a time when you started drifting spiritually without realizing it? What were the warning signs?
2. What are some common "small compromises" that believers justify today?
3. In what ways might the desire to be liked or accepted cause Christians to blend in with the world?

Small Group Discussion Questions

Use the following questions to examine your own walk and encourage open, prayerful conversation within your group.

1. **Why do you think Satan often chooses subtle traps rather than obvious sin to lure Christians?**
   - How do subtle traps work on mature believers compared to those new in the faith?
2. **What are some common modern-day examples of Satan's subtle traps?**
   - Are there any that are widely accepted—even in the church?
3. **How can we tell the difference between God's voice and Satan's imitation of it?**
   - What role does Scripture and the Holy Spirit play in that discernment?
4. **What makes a believer more vulnerable to spiritual deception?**
   - Are there certain seasons or emotions that make us more susceptible?
5. **Have you ever realized you were caught in a subtle trap?**
   - What helped you recognize it, and how did you break free?
6. **What does it look like to "resist the devil" in your everyday life?** *(James 4:7)*
   - What spiritual disciplines strengthen our resistance?
7. **How can Christian community help guard against deception?**
   - What happens when believers isolate themselves or avoid accountability?
8. **In what ways does pride make us more vulnerable to Satan's schemes?**
   - Why is humility essential to spiritual discernment?
9. **Are there popular "Christian" teachings or movements today that might actually be Satan's bait?**
   - How should we approach them with biblical wisdom and grace?
10. **How can we train ourselves—and others—to be more spiritually discerning?**
    - What habits or practices sharpen our sensitivity to truth and error?

Chapter 5

The Crisis of Churches Being Conformed to Worldly Cultures

In today's rapidly changing world, a growing concern among faithful believers is the extent to which many churches are conformed to the cultural values and trends of the world. Instead of being a countercultural beacon of truth, holiness, and righteousness, numerous churches have adopted worldly standards in an attempt to remain relevant, attractive, or acceptable in a secular society. This dangerous compromise has weakened the church's spiritual authority, blurred the lines between truth and deception, and led many believers into spiritual confusion.

When the church compromises, it ceases to be the light of the world and becomes part of the darkness. Churches that trade holiness for popularity lose both their distinction and their purpose. When the lines between the sacred and the secular are blurred, the message of repentance becomes muted.

"Her priests do violence to My law and profane My holy things; they do not distinguish between the holy and the common... So I am profaned among them." - Ezekiel 22:26

Many churches now promote lifestyles that God has clearly condemned, all in the name of love and inclusion. But love that leads people into sin is not love, it is deception.

One of the enemy's most effective lies is that speaking truth equals hatred. But in reality, truth is the most loving thing we can offer.

- Warning someone about a cliff is not hate.
- Telling a friend the truth about their addiction is not judgment.
- Sharing biblical truth about sin is not bigotry, it is mercy.

Ephesians 4:15 says we are to speak the truth *in love*. That means truth must be delivered with gentleness, humility, and compassion, but it must still be spoken.

We have far too long witnessed and been held hostage to a soft Christianity, one that avoids offense at all costs. This version of Christianity:

- Replaced repentance with affirmation.
- Preaches acceptance but avoids accountability.
- Downplays sin to appear more inclusive.

The gospel was never meant to be safe, it was meant to be *saving*. And salvation requires confrontation. Jesus didn't die to make us feel good. He died to save us and to make us *new*.

In today's church culture, the line between the sacred and the secular has become increasingly blurred. The distinction that once set believers apart as the "light of the world" and the "salt of the earth," as witnessed in the first-century apostolic church, has faded as professing Christians adopted the behaviors, attitudes, values, and appearance of the very world they were called out of. This phenomenon, professing Christians who look like the world, is not merely a cosmetic issue; it remains a spiritual crisis.

The Church was never called to blend in. It was called to stand out, not with arrogance, but with holiness, love, and truth. From the beginning, God's people were set apart, distinct in their worship, values, and lifestyle. Yet today, the lines between the Church and the world have become increasingly blurred. What once was sacred is now casual. What once was holy is now trendy. The Church, in many instances, has lost its distinctiveness as an obedient, holy, faith-living, and power-filled body of Christ.

Many professing believers are conforming more to the standards of this world's culture than to the character of Christ. This conformity isn't limited to fashion or entertainment choices, it is deeper than appearance. It reveals a heart that does not reflect holiness.

One of the clearest signs of a compromised Church is when professing Christians are indistinguishable from the world. When the values, speech, priorities, and lifestyles of professing

Christians mirror those who don't know Christ, the salt has lost its saltiness and the light is dimmed.

The Apostle Paul's exhortation is clear:

"Do not be conformed to this world, but be transformed by the renewing of your mind… — **Romans 12:2**

Yet, instead of transforming the culture, the modern Church is often being conformed by it.

The Church must reclaim its role as both a hospital for the broken and a pillar of truth. We must love deeply, but without compromising the standard of God's Word. The gospel does not just comfort the sinner, it transforms the sinner.

Let us be known for our compassion, but also for our courage. Let us speak truth, not with arrogance, but with tears. Let us love others, not by lowering God's standard, but by lifting them up to meet it through the power of grace.

This is the compassion that saves. This is the love that heals. This is the truth that sets people free.

Jesus perfectly modeled what it means to love without compromise. Consider His interaction with the woman caught in adultery (John 8):

- He protected her from condemnation.
- He refused to shame her publicly.
- But He also said, ***"Go and sin no more."***
- Often, believers compromise not because they lack conviction, but because they fear rejection. They don't want to lose friends, alienate loved ones, or be labeled as hateful. But Jesus told us this would happen:
"You will be hated by all for My name's sake" (Matthew 10:22).
- The approval of man is fleeting. The approval of God is eternal. We must decide who we are living to please.

Jesus never left people the way He found them. His compassion was real—but it was always connected to a call to righteousness.

The church must be "Christlike," reflections of His character to an unbelieving and doubtful world.

What Does It Mean to "Look Like the World"?

Looking like the world is not just about outward appearance. It's about adopting the world's mindset, priorities, and affections. Here are some key indicators of worldliness among professing Christians:

1. Compromise in Holiness

The pursuit of holiness is replaced by the pursuit of relevance. Many Christians now downplay or dismiss biblical convictions to avoid being labeled judgmental, legalistic, or "too spiritual." Sexual purity, modesty, language, and lifestyle choices that once set believers apart are increasingly indistinguishable from those of unbelievers.

"But just as he who called you is holy, so be holy in all you do; for it is written: 'Be holy, because I am holy.'" (1 Peter 1:15-16)

2. Adoption of Secular Morals

Worldly cultural values are often accepted without biblical testing. Christians support ideologies that directly contradict Scripture, whether it's views on sexuality, gender, greed, or justice, because they want to be in step with the culture of this world rather than be faithful to Christ.

"They are from the world and therefore speak from the viewpoint of the world, and the world listens to them." (1 John 4:5)

3. Worldly Ambitions and Success

Instead of seeking the kingdom of God first, many Christians chase fame, wealth, influence, and status. These pursuits in themselves are not sinful when pursued for God's glory and held in alignment with His Holy Word, but when they become self-focused, they reveal a worldly heart.

"Do not love the world or the things in the world... the world is passing away along with its desires, but whoever does the will of God abides forever." (1 John 2:15-17)

4. Entertainment and Media Choices

The content Christians consume often mirrors the world—filled with immorality, violence, and ungodliness. There is little to no filter. What used to grieve the Spirit now amuses the flesh. This erosion of discernment has led to less sensitivity.

"I will set no wicked thing before mine eyes..." (Psalm 101:3)

5. Speech That Mirrors the Culture

Crude jokes, gossip, profanity, and sarcasm have crept into Christian vocabulary. Rather than speaking with grace and truth, many believers echo the language of the world without conviction.

"Let your speech always be gracious, seasoned with salt..." (Colossians 4:6)

6. Grace has Become a License to sin

Grace is God's unmerited favor—but it is not permission to live in sin. Yet in many pulpits today:

- Sin is minimized.
- Repentance is optional.
- Conviction is avoided.

True grace doesn't leave us where it found us. It transforms us. As Titus 2:12 says:

"Grace teaches us to say 'No' to ungodliness."

If our version of grace never challenges us and points us toward righteousness, it's not the grace of God—it's a counterfeit.

Why This Matters

When Christians look like the world, the power of their witness is weakened. Jesus said His followers are to be *"a city on a hill"* and the *"light of the world."* If that light is dimmed by worldliness, the lost will have no compass. Christianity becomes a hollow label, not a transformative life.

"If the salt loses its saltiness, how can it be made salty again?" (Matthew 5:13)

It also grieves the heart of God. He has called His people to be "a peculiar people" (1 Peter 2:9): distinct, holy, and set apart. Blending in with the culture of this world is not evangelism; it's compromise.

The Root Issue: A Heart Divided

Jesus taught that no one can serve two masters (Matthew 6:24). Many professing Christians attempt to love God on Sunday and love the world the rest of the week. This duality creates lukewarmness, which Christ condemns in Revelation 3:15-16.

"I know your deeds, that you are neither cold nor hot... So because you are lukewarm, neither hot nor cold, I am about to spit you out of my mouth."

The issue is not just behavior, it's affection. What do we truly love? What captures our time, energy, and loyalty?

---

1. The Biblical Call to Non-Conformity

The Bible is explicit in its instruction for the Church to remain distinct from the world:

"Do not conform to the pattern of this world, but be transformed by the renewing of your mind." - Romans 12:2 (NIV)

Christians and the Church are called to be "set apart" (1 Peter 2:9), "salt and light" in a dark world (Matthew 5:13-16), and ambassadors of Christ (2 Corinthians 5:20). This means representing God's values and truth even when they are unpopular or countercultural. Instead of confronting the world's sins with the hope and correction of the gospel, many churches have opted to blend in, silence hard truths, and dilute doctrine to avoid offense.

Churches conform:
- By avoiding controversial topics like sin, judgment, and repentance.

- By embracing popular ideologies under the banner of love.
- By redefining success through numbers rather than spiritual maturity.

When the Church tries to blend in, it loses its power to stand out. The early Church didn't grow because it looked like Rome. It grew because it looked like Jesus, radically different, uncompromising, and holy.

2. Compromising the Gospel for Cultural Acceptance

There are several reasons believers compromise:
- **Fear of rejection** – We want to be liked, so we hide our faith.
- **Desire for success** – We pursue worldly recognition at the expense of obedience.
- **Lack of discipleship** – Many have not been taught to live set apart.
- **Neglect of the Word** – Without Scripture, our convictions weaken.

Jesus didn't die to make us *popular*. He died to save us and to make us *holy*.

One of the most tragic signs of worldliness in the modern church is the watering down of the gospel message. Churches, in an effort to attract larger audiences, have often replaced messages of repentance, judgment, and holiness with motivational speeches, self-help advice, and messages of tolerance.

This "feel-good gospel" often avoids topics like sin, hell, the wrath of God, or the sacrificial cost of discipleship. Instead, it emphasizes personal success, emotional healing, and worldly prosperity. While these topics may have a place within a biblical context, they cannot replace the central message of the cross:

"If anyone would come after Me, let him deny himself and take up his cross daily and follow Me." - Luke 9:23

3. The Church's Obsession with Entertainment

In today's culture, entertainment is king, and sadly, many churches have adopted this model. Worship services have become more like concerts, with dramatic lighting, elaborate stage designs, and performances meant to captivate rather than convict. Sermons are often brief, designed not to teach or disciple deeply, but to retain attention spans shaped by social media and streaming culture.

The danger here is not in music or excellence itself, but in replacing genuine worship and Spirit-led conviction with emotional hype and superficial spirituality. A church may appear "alive" due to the excitement of the service, but in reality, it can be spiritually dead (Revelation 3:1).

4. Moral Compromise and Silence on Sin

As society becomes more permissive and progressive, many churches have chosen silence or outright endorsement on issues that contradict Scripture. Rather than stand firm on biblical morality, by their liberal allowances within its professing body, churches are embracing:

- **Sexual immorality** — including cohabitation, fornication, and the normalization of homosexuality and transgender ideologies.
- **Materialism and greed** — promoting prosperity teachings over sacrificial living.
- **Social approval over divine approval** — avoiding controversy to protect reputation.

This is not love, it is spiritual cowardice. Love does not withhold truth. A church that refuses to address sin is complicit in people's destruction.

"They have healed the wound of my people lightly, saying, 'Peace, peace,' when there is no peace." — Jeremiah 6:14

One of the saddest results of this shift is that many churches have gone silent on the most pressing moral issues of our time. Topics like sexual purity, gender identity, abortion, and marriage are either ignored or addressed vaguely to avoid pushback.

The fear of being called intolerant has led many pastors to become passive. But silence does not equal compassion. When the Church refuses to speak truth, it leaves people bound in the chains that Christ came to break.

Ezekiel 33 describes watchmen who are responsible for warning the people of coming danger. If they stay silent, blood is on their hands. Sadly, too many spiritual leaders today have gone quiet—not because they don't see the danger, but because they fear backlash and losing influence.

- They don't want to offend.
- They don't want to lose members.
- They don't want to be labeled intolerant or outdated.

Silence in the face of sin is not love, it's abandonment. A shepherd who refuses to confront the wolves leaves the sheep defenseless.

5. The Influence of Political and Social Ideologies

Some churches have become so entangled in the political spirit of the age that they no longer discern what is biblical versus what is ideological. Some swing so far into nationalism that the cross is overshadowed by the flag. Others are so steeped in progressive activism that Christ is overlooked as the only Lord and Savior of the world.

The Church's job is not to be the echo of any political party, but the prophetic voice of God to a spiritually confused and rebellious world. While the Church must be engaged in justice, mercy, and truth, it must do so under the authority of Scripture, not the pressure of culture (Reference the book, *"Justice, the Deception of Christianity in America" by this same writer.)*

When the Church adopts the world's systems, it often loses its spiritual authority. We cannot defeat darkness with darkness. We cannot win souls by compromising truth. Jesus never diluted His message to gain followers. Neither should we.

The early Church changed the world because it refused to look like the world. They were bold, distinct, and Spirit-filled. They suffered persecution but walked in power. They didn't need to imitate culture, they transformed it.

6. Worldly Leadership Models in the Church

In some modern churches, pastors have become celebrities. Success is measured not by holiness, faithfulness, or discipleship, but by social media followers, book sales, or the size of a congregation. Leadership is modeled after corporate executives or influencers rather than shepherds who lay down their lives for the sheep (John 10:11).

Jesus gave a clear model of servant leadership, humility, and sacrifice. When churches embrace worldly leadership values, they often drift into pride, scandal, and exploitation.

7. A Call to Return to Biblical Christianity

Jesus warned that in the last days, many would fall away from the truth. Paul warned that people would gather around teachers who tell them what they want to hear (2 Timothy 4:3). But faithful believers must remain anchored in God's Word, regardless of the cultural climate.

What the church needs is not more innovation but more **repentance**, a turning back to God's Word, a hunger for holiness, and a rejection of compromise. Revival will not come through copying the culture of this world but through spiritual purity and bold proclamation of the holy word.

As earlier noted, the Church was never meant to fit in. It was designed by God to stand out. In every generation, the people of God have been called to live in contrast to the world around them. But in recent years, a dangerous shift has occurred: many churches have stopped being the light that exposes darkness and have become mirrors that reflect the culture of this world.

This is not a critique born from bitterness. It is a cry of concern for the harlot Bride of Christ. Also, as earlier noted, the line between the sacred and the secular has become blurred. In many pulpits, truth has been softened, holiness has been sidelined, and compromise has been confused as compassion. The result? A Church that looks more like the world than like Jesus.

Living a Consecrated Life

To be a Christian is to be marked by courage and conviction:
- Refusing to laugh at sin
- Choosing purity when the crowd mocks it
- Standing for truth even when it costs us

Our goal is not to appear spiritual, but to live a totally surrendered life to Almighty God.

Christians who look like the world are in danger of losing their testimony, their intimacy with God, and their eternal reward. Blending in may be easier in the short term, but it will cost far more in the end. The world doesn't need more of itself, it needs a holy, radiant, uncompromising church. Let us not be content with a faith that looks good on the outside but is hollow within. Let us be truly transformed, not just in appearance but in heart, mind, and soul.

The world doesn't need a Church that looks just like it. It needs a Church that reflects Christ, a Church that burns with holiness, that speaks truth in love, that walks in humility and power, and one that refuses to blur the line between sacred and secular.

Let us return to the call of Scripture:

"Come out from among them and be separate, says the Lord." — 2 Corinthians 6:17

God is calling His people back to a consecrated life of holiness and obedience, back to the narrow path, back to living lives that reflect Christ, not world culture. This call is not to live in isolation from the world, but to live in distinction from it. We are to engage the world as ambassadors of heaven, not assimilate into it as if we belonged here.

We were not saved to fit in. We were saved to shine. **Let your life preach Christ: loudly, clearly, and without apology.**

Because when the Church is truly different, the world will take notice, and God will be glorified.

It's time to redraw the line and become fully consecrated to Christ.

Let us be bold in our witness for Christ. Let us be holy as Christ is holy (1st Peter 1:16). Let us be faith-filled in a pleasing manner to God (Hebrews 11:6). Let us love sacrificially as Jesus did, loving others more than we love ourselves (John 13:34). Let us be unmistakably Christian.

In a world full of compromise, may the Church rise in consecration (Reference Appendix 1&2). For when we look like Jesus, the world will see who He truly is by observing us.

The Uncompromising Call for Holiness

In every age, the true Church has been marked by one defining trait, **holiness**. It is the visible fruit of an invisible allegiance to God. Holiness is not an outdated concept or a distant goal, it is a command and a calling. When the world darkens and many churches dim their light to blend in, God's people are still commanded to shine in purity, truth, and love.

Holiness has become an unpopular word. It's been replaced with comfort, convenience, and coolness. But Scripture tells us plainly:

"Without holiness no one will see the Lord." - Hebrews 12:14

When churches remove the call to holiness, they may gain crowds but lose power. Holiness is not legalism, it is the natural fruit of love for God. A Church that abandons holiness will soon embrace worldliness to its detriment.

Moral compromise has always threatened God's people. Israel was warned repeatedly not to imitate the nations around them. Yet, they constantly turned aside to idols, foreign practices, and cultural appeasement. The church today faces the same pull from the culture outside and the corruption creeping within.

Instead of standing firm, many churches today are redefining sin to align with social trends, substituting solid preaching with entertainment, and replacing reverence with relatability.

A church that conforms cannot transform. A people that compromise cannot conquer.

As noted, God never intended His church to be removed from the world, but to be **set apart within it**. Jesus never prayed for His disciples to be removed from the world, but He prayed that God would:

"Sanctify them by the truth; Your word is truth." — John 17:17

Holiness is Christlikeness, reflecting His character. We are called to:

- Speak differently
- Love differently
- Dress differently
- Forgive differently
- Live differently

When the Church looks like the world, the world sees no need for the Church. But when we live in obedience to Christ, our light exposes darkness, and our lives point to a better way.

"You are the light of the world. A city set on a hill cannot be hidden." — Matthew 5:14

Holiness is the result of being washed, renewed, and transformed by God's Word and Spirit. It's a refusal to accept what God has rejected. It's choosing to obey when others choose to blend in.

"Therefore, come out from among them and be separate, says the Lord. Do not touch what is unclean, and I will receive you." — 2 Corinthians 6:17

Holiness doesn't mean isolation, it means **influence without contamination**. The church should live among the lost, but not live like the lost.

In a world where many churches are drifting, the faithful must anchor themselves in truth. The holy must remain holy. We must never forget that **holiness is not an option for the Church, it is the identity of the Church**.

If we want to see revival in this generation, it will not come through compromise. It will come when God's people choose consecration over convenience, obedience over applause, and holiness over hype.

In an age of compromise, tolerance, and moral relativism, the call to holiness has never been more urgent or more resisted. Holiness is often misunderstood as harsh or outdated, but in reality, it is the very reflection of God's character and the standard for His people.

Holiness is not perfectionism. It is not self-righteousness. It is a life set apart, marked by purity, love, and obedience to God.

We live in a world where sin is celebrated and righteousness is ridiculed. The line between good and evil has not just been blurred, it has been erased in many circles.

- Evil is called good.
- Truth is labeled hate.
- Sin is marketed as freedom.

But God's standard has not changed. His Word is still the final authority. And He is still calling His people to come out and be separate.

Holiness is not optional for the believer, it is essential. Without holiness, there is no intimacy with God, no power in our witness, and no growth in our walk.

We pursue holiness not to earn God's favor, but because we already have it. It is our response to grace.

- Holiness protects intimacy with God.
- Holiness preserves the testimony of the Church.
- Holiness prepares us for eternity.

To be holy is to be different in thought, in speech, in action, and in desire.

What keeps believers from walking in holiness?

1. **Compromise** – Little sins slowly numb the conscience.
2. **Cultural pressure** – The fear of being labeled judgmental keeps many silent.
3. **Lack of discipleship** – Many Christians have never been taught what holiness truly means.
4. **Neglect of Scripture** – Without the Word, holiness is replaced by self-made morality.

We cannot walk in holiness apart from the Holy Spirit. It is not self-effort, it is Spirit-empowered transformation.

"Since we live by the Spirit, let us keep in step with the Spirit." — Galatians 5:25

Holiness affects every area of life:

- **Speech** – Refusing gossip, slander, and profanity.
- **Media** – Guarding our eyes and ears from ungodly content.
- **Relationships** – Pursuing purity, integrity, and forgiveness.
- **Time** – Prioritizing God over entertainment or distractions.

Holiness is not just about what we avoid, but what we pursue: love, joy, peace, patience, kindness, faithfulness, and self-control.

A holy life speaks louder than a thousand sermons. It convicts without condemning. It attracts without compromising.

- Holiness testifies to a changed heart.
- Holiness draws others to Jesus.
- Holiness honors the God we serve.

The Pressure to Be Relevant

In the name of relevance, many churches have adapted the language, style, music, and methods of the world. But relevance without righteousness leads to compromise. Instead of being salt and light, the Church begins to mirror the very darkness it was sent to confront.

- Sermons are shaped by pop culture, not Scripture.
- Worship mirrors concerts, not consecration.
- Leaders seek popularity over prophetic truth.
- Musicians seek recognition over humility.
- Pastors seek wealth and recognition over charity.

The Church is not called to be trendy; it's called to be timeless

In an age where attention is currency, many churches have fallen into the trap of entertainment over edification. There is nothing wrong with creativity, technology, or excellence. But when relevance replaces reverence, something essential is lost.

- Worship becomes a performance instead of a sacrifice.
- Sermons become motivational talks instead of prophetic truth.
- Discipleship becomes optional instead of essential.

The goal shifts from transformation to attendance, from holiness to happiness, and from conviction to comfort.

But the gospel was never meant to be acceptable to the flesh. It is a message that crucifies self, confronts sin, and calls for repentance. When we dilute that message, we are no longer preaching Christ, we are promoting this world's culture.

Redefining Love

Love is one of the most powerful forces in the Christian faith. The Bible tells us that God is love (1 John 4:8), that love fulfills the law (Romans 13:10), and that the world will know we are Christ's disciples by our love for one another (John 13:35).

Compassion without truth may feel good, but it leads to destruction. True compassion is willing to endure awkward conversations, risk offense, and speak difficult truths because it wants what's best for the other person.

The prodigal son's father loved him deeply, but he didn't follow him into the far country. He waited. He prayed. And when the son returned in repentance, he embraced him fully.

Love waits. Love prays. Love tells the truth and welcomes repentance.

But in our modern culture, love has been redefined. And in many churches, this redefinition has led to a dangerous compromise: truth sacrificed on the altar of compassion.

The deception is subtle. In an effort to show the love of Christ, many believers have stopped preaching the truth of Christ. But love without truth is not love at all. It is sentimentality. True love does not excuse sin; it exposes it and offers a better way.

Modern culture tells us that love means full acceptance, unconditional affirmation, and emotional comfort. It says, "If you love me, you'll support my choices, celebrate my identity, and never make me feel bad about myself."

But Scripture paints a different picture:

- Love is patient and kind (1 Corinthians 13:4)—but it also *rejoices in the truth* (v. 6).
- Love covers a multitude of sins (1 Peter 4:8)—but it never condones them.
- Jesus showed compassion to sinners—but also said, *"Repent, for the kingdom of heaven is at hand"* (Matthew 4:17).

When love is separated from holiness, it becomes permissive, compromising, and powerless. It no longer reflects the character of God, but enables sin under the appearance of compassion.

The cultural gospel preaches tolerance above all. But Jesus never tolerated sin. He forgave it, yes, but He also said, *"Go and sin no more"* (John 8:11). The modern Church is in danger of offering grace without transformation, love without truth, and inclusion without repentance.

This is not the gospel. This is a counterfeit that comforts people all the way to destruction.

Called to Be Set Apart

Many professing Christians today live in a gray area, where the boundaries between sacred and secular are faint. Cultural compromise is often justified under the banner of relevance:

- We excuse profanity in the name of authenticity.
- We ignore immodesty in the name of freedom.
- We adopt worldly priorities and call it ambition.

Instead of influencing culture, we've allowed culture to influence us.

Jesus was a friend of sinners, but He never sinned to befriend. He loved without compromising truth. He walked among the world, but the world never walked in Him.

Carnal Christians live according to their fleshly desires while professing faith. Their lives are marked more by:

- Entertainment than edification
- Popular opinion than biblical truth
- Comfort than conviction

They may go to church, but they won't go to the cross. They may quote Scriptures, but not live by them. Paul wrote:

"For you are still of the flesh. For while there is jealousy and strife among you, are you not of the flesh and behaving only in a human way?" - 1 Corinthians 3:3

The cross is not an accessory to be worn as jewelry; it is a lifestyle to be lived.

God is calling His people to return to consecration, to be set apart again. The Church must recover her identity as:

- A **holy bride**, not a cultural chameleon.
- A **house of prayer**, not a platform of personalities.
- A **light in darkness**, not a mirror of it.

To do this, we must:

- Preach the **whole counsel** of God.
- Call sin what it is, with compassion and clarity.
- Make **disciples**, not just attendees.
- Pursue purity over popularity.

The word "church" comes from the Greek *ekklesia*, which means "the called-out ones." We are not called to blend in. We are called to be set apart. We are the salt of the earth, and when salt loses its flavor, it becomes useless (Matthew 5:13).

Being set apart means:

- Preaching truth even when it's unpopular.
- Pursuing holiness even when it's mocked.
- Disciplining believers even when it's uncomfortable.

This isn't cruelty, it's love. It's what Jesus did. It's what His Apostles did. And it's what we must return to if we want to see true revival.

To be set apart is to:

1. **Renew the Mind Daily** – Spend time in God's Word to reshape your thoughts and desires.
2. **Evaluate Influences** – Assess what you're watching, listening to, and engaging with.
3. **Pursue Holiness** – Make decisions that align with the character of Christ, not the culture of this world.
4. **Be Accountable** – Surround yourself with mature believers who will challenge and encourage you.
5. **Remember Your Identity** – You are not of this world; you are a citizen of heaven.

Being set apart doesn't mean being weird, it means being holy. It means living by different values, speaking with grace and truth, loving radically, refusing to compromise, and standing firm when others bow to cultural idols.

The Church is not meant to blend into the background. We are meant to shine.

In a time when culture is quick to cancel anything that offends, the Church must become unshakable. Not through political power or social influence, but through unyielding faithfulness to the Word of God.

Cancel culture may silence some voices, but it cannot silence the Holy Spirit. A remnant Church is rising, one that refuses to bow to Baal, that still weeps between the porch and the altar, and that burns with holy fire.

Conclusion

Churches must reclaim their prophetic voice. Rather than mirror the world, they must expose the darkness and offer the light of Christ. Jesus did not die for a comfortable, culturally-approved Church. He died to create a holy, powerful, countercultural people who live for eternity, not for the applause of men.

Let the Church rise—not in conformity, but in **conviction**. Revelation 2 contains Jesus' rebuke to the church at Ephesus:

"I know your works, your labor, your patience...Nevertheless I have this against you, that you have left your first love."

The Church may be active. It may be busy. It may be popular. But if it has lost its first love, its burning devotion to Christ, it has lost everything.

This is a call to return to the apostolic church model which encompasses a call to purity, a call to boldness a call to biblical preaching, a call to prayer, a call to power, and a call to fear the Lord.

The world doesn't need a Church that imitates it. It needs a Church that shines like a city on a hill.

We were never called to conform. We were called to confront with truth, with love, and with lives that reflect the holiness of our Savior.

God is calling His people back to truth, to reverence, and to holiness. This is not a call to be trendy, but to be **set apart**. It is not a call to grow crowds, but to grow in Christlikeness. It is not a call to be admired by the world, but to be pleasing to God.

"Christ loved the church and gave Himself for her to make her holy, cleansing her by the washing with water through the word... without stain or wrinkle or any other blemish, but holy and blameless."— Ephesians 5:25–27

God is not coming back for a popular Church. He is returning for a *pure* one.

Let us reject compromise and embrace the call to holiness. Let us no longer flirt with sin, but flee from it. Let us be a Church that shines with purity in a darkened age.

The world needs to see what holiness looks like—not in judgment, but in love.

Holiness is the mark of those who truly belong to God. And it's time for that mark to be visible once again.

The Church Christ is returning for is not one that compromised its values to stay relevant. He is coming for a **spotless Bride**, radiant in righteousness.

<u>Closing Prayer</u>

Heavenly Father,

We come before You with heavy hearts, burdened by what we see in Your church. You have called us to be set apart, a light on a hill, salt in a flavorless world. But Lord, too often we have exchanged holiness for popularity, truth for tolerance, and conviction for comfort. We have imitated the patterns of this world instead of being transformed by the renewing of our minds. Forgive us, Lord.

Forgive us for allowing entertainment to replace worship, for seeking the applause of men more than the approval of God. Forgive us for compromising biblical truth in order to avoid offense. Forgive us for prioritizing programs over prayer, performance over presence, and relevance over righteousness.
O God, awaken Your church.

Revive us again with a hunger for Your Word, a love for Your holiness, and a boldness to stand for truth in the face of pressure. Purify our pulpits. Stir the hearts of pastors, leaders, and congregations to repent and return to our first love. Let the fear of the Lord once again grip our hearts.

Help us to shine as distinct in a dark world—not blending in, but standing out for Your glory. Teach us to love the lost without becoming lost ourselves. Strengthen us to resist the seduction of cultural acceptance, and to embrace the cross, even when it costs us.

We pray for courage, clarity, and conviction. May Your Spirit move mightily among us, breaking every chain of worldliness and compromise. Set Your church ablaze with holiness, humility, and heavenly power.

In the mighty name of Jesus we pray, Amen.

Prayer of Commitment

Heavenly Father,

You have called Your Church to be holy, set apart, and a shining light in a dark world. But too often, we have compromised. We have exchanged Your glory for popularity. We've diluted truth for comfort. We've turned worship into performance, and conviction into entertainment.

Lord, forgive us. Cleanse us. Renew us.

Today, I commit my heart back to You. I don't want to be entertained, I want to be transformed. I don't want a church that reflects the world, I want a church that reflects Christ. Start with me.

Cleanse my heart from compromise. Create in me a hunger for Your Word, a passion for prayer, and a holy fear of You.

Help me be a faithful part of Your bride, pure and spotless, ready for Your return. Let my life and my church be a testimony that we belong to You, and not to this world.

In Jesus' holy name I pray,

Amen.

Discussion Questions

1. **What does biblical holiness look like in a modern world filled with compromise?**
(1 Peter 1:15–16; Hebrews 12:14)
2. **Why is it difficult for some churches to resist the pull of cultural trends?**
(Galatians 1:10; 2 Timothy 4:3–4)
3. **How can individual believers maintain personal holiness when others around them, even in the church, are compromising?**
(Romans 12:1–2; Ephesians 6:10–13)
4. **What are some practical ways a church can remain holy and set apart without becoming judgmental or isolated?**
(John 17:15–18; Matthew 5:14–16)
5. **What does God's Word say about churches that no longer distinguish between what is holy and what is not?**
(Ezekiel 22:26; Revelation 3:15–17)
6. **What signs would show that a church is growing in holiness rather than compromising with the world?**
(Ephesians 4:11–16; 1 Thessalonians 4:7)

Individual Reflection Concerns

Ask yourself prayerfully and honestly:

- Am I more concerned with how church makes me feel than with whether I am being spiritually transformed?
- Do I get uncomfortable when the Word of God confronts my lifestyle, or do I welcome correction?
- Am I drawn to churches that look more like concerts or social clubs than houses of prayer and truth?
- Have I personally adopted worldly values in the name of being "relevant" or "modern"?
- Do I evaluate churches by how well they reflect Christ—or by how much they reflect my personal preferences?

- Am I contributing to my church being more worldly—or more holy—by the way I serve, give, and worship?
- Have I lost a burden for the lost, the holy, and the eternal because I've become too familiar with the worldly?

Small Group Discussion Questions

1. What are some clear signs that a church is beginning to look like the world? *(Think about entertainment-focused services, worldly leadership models, watered-down preaching, etc.)*
2. Why do you think churches begin to imitate the world instead of influencing it?
3. How does a church's compromise with worldliness affect its testimony to the community?
4. What are the dangers of measuring a church's success by worldly standards (e.g., attendance, money, popularity)?
5. How can we distinguish between being "relevant" and being "worldly"?
6. What Scriptures can help a church stay grounded in holiness and truth rather than conforming to culture?
7. Have you ever been part of a church that seemed to be conforming to the world? How did it affect your spiritual life?
8. What role does leadership play in either guarding or allowing worldliness in the church?
9. How can individual believers resist the pull to want church to "entertain" rather than to convict and equip?
10. What practical steps can our church take to remain spiritually distinct and Christ-centered?

Chapter 6

The Spiritual Dilemma of Trusting in Man vs. Trusting in God

One of the most difficult and ongoing struggles in the Christian life is the tension between trusting in God and trusting in man. This dilemma often arises in subtle and deceptive ways, manifesting in our relationships, decisions, church leadership, finances, and even in our own self-reliance. While Scripture repeatedly warns against placing ultimate trust in human beings, our fallen nature gravitates toward the tangible, the immediate, and the familiar—often elevating human wisdom above divine guidance.

Biblical Foundations

The Word of God is clear:

"Thus says the Lord: Cursed is the man who trusts in man and makes flesh his strength, whose heart turns away from the Lord." — Jeremiah 17:5 (ESV)

This powerful declaration is not merely a rebuke; it is a spiritual diagnostic. To trust in man—whether in political leaders, religious figures, friends, or ourselves—is to subtly divert our heart from the Lord. In contrast:

"Blessed is the man who trusts in the Lord, whose trust is the Lord." — Jeremiah 17:7

This contrast outlines two divergent spiritual paths: one cursed and filled with dryness and deception, the other blessed and rooted like a tree planted by water.

The Allure of Human Trust

Human beings crave certainty, affirmation, and visible leadership. In times of trouble, we naturally look for someone to fix our problems. Kings, presidents, pastors, politicians, doctors, and charismatic influencers all seem to offer solutions to the chaos we fear. The danger comes when these individuals begin to occupy a space in our hearts that should be reserved for God alone.

We don't always realize we are trusting in man until that man fails us. A spiritual leader falls into scandal. A politician betrays moral principles. A friend disappoints us. These painful moments are not only tests of our endurance—they are tests of our foundation. Whom have we truly trusted?

The Deceptive Nature of Self-Trust

Equally dangerous is the misplaced trust we put in ourselves. Proverbs 3:5 commands:

"Trust in the Lord with all your heart, and do not lean on your own understanding."

Yet, we often lean on our intellect, our experiences, or our feelings when making decisions, and only turn to God when those efforts fail. This inward self-trust is the quiet root of pride, a spiritual arrogance that competes with the sovereignty of God.

Consequences of Trusting Man Over God

1. **Spiritual Dryness:** Trusting in man often leads to spiritual emptiness. The more we rely on human strength, the less we experience God's supernatural provision.
2. **Disappointment and Betrayal:** Humans are fallible. When we elevate people beyond their rightful place, we set ourselves up for heartache and spiritual disillusionment.
3. **Compromise and Idolatry:** Over time, misplaced trust can morph into idolatry. We begin to serve the opinions and approval of man rather than the will of God.

How to Cultivate Trust in God

- **Daily Surrender:** Trusting God is not a one-time decision but a daily surrender of will, plans, and emotions.
- **Immersing in His Word:** The more we know God through Scripture, the easier it is to trust Him over the voices of man.
- **Prayerful Dependence:** Prayer keeps us aligned with God's wisdom and protects us from impulsively running to human solutions.

- **Discernment and Accountability:** Not all counsel from man is wrong. But spiritual discernment helps us filter human advice through the lens of God's Word.
- **Remembering God's Faithfulness:** Looking back on how God has come through in the past strengthens our resolve to trust Him in the present.

Example: Trusting a Political Leader to "Save the Nation"

Imagine a professing Christian who is deeply concerned about the moral decline, economic struggles, the influx of undocumented aliens, and political instability in their country. A new political figure rises promising to restore righteousness, stop the influx of undocumented aliens, bring back jobs, defend religious liberty, and "make the nation great again." The professing Christian begins to feel hopeful—not because of prayer or God's promises, but because this leader seems like the answer to everything.

They spend hours defending this leader online, justifying questionable behavior, and putting faith in campaign slogans more than Scripture. Their hope, confidence, and even joy rise or fall based on the success or failure of this person. They start to believe that if this political figure loses power, all hope is lost. In doing so, they may have unintentionally shifted their trust—from God, who rules over nations and kings, to a human being with charisma and influence.

Spiritual Insight:

While political engagement is important, Scripture reminds us:

"Do not put your trust in princes, in a son of man, in whom there is no salvation." — Psalm 146:3

True hope and salvation for a nation don't come from politicians, parties, or platforms—but from repentance, righteousness, and God's sovereign hand. When we place our ultimate trust in man, even for good intentions, we risk spiritual blindness and eventual disappointment.

A Story of Misplaced Trust: When Politics Replaces Prayer

Derrick was a faithful churchgoer, respected in his community, and deeply troubled by the direction his country was headed. Every day, he watched the news and grew more anxious about rising crime, cultural confusion, the influx of undocumented aliens, and the rapid moral decay in the nation. "This country needs to turn back to God," he would often say at men's Bible study, shaking his head with concern.

When a bold, charismatic political figure emerged on the scene promising to restore the nation's values, Derrick felt a renewed sense of hope. This candidate spoke about faith, patriotism, and protecting religious freedom. He wasn't perfect—he had a criminal record and many moral deficiencies, a reputation for arrogance and sharp rhetoric—but Derrick told himself, *"God can use anyone. Maybe this is who we've been praying for."*

As the campaign heated up, so did Derrick's devotion. He began watching rallies more than he read Scripture. His conversations slowly shifted—from the gospel to politics. At church, he quoted his favorite candidate more than he quoted Jesus. He defended him online, even when the man made unethical decisions, explaining them away as "tough leadership" or "strategic compromise."

Prayer meetings became less attended. The nation's revival seemed to hinge, in Derrick's mind, not on repentance or spiritual awakening—but on winning the next election.

When the candidate lost, Derrick was crushed. He was angry, bitter, and confused. *"How could God let this happen?"* he asked. His faith was shaken—not because God had failed, but because Derrick had placed more trust in a man than in the Lord who raises up and tears down kings.

In the quiet that followed, Derrick began to see how far his heart had drifted. He repented. Slowly, God brought him back to the Scriptures. He was reminded of Psalm 20:7:

"Some trust in chariots and some in horses, but we trust in the name of the Lord our God."

Derrick had mistaken human strength for divine salvation. But now, his confidence was no longer in political outcomes—it was in Christ alone.

Spiritual Reflection:

This story is a sobering reminder that while God can use leaders for His purposes, He alone is our Deliverer. Political engagement should never replace prayerful dependence. When Christians put their trust in human systems and charismatic leaders more than in the Sovereign Lord, they risk building their hope on shifting sand.

True transformation begins not in Washington or the courts—but in the hearts of God's people who choose to trust Him, obey His Word, and seek His kingdom above all else, combined with unconditional sacrificial love for all humanity regardless of differences.

Back to the Heart of the Issue

Derrick's story is not unique. Many believers, often with good intentions, slip into the dangerous habit of replacing dependence on God with dependence on man - whether in politics, spiritual leaders, or even their own reasoning. It begins subtly, with hopes and desires aimed at earthly change. But slowly, trust migrates from the eternal to the temporal.

When our hope is tethered to men instead of anchored in God, disappointment is inevitable. The challenge is not to disengage from the world entirely, but to stay spiritually alert. We must ask ourselves regularly: ***Am I seeking God's will or man's approval? Am I trusting God's sovereignty, or am I relying on human power to bring about what only God can do?***

True faith demands that we walk by trust in God—even when man seems more visible, more practical, and more persuasive. And it is in this very tension that the spiritual war is fought.

Final Reflection

The spiritual life demands radical trust in an unseen God. This kind of faith challenges our instincts and calls us to walk not by sight but by truth. As believers, we must continually resist the temptation to replace divine authority with human charisma. The dilemma is real, but the choice is clear:

"It is better to take refuge in the Lord than to trust in man." — Psalm 118:8

In every season of life, in every trial, in every decision, let us choose to trust in the One who never fails, who sees the end from the beginning, and who works all things together for our good.

Group Discussion Questions

1. **Why do you think people, even Christians, tend to trust in man more than in God?**
   - Can you share an example where this happened in your life or someone else's?
2. **What are some modern ways that Christians unknowingly place their trust in man rather than in God?**
   - (e.g., political leaders, doctors, celebrity pastors, influencers, self-help culture, etc.)
3. **Jeremiah 17:5 says, "Cursed is the man who trusts in man." What do you think this "curse" looks like in today's world?**
4. **What is the difference between trusting a godly person and placing your ultimate trust *in* that person? How do we maintain the right balance?**
5. **What happens when someone you looked up to spiritually lets you down? How can God use that experience for growth?**
6. **How does self-trust (leaning on your own understanding) show up in decision-making? How can we shift that trust to God?**
7. **How can a community of believers help one another develop deeper trust in God rather than man?**
8. **How does trusting in man lead to idolatry, and how can we guard against this spiritually?**

Personal Reflection Questions

1. Who or what do I turn to first when I'm afraid, uncertain, or in need of help—God or someone/something else?
2. Have I ever made a major decision based more on human advice or pressure than on prayer and Scripture? What was the result?
3. Do I secretly trust in my own ability to solve problems instead of depending on God's wisdom and timing? Why?
4. Have I elevated a person—whether a leader, family member, doctor, or friend—to a position in my heart that only God should hold?
5. What fears or insecurities make it hard for me to fully trust in God?
6. In what ways has God proven Himself faithful when I chose to trust Him over man?
7. What specific steps can I take this week to surrender more of my trust to God—especially in an area where I'm struggling?
8. Is there an area in my life where God is asking me to let go of human reliance and walk by faith? What's stopping me?

Prayer of Repentance

Heavenly Father,
I come before You with a heavy heart, acknowledging that I have sinned against You.
I have put my trust in man—seeking approval, relying on human wisdom, leaning on the strength of others—while neglecting to trust fully in You, my Creator, my Sustainer, and my Redeemer.

Forgive me, Lord, for looking to people for what only You can provide.
Forgive me for allowing fear, pride, and impatience to lead me astray from total dependence on You.
Your Word says, *"Cursed is the man who trusts in man and makes flesh his strength, whose heart turns away from the Lord."* (Jeremiah 17:5)
I do not want to live under that curse, Father. I want to return my heart to You.

Cleanse me from this sin, O God.
Renew a steadfast spirit within me.
Help me to place my full confidence in Your power, Your promises, and Your perfect will.

When I am tempted to rely on others more than You, remind me that You alone are my rock and refuge.
Teach me to walk by faith and not by sight, trusting You even when I don't understand the path before me.

Lord, I surrender my will, my fears, and my dependencies into Your hands.
Help me to seek You first in all things, and to wait patiently for Your direction.
Let me not be swayed by the voices of man, but let Your voice be the one I hear and follow.

Thank You for Your mercy, Your patience, and Your grace.
Thank You for not giving up on me when I have misplaced my trust.
Today, I recommit my heart to You.
Be my strength, my guide, and my confidence—forevermore.

In the mighty name of Jesus I pray,
Amen.

Chapter 7

Double-Minded Christians: Trapped Between Worldliness and Holiness

"A double minded man is unstable in all his ways."
— James 1:8 (KJV)

The church today faces not only external pressures from a fallen world but internal confusion caused by Christians who live in a constant tug-of-war between holiness and worldliness. These are individuals who declare loyalty to Christ with their lips while their lifestyles reflect a love affair with the world. They sing in the choir on Sunday but party or perform in clubs on Friday night. They lift their hands in worship while simultaneously promoting music or messages that glorify immorality, pride, or vanity. These are **double-minded Christians**—individuals who are **trapped between two conflicting lifestyles** and dangerously unaware of the eternal consequences.

The Hidden Danger of Double-Mindedness

To be double-minded is not merely a flaw in character—it is a spiritual danger zone. James tells us that a double-minded person is *unstable* in all their ways.

The Greek term for "double-minded" (δίψυχος, *dipsuchos*) literally means "two-souled." This suggests a person with conflicting loyalties—a soul torn between the kingdom of God and the kingdom of this world.

Jesus warned against this kind of split allegiance:

"No man can serve two masters..." (Matthew 6:24).

Yet many believers attempt to do just that. They want the blessings of God without the sacrifice or total commitment to God. They want the appearance of holiness without the lifestyle. They want to be in the presence of God but not **spiritual vitality** while the heart remains divided.

The Example of Christian Musicians: Serving Two Altars

Consider the case of a Christian musician named *Darius*. Raised in the church, Darius developed an exceptional musical talent. He plays the keyboard at his local church, leading the congregation in powerful worship. His voice brings tears to the eyes of saints on Sunday morning. But during the week, Darius performs in secular venues—clubs, weddings, hotels, and parties—singing songs that glorify lust, drunkenness, greed, and pride.

He justifies this by saying, "It's just music. I'm not doing anything sinful. I'm just using my gift." But his "gift" is being used to **build two kingdoms**—one that exalts Christ, and another that entertains the flesh.

When Darius sings *"I Surrender All"* on Sunday and *"Let's Get It On"* on Friday, he isn't just performing different genres—he is **testifying to two different allegiances**. One calls people to repentance; the other stirs up carnal desires. The same mouth that blesses God is being used to promote the very world system Christ came to rescue us from. James 4:10-12 states,

"Out of the same mouth proceed blessing and cursing. My brethren, these things ought not to be so. Does a spring send forth fresh water and bitter from the same opening? Can a fig tree, my brethren, bear olives, or a grapevine bear figs? Thus no spring can yield both salt water and fresh."

This duplicity not only **confuses the hearers** but dulls Darius's own spiritual sensitivity. Over time, his conviction weakens. What once grieved him, now excites him. What once made him feel guilty, now feels normal. He has become numb—still appearing gifted and anointed, but **spiritually adrift**.

An example of a **pastor serving two altars**—being **double-minded**—can be seen in a minister who publicly preaches holiness, righteousness, and separation from the world, yet privately or even subtly **promotes worldly values, seeks the approval of men**, and **compromises truth for personal gain or popularity**.

Example: Pastor Marcus – Serving Two Altars

Public Altar – God's Truth:
Pastor Marcus preaches with passion every Sunday. He quotes Scripture about denying the flesh, warns against worldliness, and tells the congregation to be "in the world but not of it." He teaches about the narrow path, fasting, prayer, and avoiding ungodly influences.

Private Altar – The World's Approval:
However, behind the scenes:

- He **partners with secular organizations** that promote ungodly agendas in exchange for large donations to his church.
- He **compromises biblical truth** when speaking in public forums or media interviews so as not to offend.
- He invites **entertainers** as well as anointed ministers, to church events to increase attendance.
- He **promotes himself** on social media with designer suits, flashy cars, and luxurious vacations, while his congregation struggles financially.
- He hesitates to preach on controversial topics like sin, repentance, or judgment, fearing it might shrink the crowd or cost him influence.

As noted, not all worldliness is obvious. Sometimes, it appears under the guise of "just being social," "fitting in," or "harmless fun." But compromise begins subtly. For many believers—especially those in spiritual leadership—the greatest danger is not open rebellion against God but private justification of worldly behavior.

Consider the example of Pastor Terrence

Pastor Terrence is a well-known preacher who leads a mid-sized suburban church. He was known in his community as a solid Bible teacher and a caring shepherd. So when his 25-year high school class reunion came around, he didn't hesitate to attend. He wanted to reconnect and reflect among his old peers.

At the class reunion banquet on Saturday night, Terrence arrives sharply dressed. The evening begins with a formal dinner, followed by music and dancing. At first, Pastor Terrence simply observed as the worldly-inspired DJ plays songs from the 90s and early 2000s—many of them filled with sensual lyrics and worldly themes. Soon, Pastor Terrence begins to loosen up.

Laughter flows. Though he doesn't drink alcohol, he doesn't distance himself from his old classmates that do. He joins in dancing to songs that glorify promiscuity, partying, and materialism. Classmates cheer him on, saying things like, "Wow, Terrence, I thought you were a pastor!" He laughs it off, saying, "Hey, I'm just enjoying the moment."

The next morning, Terrence is the guest preacher for a worship service organized for the reunion. He opens in prayer, preaches a fiery sermon on God's love, and leads the group in singing "Amazing Grace." People clap and say how "real" he is.

Pastor Terrence, like so many spiritual leaders who blur the lines between worldliness and holiness, is unaware of the spiritual pitfalls of his behavior of compromising with the world. By participating in the worldly dancing and music, Terrence blurs the line between holiness and worldliness.

"Do not love the world or anything in the world. If anyone loves the world, the love of the Father is not in him."
— *1 John 2:15*

"Therefore, come out from them and be separate, says the Lord. Touch no unclean thing, and I will receive you."
— *2 Corinthians 6:17*

Terrence shows one face on Saturday night and another on Sunday morning. This kind of inconsistency reflects a heart that is not fully surrendered.

While his classmates find him relatable, he has sacrificed his distinctiveness as a sanctified man of God. His actions suggest that faith is flexible and that holiness is optional.

"You are the salt of the earth. But if the salt loses its saltiness... it is no longer good for anything..."— *Matthew 5:13*

"Let your light so shine before men, that they may see your good works and glorify your Father which is in heaven." — *Matthew 5:16*

Leading worship the morning after engaging in behavior that contradicts his calling is a form of spiritual hypocrisy.

"These people honor me with their lips, but their hearts are far from me."— *Matthew 15:8*

"Having a form of godliness, but denying the power thereof: from such turn away."— *2 Timothy 3:5*

A pastor—like all believers—is called to be **set apart**. The danger of being double-minded is not just in public perception but in the spiritual erosion it causes. Pastor Terrence may not have meant harm, but his compromise diluted his spiritual authority. Worse, it sent the message that Christ can be mixed with carnality without consequence.

What seemed like a light-hearted weekend gathering was actually a serious display of spiritual inconsistency. Terrence's actions, though socially accepted, revealed deeper spiritual dangers:

By joining in with the world's ways—its music, behaviors, and values—Terrence blurred the line between sacred and profane.

Terrence's ability to shift between the world and the pulpit shows a heart pulled in two directions.

Instead of standing out as a light in the darkness, Terrence became indistinguishable from the worldly-focused crowd.

The Spiritual Conflict

According to the Bible, Pastor Darius and Pastor Terrence are **double-minded** (James 1:8), serving **both God and mammon** (Matthew 6:24). They have **one foot on the altar of God** and the **other on the altar of worldliness and are glorifying the kingdom of Satan**.

Just like the prophets of Baal in 1 Kings 18, they are blending two opposing spiritual systems. But as Elijah said, "**How long will you halt between two opinions? If the Lord is God, follow Him**; but if Baal, then follow him" (1 Kings 18:21).

The Danger

Such pastors may appear successful outwardly - large church, media presence, community influence - but in God's eyes, they are **lukewarm** (Revelation 3:16) and leading others into compromise by their lifestyles. They are caught in the snare of **pleasing man rather than God** (Galatians 1:10), which leads to spiritual ruin.

✶✶✶✶✶✶✶✶✶✶✶✶✶✶✶✶✶✶✶✶✶✶✶✶✶✶✶✶✶✶

These commonly seen realities of double-mindedness among professing Christian leaders often leads to a development of satanic strongholds that can not only cause physical or mental maladies, but will open a door of access for Satan to destroy ministries that they are serving and the lives of those to whom they minister.

✶✶✶✶✶✶✶✶✶✶✶✶✶✶✶✶✶✶✶✶✶✶✶✶✶✶✶✶✶✶

A Slow Drift with Eternal Consequences

The most tragic part of the double-minded life is not how it looks in the moment, but **where it ultimately leads**.

Jesus spoke plainly in Revelation 3:16:

"So then because thou art lukewarm, and neither cold nor hot, I will spue thee out of my mouth."

This warning is not for atheists or pagans, it is for those in the church who have become lukewarm, trying to balance worldliness and righteousness. A lukewarm professing Christian is dangerous because they look saved, sound spiritual, and speak religious language, but **lack wholehearted and total devotion to God**. The greatest deception is not from outside the church, it is **from within**, when professing Christians are self-deceived about the state of their souls.

Musicians like Darius and pastors like Pastor Marcus and Pastor Terrence are not alone. There are many professing Christians who live double lives: pastors, worship leaders, Bible study and Sunday School teachers who preach and teach against sin but harbor secret addictions, choir members who sing praises on Sunday but live promiscuously during the week, entrepreneurs who tithe with one hand while exploiting others with the other. They do not see the contradiction because **their conscience has been dulled by the ways of this world**, and the applause of people has replaced the approval of God.

The Call to Choose

Elijah's words on Mount Carmel still echo today:

"How long halt ye between two opinions? If the LORD be God, follow him: but if Baal, then follow him." (1 Kings 18:21)

God is not interested in part-time, half-hearted devotion. He wants the whole heart. God's "Great Commandment" to all believers states,

*"And you shall love the LORD your God with **all** your heart, with **all** your soul, with **all** your mind, and with **all** your strength"* (Mark 12:30).

God requires that we love Him with all of our being. Being double-minded is not a neutral zone—it is a dangerous middle ground that leads to spiritual instability and potentially eternal separation and eternal damnation.

Jesus does not call us to balance worldliness and holiness. He calls us to **die to the world** (Galatians 6:14), to **crucify the flesh** (Romans 8:13), and to **be holy** as He is holy (1 Peter 1:16). There is no middle ground that pleases Him.

A Heart Check for Every Believer

Are you like Darius, or Marcus, or Terrence? Do you serve two altars? Have you justified your compromise in the name of talent, business, profit, or cultural relevance? Examine yourself.

Ask yourself:

- Does my lifestyle reflect total surrender to Christ?
- Do I honor God with my gifts in every environment?
- Am I living one life on Sunday and another during the week?

Repentance is still possible. The grace of God reaches to those who are willing to turn from their double-mindedness. But the time to choose is now—not later.

Final Warning

The greatest tragedy is not simply living a double life. It is **dying in one**—never having made a clear decision for Christ. Don't be like the foolish virgins who had lamps with no oil, religious appearance with no relationship. Eternity is too long, and the soul is too precious, to gamble with compromise.

"Choose you this day whom ye will serve..." (Joshua 24:15)

Summary

This chapter exposes the spiritual danger of being a **double-minded professing Christian**, a person who attempts to live both for God and the world. Using the example of a Christian musician who performs both sacred and secular music, and pastors who alternate between conflicting altars, we see how living a divided life can lead to spiritual dullness, confusion, and eventually, eternal loss. The Holy Bible warns that such instability is unacceptable to God, who desires total devotion, not part-time allegiance. This chapter calls for personal examination, repentance, and a clear decision to live fully for Christ without compromise. Being "lukewarm" is not a safe middle ground—it is a path that leads away from God's presence. The time to choose holiness over worldliness is now.

Closing Thought:

"Draw near to God, and He will draw near to you. Cleanse your hands, you sinners; and purify your hearts, ye double minded."— James 4:8

Prayer of Commitment

"Search me, O God, and know my heart: try me, and know my thoughts."— Psalm 139:23

Heavenly Father,

I come before You today with honesty and humility. I confess that I have tried to live in both worlds—seeking Your blessing while entertaining worldly desires. Forgive me for the times I have been double-minded, unstable, and spiritually distracted.

Lord, I do not want to live a life of compromise. I do not want to worship You with my lips while my heart is far from You. I surrender every area of my life to Your control—my thoughts, my words, my music, my gifts, my time, and my choices.

Cleanse my heart, renew my mind, and make me single-minded in my devotion to You. Let there be no part of me reserved for the world. Set me apart for Your glory. Help me to resist temptation, to flee from compromise, and to pursue holiness with passion.

I choose today to follow You fully—no turning back, no double life, no divided heart. Empower me by Your Spirit to walk in truth, live in righteousness, and love You above all else.

In Jesus' name I pray,
Amen.

Small Group Discussion Questions

Reflection and Heart Check

1. **What does it mean to be "double-minded" according to James 1:8?**
   How have you seen this play out in real-life situations?
2. **Have you ever felt torn between living for God and pleasing the world?**
   What emotions or situations trigger that internal conflict?
3. **Why do you think double-mindedness is so dangerous spiritually?**
   How can it affect our witness, worship, and relationship with God?

Real-World Application: Music and Ministry

4. **What are the dangers of using your talents or ministry commitments for both worldly and sacred purposes, as seen in the story of Darius, Marcus, and Terrence?**
   Can someone effectively minister while also promoting worldly values?
5. **Can Christians listen to or participate in secular music without compromising their faith?**
   Where should we draw the line? What principles can help guide these decisions?

Spiritual Consequences

6. **Why is lukewarm Christianity so offensive to God (Revelation 3:16)?**
   What does Jesus' warning about lukewarm believers teach us about eternal outcomes?
7. **How does the world subtly encourage double-minded living today?**
   What role does social media, television, culture, or even some churches play in this?

Commitment and Change

8. **What would it look like for you to be "single-minded" in your devotion to Christ?**
   What changes might God be asking you to make right now?
9. **Have you justified compromise in your own life under the banner of "freedom," "talent," or "opportunity"?**
   How can you surrender those justifications to God?
10. **How can we lovingly hold one another accountable in small groups or church to avoid spiritual double-mindedness?**
    What does healthy accountability look like?

Personal Reflections: Taking Inventory of the Heart

Use this guide during your quiet time or journaling. Take your time. Be honest. Let the Holy Spirit lead.

1. The State of My Heart

- Is my heart fully surrendered to Christ, or are there areas I've withheld?
- What worldly influences have I allowed to shape my thinking, music, habits, or values?

2. My Daily Choices

- Are my daily choices drawing me closer to God or slowly pulling me away?

- Where am I compromising in the name of entertainment, popularity, or opportunity?

3. My Use of Talents and Gifts
- Am I using my God-given talents (like music, speech, or leadership) to glorify God and God only?
- Have I justified using my gifts in ungodly environments? What changes need to be made?

4. My Private vs. Public Life
- Is who I am in private the same as who I present in church or online?
- Are there secret behaviors or attitudes that conflict with my Christian witness?

5. Eternal Perspective
- If I stood before Christ today, would He see a heart fully committed or divided?
- What would He say about the direction of my life—toward Him or toward the world?

6. Steps of Surrender
- What practical steps can I take this week to turn from double-mindedness?
    - ☐ Cut out certain music, media, or environments
    - ☐ Confess to a trusted believer for accountability
    - ☐ Spend focused time in prayer and God's Word
    - ☐ Use my talents exclusively for God's glory
    - ☐ Write out a personal commitment to holiness

"If your worship is not directed to God on Saturday night, it is not received by Him on Sunday morning."

~ Walter B. Pennington ~

Chapter 8

Trapped by the Hunger for Entertainment

In recent decades, a significant shift has taken place in many modern churches. What was once considered sacred space for reverent worship, biblical instruction, and spiritual transformation is increasingly being replaced by stages, spotlights, and spectacle. The rise of "churches as entertainment" reflects a concerning trend where the line between spiritual edification and worldly amusement has been dangerously blurred.

In modern Christianity, a growing number of churches have shifted their focus from spiritual edification to emotional stimulation. Pews once filled by seekers of truth are now captivated by flashing lights, concert-style music, and feel-good messages carefully curated for maximum applause. This trend—often labeled *entertainment worship*—has created an illusion of spiritual vitality, but its long-term consequences are spiritually devastating.

We live in an age of distraction. Screens glow. Music blares. Content streams 24/7. The modern world is saturated with entertainment—designed not to inform or transform, but to amuse and consume precious God-allotted time. Sadly, this culture has not just crept into the church; in many places, it has taken center stage.

Of all the snares the enemy uses to entangle modern believers, few are as underestimated—and as effective—as entertainment. In our digital, distraction-driven world, many Christians are not falling away through heresy or persecution but through amusement.

Entertainment-driven faith is a subtle but serious form of worldliness. It prioritizes excitement over engagement, amusement over awe, and stimulation over sanctification. It reduces the Church from a place of reverence to a stage for performance. In doing so, it changes not only how we worship, but disguises whom we worship.

Entertainment itself is not evil. God designed us with the capacity for joy, beauty, music, creativity, and laughter. But when what was meant to refresh the soul begins to rule it from a worldly perspective, we step into dangerous territory. Entertainment becomes a snare when it replaces intimacy with God, dulls our spiritual senses, or subtly promotes values that oppose the gospel.

A Culture Obsessed with Amusement

The word "amuse" comes from the prefix "a-" meaning "not," and "muse," meaning "to think." So, to amuse is literally "not to think" which is contrary to the Word of God.

In Philippians 4:8, Paul instructs believers to focus their thoughts on things that are true, honorable, just, pure, lovely, of good report, virtuous, and praiseworthy. This verse is a call to cultivate a positive and constructive mindset by dwelling on what is good and excellent. Paul says, "Think on these things."

We now live in a culture obsessed with amusement:

- Endless scrolling.
- Binge-watching shows.
- Constant gaming.
- Addictive social media cycles.

These things are not inherently sinful, but when they dominate our time, distract us from prayer and the study of the Word of God, and desensitize us to sin, they become spiritually dangerous.

Paul warns in Ephesians 5:15-16:

"Be very careful, then, how you live—not as unwise but as wise, making the most of every opportunity, because the days are evil."

Wasted time is not just unproductive—it's a gateway for spiritual erosion.

Many churches today mirror the look and feel of a concert venue or a TED (Technology, Entertainment, and Design) Talk stage more than they do the reverent atmosphere of early Christian worship. With high-powered sound systems, dynamic light shows, multimedia presentations, and charismatic speakers delivering carefully crafted messages with humor and flair, the experience is increasingly catered to the consumer. Congregants have become spectators, and pastors have become performers.

This shift did not happen overnight. As culture became more entertainment-driven—through television, social media, and instant gratification—many churches responded by adapting their methods to keep people's attention. In an effort to appear "relevant" and draw crowds, churches adopted techniques from the entertainment industry: themed sermon series with catchy titles, worship leaders who resemble pop stars, and sanctuaries redesigned to look like performance halls.

While innovation and creativity are not inherently wrong, the underlying motivation is critical. When the aim of church services becomes audience satisfaction rather than God's glorification, the result is a distortion of the biblical mission of the church.

When Worship Becomes a Show

Many believers spend hours consuming entertainment daily but struggle to spend even minutes in God's Word. We are overfed by the world and undernourished in truth without discernment to spiritually evaluate our dilemma. The result is a spiritually weak Church that knows the plot lines of shows and the scores and stats of sports competition better than the promises of Scripture.

Entertainment isn't neutral. Every story, every song, every post is shaping how we think, feel, and believe. The values of the world are often delivered through humor, drama, or music in a way that makes them easier to accept and harder to resist. What we repeatedly watch, we begin to tolerate. What we tolerate, such as lies and immorality among political leaders, we begin to normalize. What we normalize, we eventually accept and practice.

In many churches today, the line between worship and entertainment is blurry. Lights flash. Stages are elaborate. Music is loud and professionally produced. The intent may be to create a "relevant" experience—but relevance without reverence quickly becomes irreverent.

- Worship becomes a concert.
- Sermons become motivational speeches.
- Altar calls become emotional moments with no lasting repentance.

God is not against excellence in creativity. But He is grieved when our pursuit of excellence overshadows His presence. The question must not be, "Did I enjoy the service?" but "Did God receive my worship?"

The Danger of Spectator Christianity

Entertainment breeds passivity. Instead of engaging with the presence of God, believers become spectators:

- Watching rather than worshiping.
- Consuming content rather than communing with Christ.
- Grading sermons like movie critics instead of receiving them with humility.

When faith becomes entertainment, discipleship suffers. The cross is no longer central. Suffering is avoided. Conviction is offensive. And spiritual maturity is replaced by emotional experience.

Trading Depth for Hype

Depth takes time. It requires silence, study, prayer, and patience. But hype is instant. It's loud. It's flashy. It keeps people "coming back for more." And so, many churches cater to consumer tastes:

- Short, upbeat messages.
- Services designed to entertain.
- Programs built around comfort and convenience.

But hype never sustains hunger. What draws people in with excitement often leaves them empty in the long run. Faith becomes shallow, easily shaken, and rooted in feelings rather than truth.

The Desensitizing Effect

One of the devil's greatest strategies is not to shock you but to slowly desensitize you.

- The first time you hear profanity, it bothers you.

- The tenth time, it annoys you.
- The hundredth time, you don't even notice it.

That's how spiritual dullness happens. Not in a moment, but over time.

The more time we spend entertaining our flesh, the less hunger we have for the things of the Spirit. The result? Prayerlessness. Passivity. Powerlessness, as revealed in far too many of our twenty-first-century professing churches of God in Christ.

Hidden Messages and Open Doors

Many forms of entertainment carry hidden messages. Shows and music normalize rebellion, sexual immorality, materialism, dishonor, witchcraft, and other unbiblical behaviors. These things aren't just fictional—they are spiritually real, and they influence the heart more than we realize.

Psalm 101:3 says:

"I will set no wicked thing before my eyes."

Can you say that about your favorite shows, music, or games? If what we consume contradicts God's truth, why are we feeding it to our souls?

Addiction to Stimulation

Entertainment often becomes addictive because it offers constant stimulation. The brain releases dopamine in response to pleasure, and over time, we crave more.

- More laughs.
- More drama.
- More romance.
- More action.

This creates a dependency that makes silence feel uncomfortable and spiritual disciplines feel boring. But God often speaks in the quiet. If we are never still, we will rarely hear Him.

Is It Lawful or Is It Beneficial?

Paul said in 1 Corinthians 6:12:

"All things are lawful for me, but not all things are helpful."

Just because it's not a sin doesn't mean it's helping you.

- Is it drawing you closer to Christ or dulling your desire for Him?
- Is it encouraging holiness or stirring up your flesh?
- Is it redeeming your time or wasting it?

Entertainment becomes a snare when we no longer control it—but it controls us.

Consequences of Entertainment-Driven Churches

1. Shallow Discipleship

Entertainment-driven worship centers on experience, not depth. It conditions believers to associate spiritual encounters with emotional highs, rather than the deep truths of God's Word. As a result, discipleship becomes shallow and not sacrificial. People leave services having been entertained but not transformed. Sermons are increasingly motivational talks rather than convicting, Bible-saturated exhortations. There is little call to repentance, no confrontation of sin, and rarely a mention of suffering or sacrifice—the very marks of genuine Christian growth and Christian Discipleship (Reference *"The Fanaticism of Christian Discipleship"* by this same writer).

When feelings fade, so does the supposed "faith" of those discipled in entertainment. Like the seed on rocky ground (Mark 4:16–17), they receive the word with joy but have no root. They quickly fall away when trials come because their foundation was emotional, not doctrinal.

2. Misplaced Worship

The purpose of Christian worship is to glorify God and reorient the heart toward Him. But entertainment worship often reverses that direction. It seeks to please people rather than God. Churches become audience-focused instead of Christ-centered. The congregation turns from being participants in worship to spectators of a performance. The band becomes the focus, the preacher becomes a celebrity, and Jesus is relegated to a footnote.

God warned of this kind of worship through the prophet Isaiah: ***"This people honors me with their lips, but their hearts are far from me. In vain do they worship me..."*** (Isaiah 29:13; cf. Matthew 15:8–9). Worship that entertains the flesh but starves the spirit is ultimately offered in vain.

3. Sensory Addiction and Spiritual Apathy

Entertainment worship cultivates an addiction to stimulation. Lights, fog machines, moving graphics, and emotionally charged music create a carefully controlled environment that mimics the world's concerts and media productions. This stirs the senses but not the soul. Over time, people become dependent on the spectacle. Quiet, reverent, Scripture-based worship begins to feel boring. Truth without theatrics is dismissed as "dead."

This addiction leads to apathy toward biblical preaching, serious prayer, and personal holiness. Worship becomes something to "feel" rather than a lifestyle to live. In this state, spiritual disciplines are neglected. There's no hunger for God's Word, no weeping over sin, no desire for Christlikeness—only a craving for the next emotional rush.

4. False Assurance of Salvation

One of the most dangerous outcomes of entertainment worship is that it can provide false assurance. People equate good feelings with salvation. If they cried during a song, raised their hands, or felt goosebumps during a service, they may believe they've encountered God—even if their lives bear no fruit of true repentance.

This emotionalism without regeneration is deceptive. Jesus warned, ***"Not everyone who says to me, 'Lord, Lord,' will enter the kingdom of heaven"*** (Matthew 7:21). A faith that is built on entertainment, but not the cross, leads people to eternal ruin while making them feel spiritually safe.

5. Man-Centered Christianity

At its core, entertainment worship shifts the focus of the gospel from God to man. Messages become centered on *your victory*, *your blessing*, *your breakthrough*—rather than God's holiness, Christ's atonement, and the call to die to self. The church becomes a place to *consume*, not a body in which to *serve* and *be sanctified*.

This man-centered model breeds entitlement rather than humility. It creates consumers instead of disciples. People attend church to be pleased rather than to be purified. When entertainment fades or fails to meet expectations, they leave, looking for the next "spiritual show."

6. Consumer Christianity

In entertainment churches, attendees are subtly trained to be consumers, not participants. The focus becomes: "What did I get out of the service?" rather than "How did I worship and serve the Lord?" Church-hopping becomes prevalent, as people shop around for the best "experience," treating churches like spiritual theme parks.

7. Loss of Reverence

True worship involves reverence, humility, and awe before a holy God. When church services become indistinguishable from secular concerts or comedy shows, the sense of God's holiness is diluted. Sacred moments become performances. The cross becomes a backdrop, not the central message.

What we need is not more spectacle, but more *sacredness*. We need awe. We need repentance. We need preaching that pierces the heart. We need worship that draws heaven to earth.
The Church must return to what matters most:

- Prayer over programs.
- Presence over performance.
- Holiness over hype.

Only then will we see transformation—not just attendance.

8. Personality-Driven Ministries

Entertainment-based churches often elevate the personality of the pastor over the power of the Word. Dynamic communicators become celebrities. The focus shifts from "Thus saith the Lord" to "Let me tell you a story." When these personalities fall from grace—as many inevitably do—the faith of many is shaken because their trust was in a person, not in God.

The Biblical Model for the Church

Jesus often had large crowds, but He didn't cater to them. In fact, many walked away when He preached hard truth (John 6:66). He didn't water down the message. He didn't chase popularity. He told the truth—even when it hurt.

- He called for repentance.
- He exposed hypocrisy.
- He demanded surrender.

Jesus wasn't building a fan base—He was forming disciples.

The early church, as seen in Acts 2:42, was devoted to "the Apostles' teaching and to fellowship, to the breaking of bread and to prayer." Their gatherings were marked by simplicity, devotion, and spiritual hunger—not entertainment. Paul exhorted Timothy to *"preach the word... in season and out of season"* (2 Timothy 4:2), not to entertain the crowd or keep their attention with clever speech.

Worship in the Bible was never about personal amusement—it was about honoring God. Singing was congregational and Christ-centered. Preaching was bold and grounded in truth. Prayer was fervent and corporate. And the sacraments were sacred acts, not stage props.

Entertainment in itself is not evil. God is a creative God. He delights in beauty, artistry, and expression. But our creativity must be submitted to His Lordship.

- Music should exalt God—not the musician.
- Drama, media, and art should tell the gospel—not just stir emotion.
- Technology should serve the mission—not replace the Spirit.

The early Church had no lights, microphones, or media teams—but they had revival. Why? Because they had the presence of God.

A Call to Discernment

God is not calling us to legalism, but to discernment. We must guard what we allow into our minds and hearts. As earlier noted, Philippians 4:8 gives us a filter:

"Whatever is true, noble, right, pure, lovely, admirable—if anything is excellent or praiseworthy—think about such things."

Imagine applying that verse to your media habits. What would stay? What would need to go?

Keeping the Main Thing the Main Thing

The Church is not a theater. The gospel is not a product. The pulpit is not a platform for performers.

The Church is the body of Christ. It is the dwelling place of the Holy Spirit. Its purpose is to glorify God, equip the saints, and preach the Word.

When entertainment becomes the focus, Christ is pushed to the background. And we must ask: If Jesus isn't the center, what are we really building?

How the Church Must Respond

1. **Return to the Word**
   Churches must re-center themselves on the authority and sufficiency of Scripture. Teaching should be deep, convicting, and faithful to the text—not merely inspirational or therapeutic.

2. **Pursue Reverent Worship**
   Worship must glorify God, not entertain people. Music should lead the congregation to reflect on God's greatness and holiness, not mimic the culture's musical trends for applause or performance.

3. **Equip the Saints**
   The church exists to make disciples, not spectators. Every sermon, small group, and ministry should equip believers to live holy lives and to share the gospel with a dying world.

4. **Reject Worldly Models of Success**
   Success is not measured by attendance numbers, likes, or media impact. Success is measured by faithfulness to God's Word and the transformation of lives by the Spirit of God.

Entertainment-driven faith is a counterfeit. It numbs instead of convicts. It thrills the senses but starves the spirit. And in the end, it cannot withstand the pressures of life or the trials of faith. Let us return to the ancient paths. Let us build altars, not stages. Let us produce disciples, not audiences. Let us preach Christ crucified—not watered-down comfort.

The world needs a Church ablaze with God's presence—not flashing lights. It needs truth, not trends. It needs holiness, not hype.

Let us be that Church.

Let us be faithful.

Let us be different.

What the world desperately needs cannot be found in entertainment—it can only be found in Christ.

A Call to Return to True Worship

As noted, true Christian worship is not about entertainment—it is about encountering the living God in spirit and in truth (John 4:23–24). It is reverent, rooted in Scripture, centered on Christ, and led by the Holy Spirit. It exalts God, humbles man, convicts of sin, comforts the broken, and points all hearts to the cross and resurrection of Jesus.

Entertainment cannot produce what only the Spirit of God can. It cannot give new birth, grow holiness, or sustain a soul in suffering. Only truth can sanctify (John 17:17). Only the Word rightly preached and the gospel rightly believed can save.

In the face of a culture that demands amusement, the church must have the courage to resist the pressure to perform. It must reject the world's methods and cling to the old paths—prayer, preaching, deliverance, praise, repentance, fellowship, and sacrificial love. The church is not a theater. Worship is not a concert. And the Christian life is not a spectacle.

Regretfully, the lives of many professing Christian in the twenty-first century church would be seen as a deceptive spectacle, an abomination before God, and a gateway to eternal damnation.

Consider the example of Brother Joseph Martin.

Brother Joseph Martin: The Smiling Greeter with a Hidden Darkness

Each Sunday morning, Brother Martin stands faithfully at the church doors with a bright, welcoming smile. He is the first face many see—always warm, always joyful, always ready with a kind word or a handshake. His presence is a comfort to the congregation, especially the newcomers. To all outward appearances, he is a model of Christian hospitality.

Yet behind that cheerful exterior lies a secret life—a darkness he thinks is hidden from all eyes, including God's. In the quiet moments of the week, when no one is watching, Brother Martin indulges in adult movies. He tells himself it's just a private weakness. After all, it doesn't affect his church duties. No one knows. No one is harmed. But that is a lie from the enemy.

Brother Martin may believe he is spiritually unaffected, but *sin always corrupts*. Sexual immorality—whether physically acted upon or visually indulged—defiles the soul and sears the conscience.

"But I say to you that everyone who looks at a woman with lustful intent has already committed adultery with her in his heart."— *Matthew 5:28 (ESV)*

Each time he gives in to lust, he chips away at his intimacy with God. The Holy Spirit is grieved (Ephesians 4:30), and unrepented sin builds a wall between the sinner and God's presence.

"Your iniquities have made a separation between you and your God, and your sins have hidden His face from you so that He does not hear."— *Isaiah 59:2 (ESV)*

Brother Martin's inner life begins to dry up—his prayers lose power, his worship feels hollow, and his discernment becomes clouded. Though he still smiles at the church doors, he is walking with a hidden limp.

Sin never stays private in the spiritual realm. Though the congregation may not know, the body of Christ is interconnected. *"For as the body is one and has many members, but all the members of that one body, being many, are one body, so also is Christ."*- 1 Corinthians 12:12 (NKJV)

"If one member suffers, all suffer together; if one member is honored, all rejoice together."— 1 Corinthians 12:26 (ESV)

When a leader or visible servant in the church lives in secret sin, it brings spiritual defilement to the entire body. His lack of purity can dull the spiritual atmosphere at the church entrance where he serves. The very place meant to be a threshold into God's holy presence becomes subtly contaminated.

Worse, if Brother Martin's sin is ever exposed, it can cause confusion, disillusionment, and discouragement—especially among young believers. It damages the church's witness and reinforces the lie that Christians are hypocrites.

Brother Martin's bondage also hinders the advancement of God's Kingdom. His spiritual authority is weakened. Instead of being a vessel for God's glory, he becomes a tool of distraction and compromise. Every soul that passes him at the door is met by a man whose spiritual shield is cracked—whose inner man is not in alignment with the holiness of God.

"Be holy, for I am holy."— 1 Peter 1:16 (ESV)

God is calling His people to be pure vessels:
"Therefore, if anyone cleanses himself from what is dishonorable, he will be a vessel for honorable use, set apart as holy, useful to the Master..."— 2 Timothy 2:21 (ESV)

But as long as Brother Martin clings to his secret sin, he limits how useful he can be for the Kingdom. The enemy rejoices, not just because of Brother Martin's fall, but because of the ripple effect that impacts many.

Yet even in this dark situation, the mercy of God is not absent. If Brother Martin confesses and turns away from his sin, healing is possible.

"If we confess our sins, He is faithful and just to forgive us our sins and to cleanse us from all unrighteousness."
— 1 John 1:9 (ESV)

God does not expose sin to shame us, but to purify and restore us. True repentance brings not only forgiveness, but spiritual power and renewed intimacy with God. Brother Martin can still be redeemed, delivered, and become a powerful testimony of God's grace.

Also, let us consider the example of Sister Clara Smith.

The Choir member with a Spiritual Dilemma

Sister Clara Smith is a devoted member of her church. Every Sunday, her voice lifts high in the choir as she worships with sincerity. She is known for her reliability, her kind spirit, and her faithfulness in financial stewardship. Yet, every Saturday night, she makes her way to the local casino—not to engage in vice, she insists, but simply to "relax" and enjoy what she calls harmless fun. She never gambles more than her preset $100 limit and believes that since she controls her spending, it doesn't affect her spiritual walk.

But herein lies the danger: **the deception of innocence.** The enemy rarely tempts believers with full-blown wickedness; he often uses *controlled compromise.* Sister Smith may not see her casino visits as sin, but what is the spiritual cost of aligning with the world's system for entertainment?

Sister Smith believes her gambling is separate from her spiritual life. But James 1:8 warns,

"A double minded man is unstable in all his ways."

She is singing praises on Sunday while engaging in an activity on Saturday that is built on greed, risk, and the love of money. Even if she sets limits, the environment itself promotes covetousness—something Scripture warns against (Luke 12:15). She may not be addicted, but she is **normalized to a worldly mindset**, relaxing her spiritual guard in a setting driven by chance rather than trust in God.

"Abstain from all appearance of evil." – 1 Thessalonians 5:22
Her personal witness is at stake. What message does it send to others in the faith or those considering Christ?

The church is called to be *set apart* (2 Corinthians 6:17), a *city on a hill* (Matthew 5:14). But when faithful members like Sister Smith engage openly in questionable entertainment, it causes confusion within the body. Younger or weaker believers may say, "If she can go to the casino, maybe it's okay for me to…" leading to **spiritual erosion** within the church congregation over time.

It also places church leadership in a difficult position. Should they address it? Ignore it? Endorse it by silence? When churches do not confront subtle worldliness, they risk **losing their prophetic voice** in a culture that desperately needs clarity.

The kingdom of God is built on righteousness, peace, and joy in the Holy Spirit (Romans 14:17). When believers engage in worldly practices for personal amusement, they represent the Kingdom in contradiction. Sister Smith's actions may seem small, but they reinforce a **larger cultural lie**—that Christians can serve two masters (Matthew 6:24).

Every believer is an ambassador for Christ (2 Corinthians 5:20). When ambassadors mix their allegiance, the **message of the Kingdom becomes muddled**. Sister Smith's behavior—though well-intentioned—contributes to a diluted gospel witness in a dark world.

Biblical References:
- **1 John 2:15-17** – "Do not love the world or the things in the world…"
- **Romans 12:2** – "Do not be conformed to this world…"
- **Proverbs 13:11** – "Wealth gained hastily will dwindle…"
- **Ecclesiastes 5:10** – "He who loves money will not be satisfied with money…"
- **Hebrews 12:14** – "Without holiness no one will see the Lord."

Let us also consider the example of Sister Louise McGee.

Sister Louise McGee and the Subtle Snare of Worldly Entertainment

Sister Louise McGee is a long-time member of the church, well-respected for her dedication, cheerful demeanor, and steady attendance. She loves spending her evenings watching television, especially her favorite show—*Law and Order*. She finds the courtroom drama and detective work fascinating and considers it a harmless way to unwind after a long day. Although she acknowledges that the show includes profanity, innuendos, and moments that don't align with Christian values, she brushes them off, reasoning, "The storylines are so well written—it's just entertainment." She is captivated by the suspense.

What Sister McGee doesn't realize is that her spiritual discernment is being dulled over time. The more she watches, the more desensitized she becomes to the ungodly elements—language, violence, moral ambiguity, and sexual references. Slowly, a tolerance for darkness takes root. Though she still attends church, reads her Bible, and sing songs of praise, her hunger for righteousness is compromised by her steady appetite for worldly content.

She unknowingly trades spiritual alertness for carnal amusement. The enemy's strategy often isn't to push believers into overt sin, but to subtly lure them into *compromise*. The entertainment industry excels at packaging ungodliness in attractive, engaging forms—designed to bypass our convictions and stir our emotions. Shows like *Law and Order*, while intellectually stimulating, often normalize:

- Profanity and crude speech (Ephesians 4:29)
- Blurred morality and justice defined by man, not God (Isaiah 5:20)
- Desensitization to violence and sexual content (Psalm 101:3)
- A humanistic worldview that leaves no room for divine truth (Colossians 2:8)

When believers consume this content regularly, even "innocently," it seeps into their thinking and values. The fallacy is the belief that "I can handle it" or "It doesn't affect me," when in fact, the heart and mind are being reshaped by worldly ideals (Romans 12:2).

Spiritual Damage to Sister Louise and Her Witness

1. **Weakened Spiritual Sensitivity** – Louise becomes less grieved by sin and more accepting of moral compromise. Her prayers become shallow, and her hunger for holiness wanes (1 Peter 1:14–16).
2. **Diminished Witness** – Her conversations increasingly reflect the content she watches. Younger believers and family members who look up to her begin to think, *If Sister McGee watches that, it must be okay*. Without knowing it, she becomes a stumbling block (Romans 14:13).
3. **Disobedience to God's Standard of Purity** – The Word of God calls believers to *guard their hearts* and *set no wicked thing before their eyes* (Proverbs 4:23; Psalm 101:3). Louise's casual consumption of ungodly media violates this standard.

Scriptural References

- **Psalm 101:3** – "I will set no wicked thing before mine eyes: I hate the work of them that turn aside; it shall not cleave to me."
- **Romans 12:2** – "And be not conformed to this world: but be ye transformed by the renewing of your mind..."
- **Ephesians 5:11** – "Have no fellowship with the unfruitful works of darkness, but rather reprove them."
- **Matthew 5:13-14** – We are the salt of the earth and the light of the world; when we look just like the world, our witness is diluted.
- **2 Corinthians 6:17** – "Come out from among them, and be ye separate, saith the Lord..."

Let us consider the final example of Brother Willie Stokes.

Brother Willie Stokes and the Dallas Cowboys: A Spiritual Dilemma

Brother Willie Stokes is a faithful member of Mount Olive Baptist Church. He attends Sunday service regularly, dresses sharp, and is known for his warm handshake and quick smile. But there's one thing everyone knows about Brother Stokes—**he does not play when it comes to the Dallas Cowboys.**

Every Sunday during football season, the moment church is dismissed, Brother Stokes rushes out. He skips fellowshipping, ignores ministry meetings, and avoids opportunities to serve—**all to catch the 12:00 PM kickoff.** His Sundays are built around the NFL schedule. If the Cowboys play early, church better not run long. If they play late, he mentally checks out by the benediction.

Over time, some church members began to notice a shift. Brother Stokes' once vibrant spiritual presence became **more passive and distracted.** He stopped attending mid-week Bible study. He declined leadership roles, saying, "I got too much going on." But the truth was, **he prioritized sports above the things of God.**

Brother Stokes' love for football created a *spiritual conflict*. While football isn't inherently sinful, **the idolatry of it—placing it above God—became his stumbling block.**

"You shall have no other gods before Me." – Exodus 20:3 (NKJV)

"Do not love the world or the things in the world. If anyone loves the world, the love of the Father is not in him." – 1 John 2:15 (ESV)

His passion for the Cowboys began to rival his passion for Christ. He never missed a game but began to miss opportunities for prayer, fellowship, and outreach. Even his conversations became more about stats, scores, and Super Bowls than about Scripture or salvation. He became known more as a **"Cowboys fan"** than a follower of Jesus.

Brother Stokes' spiritual life plateaued. The joy he once had in the Lord dulled. His prayer life weakened, and he no longer hungered for the Word like before. Though he still came to church, **his heart was divided** (Matthew 6:24).

His leadership potential went unused. Younger men who once looked up to him stopped seeing him as a spiritual example. Ministry opportunities were missed because of his constant unavailability.

"No one who puts his hand to the plow and looks back is fit for the kingdom of God." – Luke 9:62 (NIV)

To coworkers and friends, Brother Stokes was a **fanatic for football**, not faith. While he wore a cross and said grace at meals, his passion clearly leaned toward sports. When invited to evangelize or attend a prayer rally, he often replied, "Let me check the game schedule." His witness was **compromised by his worldly obsession.**

The issue is **priority and passion**. Anything we love more than Christ becomes an idol, even if it's wrapped in family fun, tradition, or team loyalty. Brother Stokes serves as a warning: when the things of this world consume our attention, they slowly choke our spiritual life (Mark 4:19).

"But seek first the kingdom of God and His righteousness, and all these things will be added to you." – Matthew 6:33 (ESV)

These four examples highlight the detriment of worldly entertainment and worldly passions in our personal lives and our witness for God's Kingdom. They serve as warnings to some of Satan's deceptive gateways to spiritual destruction. **Professing**

Christians must remain on guard for the spiritual distractions of evilness that can derail their spiritual walk with God.

Conclusion: Rekindle Your Hunger for God

The church was never called to compete with the world's entertainment. When churches become entertainment venues, they lose their prophetic voice, their biblical foundation, and their spiritual power. True revival will not come through more lights, louder music, or funnier sermons. It will come when churches humble themselves, return to the gospel, and seek God above all else.

Churches must ask themselves: Are we forming faithful disciples, or merely pleasing an audience? Are we building the kingdom of God, or are we building a stage?

Let us reclaim the church—not as a theater of amusement—but as a temple of worship, where Christ is exalted, the Word is preached, and lives are eternally changed.

You don't overcome the entertainment snare by gritting your teeth. You overcome it by falling in love with Jesus. When He becomes your delight, lesser pleasures lose their pull.

- Rediscover the wonder of God's presence.
- Replace screen time with Scripture time.
- Turn down the noise and tune in to His voice.

Entertainment isn't the enemy. But unchecked worldly entertainment must be avoided at all cost. Let entertainment serve you—not rule you. Keep all entertainment focused on the glory of God. Let it refresh you spiritually—not replace your relationship with Christ.

In a world that numbs the soul with amusement, may you be awakened to the joy of knowing God deeply, purely, and without distraction.

Group Study Questions

1. Have you ever allowed entertainment (sports, TV, social media) to interfere with your walk with God? How did it affect you?
2. In what ways can something like football become an idol, even if it seems harmless?
3. How can we tell when our love for entertainment is outweighing our love for Christ?
4. What boundaries can we put in place to prevent worldly passions from becoming spiritual distractions?
5. Read Mark 4:18–19. How do the "cares of this world" and the "desire for other things" choke the Word in our lives?
6. How might Brother Willie have used his passion for football as a tool for outreach instead of letting it weaken his witness?
7. What does Matthew 6:24 mean in the context of balancing faith and worldly interests?
8. Why do you think worldly entertainment is so appealing to Christians?
9. Have you ever justified watching a show or movie that includes ungodly content? How did it affect your spirit afterward?
10. What does Psalm 101:3 challenge us to do regarding our entertainment choices?
11. How can a believer guard their heart and mind when the world's entertainment is so easily accessible?
12. What boundaries can we set to help us pursue holiness in what we watch and listen to?
13. Have you ever considered how your entertainment habits affect your witness to others? What example are you setting?
14. How can a church or small group encourage one another toward media discernment and accountability?

Personal Reflection Questions

1. **Have I equated emotional experiences in church with genuine spiritual growth?**
   - Reflect on moments in worship when you felt deeply moved. Was it rooted in truth from God's Word or simply a response to atmosphere?
2. **Do I find quiet, Scripture-centered worship less appealing than high-energy, performance-driven services?**
   - What does that say about the condition of my spiritual appetite?
3. **Am I more concerned with how church makes me feel than how it changes me?**
   - Ask yourself: Do I leave worship services convicted, challenged, and committed to obedience—or merely entertained?
4. **Is my worship God-centered or me-centered?**
   - Are my prayers, praise, and expectations focused on honoring God or on what I hope to receive from Him?
5. **Has my faith been shaped more by culture or by Scripture?**
   - Consider the messages you hear in church. Are they consistent with the gospel of Christ or more aligned with pop-psychology and self-help themes?

Small Group Discussion Questions

1. **What are some signs that a church has become entertainment-focused rather than Christ-centered?**
   - Share observations from your experiences or from trends in popular church culture.
2. **Why do you think entertainment worship is so attractive, especially to younger generations?**
   - Discuss the societal influences that have shaped our expectations for church.
3. **What dangers arise when feelings become the foundation of faith?**
   - How does this affect one's response to suffering, persecution, or spiritual dryness?

4. **How can a church foster genuine, Spirit-filled worship without falling into performance-driven patterns?**
   - Brainstorm practical ways to cultivate reverence, truth, and participation in worship gatherings.
5. **What does Scripture teach about the nature and purpose of worship?**
   - Study passages such as John 4:23–24, Romans 12:1, Colossians 3:16, and Psalm 95. How do these contrast with modern trends?
6. **How can we personally and collectively return to worship that pleases God rather than entertains people?**
   - Discuss heart-level repentance, leadership accountability, and spiritual disciplines that need to be recovered.

<u>Group Prayer Focus</u>

- Pray for a renewed hunger for truth over entertainment.
- Ask the Lord to purify your heart from consumer-minded Christianity.
- Pray for your church—that it would glorify God in its worship, preaching, and priorities.
- Intercede for believers who may be spiritually numb, addicted to emotional highs but lacking deep faith.

Prayer of Rededication: Turning from Worldly Entertainment to the Living God

Heavenly Father,

We come before You with humble hearts, broken by the realization that we, Your people, have allowed the world to distract us from Your holy presence. Lord, we confess that we have not loved You with our whole hearts. We have given our affections to worldly entertainment, and in doing so, we have grieved Your Spirit. But today, O God, we come to rededicate **Your church**—back to You.

We cleanse our sanctuary of every influence that does not honor Your name. We reject the spirit of compromise, the desire to entertain the flesh, and the need to please the world. Let this our church facility no longer be a stage for performance, but an altar for worship. Let it be a house of **prayer, truth, holiness,** and **power**—not distraction.

Father, we repent for following personalities more than we follow Christ. We've celebrated actors, singers, influencers, and even false prophets more than we celebrate the risen Savior.
Forgive us for exalting man and robbing You of the glory due Your name. Help us to fix our eyes on **Jesus, the Author and Finisher of our faith (Hebrews 12:2)**, not the stars of this world. Strip away our fascination with fame, and let us pursue **Your approval above all.**

God, we confess that we have been bound by the glowing lights of screens—scrolling endlessly, binge-watching aimlessly, and giving more time to devices than to devotion.

Forgive us, Lord, for surrendering our minds to media instead of renewing them by Your Word (Romans 12:2). Break the chains of addiction to social media, television, and virtual distractions. Help us to be still and know that **You are God (Psalm 46:10).** Return us to the simplicity and depth of communion with You.

Lord, we renounce every ungodly song, lyric, and beat that exalts the flesh, glorifies sin, or mocks righteousness. We acknowledge that what we feed our spirit through music affects our walk with You.

Purify our playlists, cleanse our ears, and set a new song in our mouths—a song of praise to our God (Psalm 40:3). May we no longer dance to the rhythms of rebellion, but worship in the beauty of holiness.

Lord, we repent for putting games before Your glory. We confess that we have allowed our passion for teams, athletes, and schedules to come before our passion for Christ. Forgive us for reshaping our Sundays around kickoff times rather than communion with You.

Help us seek first the kingdom of God (Matthew 6:33), and to run the race that leads to the incorruptible crown (1 Corinthians 9:25). Let our allegiance be to Jesus, not jerseys. May we be known as disciples—not just fans.

Today, we rededicate **ourselves**, our **families**, and our **church** back to You, O Lord. We declare that You are our joy, our peace, our delight, and our portion. Let the fire of revival burn in us again. Teach us to hunger for righteousness and thirst for holiness.

May our church, family, and every heart within them, be fully surrendered to the Lordship of Jesus Christ. We cast down every idol and lift up **one name alone**—the name that is above every name: **Jesus**.

We declare:

"As for me and my house, we will serve the Lord." – Joshua 24:15

And so shall it be for our house of worship and our home of residence, forevermore.

In Jesus' mighty name we pray, Amen.

Chapter 9

Trapped by the Deception of Secret Societies

"Take no part in the unfruitful works of darkness, but instead expose them."— Ephesians 5:11 (ESV)

A Hidden Snare

In every generation, there are movements and organizations cloaked in secrecy—promising power, influence, and wisdom. Some are political. Others are philosophical. Still others are spiritual in appearance but demonic at their core. These are the secret societies—groups that often operate behind closed doors, under oaths of silence, swearing allegiance not to Christ, but to an alternate system of belief, hierarchy, and control.

What many believers fail to realize is that these groups often wear the disguise of goodness, charity, or even religion. Christians are sometimes drawn in by appeals to brotherhood, sisterhood, community service, intellectual pursuit, or professional advancement. But beneath these facades lie spiritual compromises that slowly erode a believer's allegiance to Christ.

The Allure of Secrecy

Secret societies appeal to some of the most dangerous human desires:

- **The desire to belong**
- **The desire to possess hidden knowledge**
- **The desire for influence and recognition**
- **The desire to "play both sides" of the spiritual fence**

Just like Satan in the Garden of Eden, these societies offer a subtle lie: "You can be one of us and still serve God." They whisper, *"Has God really said you can't be part of this?"* (Genesis 3:1 paraphrased). Many Christians fall into this trap because they believe they are strong enough to handle the double life—faithful to Jesus on Sunday, loyal to a secret brotherhood or sisterhood the rest of the week.

But Scripture is clear: *"No one can serve two masters"* (Matthew 6:24). The secrecy, the rituals, the hidden oaths, and the spiritual mixtures are not harmless—they are spiritual poison.

A Conflict of Allegiances

Many secret societies, whether Freemasonry or other occultic or mystical fraternities, ask members to swear oaths of loyalty that often contradict the lordship of Jesus Christ. These oaths may seem symbolic or ceremonial at first, but they represent spiritual agreements. Scripture warns us:

"But above all, my brothers, do not swear, either by heaven or by earth or by any other oath..."— James 5:12

Some secret societies invoke pagan gods or spirits during rituals. Others offer secret teachings that contradict the Bible. Still others reinterpret Scripture to fit their own focused traditions. **Any Christian who participates in such systems is, knowingly or unknowingly, putting another god alongside or, in far too many instances, before the Lord.**

Darkness Masquerading as Light

Paul wrote, *"Even Satan disguises himself as an angel of light"* (2 Corinthians 11:14). That's exactly how these societies often present themselves. They host charity events. They provide scholarships. They support community causes. But the spiritual foundation is compromised. It's not just about the deeds they do—it's about the spirit behind them.

To the undiscerning eye, these societies seem harmless, even noble. But to those who examine them through the lens of Scripture and spiritual discernment, they are systems rooted in rebellion, secrecy, and counterfeit spirituality.

Why Some Christians Remain Involved

There are a few common reasons why believers stay entangled in secret societies:

- **Fear of rejection** – Some fear losing family, friends, or business connections if they leave.

- **Ignorance** – Some genuinely do not know the spiritual implications of their involvement.
- **Pride** – Others enjoy the prestige, titles, or sense of superiority these groups offer.
- **Double-mindedness** – Some think they can maintain dual allegiance without consequence. Sadly, most do not realize that a double allegiance is inherent to their commitments.

But the call of Christ is one of exclusivity. He said, *"If anyone would come after me, let him deny himself and take up his cross and follow me"* **(Matthew 16:24). Jesus didn't offer a part-time discipleship. He didn't call us to split our loyalty. He calls for all of us—heart, mind, soul, and strength.**

"And you shall love the LORD your God with all your heart, with all your soul, with all your mind, and with all your strength" (Mark 12:30).

The Hidden Loyalties – Church Members in Secret Societies

The Body of Christ is called to be a peculiar people, set apart for the glory of God (1 Peter 2:9). Yet in many churches today, **secret society membership has crept into the pews and even the pulpits**, cloaked in cultural tradition, fraternal brotherhood and sisterhood, and charitable works. Many sincere pastors maintain membership in secret society organizations that they joined before receiving their call into Christ's ministry of salvation and committing themselves totally to Him. Many remain unaware of the spiritual conflict of their dual allegiance within God's Kingdom and the kingdom of darkness. The danger is not only in what these secret societies represent, but in how they **dilute, divide, and devour the spiritual integrity** of those who claim to follow Christ.

The Mask of Dual Allegiance

Church members who belong to secret societies are living with **divided loyalties**. On Sunday, they sing hymns and raise their hands in worship. But during the week, they attend meetings that involve oaths, rituals, and symbols that often **contradict the gospel of Jesus Christ**.

These societies—whether Masonic lodges, Greek-letter fraternities/sororities, or other organizations steeped in secrecy—often require:

- **Sworn oaths** that pledge loyalty to the organization above all else.
- **Secret rituals** that have spiritual roots not founded in Christ.
- **Symbols and language** borrowed from paganism, mysticism, or occult tradition.
- **Allegiance to "light" or "wisdom"** not defined by the Word of God.

This creates a spiritual **double-mindedness** (James 1:8), where individuals profess to follow Jesus but walk in fellowship with **hidden darkness**.

"And have no fellowship with the unfruitful works of darkness, but rather reprove them." – Ephesians 5:11

Spiritual Conflict and Compromise

The believer's life is not meant to be lived in **compartmentalization**. You cannot serve Christ and belong to an organization that spiritually binds you to worldly philosophies. These dual commitments **erode biblical conviction**, slowly normalizing compromise:

- A deacon who excuses occultic ritual as "just symbolic."
- A choir director who displays secret society hand signs in social media photos.
- A youth leader who recruits young Christians into these societies under the guise of "networking" or "legacy."

This is more than harmless fraternity—it is **a snare**. As earlier noted, these societies often require participants to **keep secrets, make vows, and follow codes of ethics** that directly oppose Scripture.

God never calls His people to secret knowledge or dual allegiance, He calls them into his universal light of one body in Christ (John 3:19-21, Romans 12:5, 1st Corinthians 12:13).

God's Jealousy and the Spirit of Idolatry

God is a jealous God (Exodus 34:14). When church members bow at two altars, **the altar of Christ and the altar of worldly brotherhood or sisterhood**, they stir up divine displeasure. These societies may promise unity, influence, or success—but underneath, they promote **idolatry**, **self-exaltation**, and **spiritual bondage**.

When Israel attempted to mix worship of Yahweh with the gods of the surrounding nations, judgment swiftly followed. The same principle applies today. You cannot sprinkle a little Jesus into an unholy system and expect it to be sanctified.

"You cannot drink the cup of the Lord and the cup of demons too; you cannot partake of the Lord's table and the table of demons." – 1 Corinthians 10:21

Deception of Good Works

Many secret societies are involved in **philanthropy**, **scholarships**, and **community service**, which may seem admirable. But **good works without the Spirit of Christ are not proof of righteousness**. Satan masquerades as an angel of light (2 Corinthians 11:14), and one of his greatest deceptions is convincing Christians that **participating in "positive" worldly systems is harmless**.

But when these works are rooted in oaths, secret codes, and spiritual compromise, they become **counterfeits of true Kingdom character and service**.

Bondage, Not Brotherhood of Sisterhood

What begins as brotherhood or sisterhood often ends in **spiritual bondage**. Some believers report **torment, confusion, and generational curses** linked to their involvement in secret societies. Because these societies often invoke names, powers, and forces that are not of God, members unknowingly open doors to demonic oppression.

True freedom is found in **Christ alone**, not in hidden alliances or man-made or woman-made rituals. **The early church did not advance by joining forces with Rome or Greek intellectual** societies—they turned the world upside down by preaching a crucified and risen Savior and remained in brotherhood and sisterhood solely in Him. Their allegiance was not divided.

A Call to Repentance and Separation

If you are a professing Christian and a member of a secret society, **come out from among them** (2 Corinthians 6:17). Renounce the oaths. Break the soul ties. Ask the Holy Spirit to cleanse and renew your mind. The cross of Christ demands full allegiance, not shared loyalty.

In the spirit of transparency, I will now share a brief testimony of my personal experience:

This was an eye-opening God-given revelation that required a personal and life-altering decision by this writer as an active member of Freemasonry and as serving as a pastor in a major man-devised denomination that God never ordained. Indeed, God truly blessed my voluntary separations. My separation from Freemasonry enabled me to break a longstanding curse that existed over my family line due to my father's membership and my reinforcing it with my commitment to the same evil-orchestrated vows. I was totally unaware of this curse and the fact that it was the spiritual foundation for many sicknesses and spiritual confusion that existed within my family line. By renouncing my vows and committing my life totally to Christ, I was able, through anointed deliverance ministry, to break the longstanding curse over my family line. I now desire that everyone will experience this same freedom and protection that exist from living under the shelter of Almighty God (Psalm 91).

Jesus said plainly:

"No one can serve two masters..." – Matthew 6:24

And again:

"He who is not with Me is against Me..." – Luke 11:23

Let the Church return to **purity, holiness**, and **truth**. Let us be known not for a divided allegiance, handshakes, colors, and symbols—but for **power, love, and a sound mind** in Christ (2 Timothy 1:7) that will only be realized through a undivided allegiance to Him.

Many pastors caught in the snare of the divided allegiance of active membership in a secret society and a commitment to Christ remain unaware of the spiritual conflict and potential spiritual damage resulting from their spiritual leadership.

Consider the example of Pastor Mike.

Pastor Mike - A Divided Allegiance

Pastor Mike is a dynamic and respected leader of a growing urban church. His sermons are biblically sound, his prayer life is consistent, and his passion for ministry is evident. He leads a weekly Bible study, counsels married couples, and often speaks at revivals.

However, Pastor Mike is also a proud, active member of the graduate chapter of a popular Greek-letter fraternity. He often wears the fraternity's paraphernalia, attends meetings and rituals, and mentors new initiates. He views his involvement as harmless and culturally valuable—a way to connect with young Black professionals and promote community service. To him, it's just "networking and legacy."

But spiritually, Pastor Mike is entangled in a **dangerous conflict of allegiance**—a conflict he does not fully perceive.

Pastor Mike has sworn oaths, participated in rituals, and upholds the traditions of a brotherhood that often invokes spiritual language and symbolism foreign to biblical Christianity. Even if done unknowingly, this places him in a **covenantal conflict**.

Matthew 6:24 (ESV) – *"No one can serve two masters, for either he will hate the one and love the other, or he will be devoted to the one and despise the other."*

By pledging loyalty to an organization with its own creeds, secrets, and sometimes occultic origins, Pastor Mike is in danger of giving **spiritual allegiance** to something other than Christ.

Because the fraternity is cloaked in positive cultural and charitable contributions, Pastor Mike fails to discern the **spiritual compromise**. Many of these societies include **secret oaths**, symbolic rituals, or acknowledgment of multiple deities—elements that are explicitly forbidden in Scripture.

2 Corinthians 6:14-17 (ESV) – *"Do not be unequally yoked with unbelievers. For what partnership has righteousness with lawlessness?... What agreement has the temple of God with idols?... Therefore go out from their midst, and be separate from them, says the Lord."*

Fraternal initiation rites often contradict the exclusivity of Christ as Lord, introducing **syncretism**—the blending of biblical faith with worldly or occult practices.

When the shepherd mixes **spiritual truth** with **worldly affiliations**, the flock is led into confusion. Members may ask:
- "If Pastor Mike can join, why can't I?"
- "If he swore a secret oath, is that okay for Christians?"
- "Can we be both spiritual and worldly at the same time?"

This double message undermines **holiness** and **spiritual separation**, setting a precedent that participation in secret, spiritual societies is compatible with biblical Christianity.

James 4:4 (ESV) – *"...Do you not know that friendship with the world is enmity with God? Therefore whoever wishes to be a friend of the world makes himself an enemy of God."*

Pastor Mike may not realize that his visible affiliation with a secret society sends a message to unbelievers: *You can serve God and the world at the same time.* The cross and the crest are both around his neck—but the world will always see the contradiction.

Romans 12:2 (ESV) – *"Do not be conformed to this world, but be transformed by the renewal of your mind..."*

His **spiritual credibility is weakened**. The world may question if his loyalty is truly to Christ, or if he's divided between two identities—one rooted in the Gospel, the other in tradition, symbolism, and secrecy.

Pastor Mike is sincere in his walk with God—but **sincerity is not the same as truth**. His divided allegiance places him in spiritual danger, blinds his discernment, weakens the church's foundation of holiness, and compromises his public witness for Christ. God calls His leaders to **full consecration**, not divided allegiance.

1 Kings 18:21 (ESV) – *"How long will you go limping between two different opinions? If the Lord is God, follow him…"*

The Call to Come Out

Just as God called His people to come out of Babylon, He is still calling believers today to ***"come out from among them and be separate"*** (2 Corinthians 6:17). The church cannot afford to be in covenant with both Christ and the kingdom of darkness.

If you are a professing Christian and involved in a secret society:

1. **Renounce it** – Break every oath, even those spoken decades ago.
2. **Repent** – Ask the Lord for forgiveness for misplaced loyalty and spiritual compromise.
3. **Remove yourself** – Leave the organization publicly and boldly.
4. **Affirm your devotion** – Affirm your allegiance to Christ alone, declaring solemnly and formally so as to be a bold example to all others.

Conclusion: Walk in the Light

God's people are called to be children of His light—not keepers of hidden darkness. Any allegiance that compromises your walk with Christ must be exposed and discarded (Ephesians 5:11). No matter how prestigious or powerful a secret society may seem, it is dust and shadow compared to the glory of knowing Christ and rededicating your life solely to bring glory to His Kingdom on Earth. (Reference Appendix 1 & 2 for Christian Consecration and Appendix 3 for more prayers.)

Let us reject every hidden snare, every double-minded allegiance, and every dark covenant. **Let us walk in the light of the Lord, whose kingdom has no secrets—only truth, freedom, and eternal life.**

"For nothing is hidden that will not be made manifest, nor is anything secret that will not be known and come to light."— Luke 8:17

Prayer for Separation, Freedom, and Deliverance

Gracious and Mighty God,

I come before You today in full surrender, seeking Your strength, Your truth, and Your freedom. Lord, I acknowledge that I have made covenants and associations that have entangled me in darkness, secrecy, and deception. But today, in the name of Jesus Christ, I renounce every vow, oath, ritual, and allegiance that I made to any secret society—knowingly or unknowingly—that conflicts with Your truth and Your kingdom.

Father, by the authority of Jesus' name, I break every chain of bondage, every spiritual stronghold, and every soul tie connected to these organizations. I plead the blood of Jesus over my mind, my spirit, and my life. Cleanse me from all defilement. Deliver me from every spiritual influence that has tried to control, confuse, or compromise my walk with You.

I declare that my only loyalty is to the Lord Jesus Christ, the One who died and rose again to set me free. I choose to walk in the light, to walk in truth, and to walk in the power of the Holy Spirit. Fill every empty place with Your presence. Guard my heart and guide my steps as I walk in newness of life.

Father, give me boldness to stand firm in this decision and not look back. Restore everything the enemy tried to steal from me— my peace, my purpose, my joy, and my identity in Christ. Surround me with godly counsel and supportive believers who will walk with me on this journey of freedom.

Thank You for Your mercy. Thank You for rescuing me. Thank You for being the God who delivers completely. In Jesus' powerful and holy name I pray, **Amen.**

Reflection Questions:

1. Have I ever compromised my faith by aligning with organizations that contradict the Bible?
2. What secret or hidden loyalties might be hindering my spiritual growth?
3. How does Scripture instruct us to respond to spiritual darkness in our own lives and in the Church?
4. What are practical steps to renounce and walk away from secret societies as a believer?
5. How can the Church create safe spaces for people to repent, be delivered, and restored? To remain free?

Small Group Discussion Questions:

1. Opening Reflection

- When you hear the term *"secret society,"* what comes to mind? Have you ever encountered or been invited into a group that operated under secrecy or hidden rituals?
- Why do you think secrecy appeals to so many people, even within the church?

2. Scripture-Based Examination

- Read **Ephesians 5:11**. What does it mean to "expose" the works of darkness rather than participate in them?
- How does **Matthew 6:24** ("You cannot serve two masters") apply to Christians involved in divided allegiances?

3. Identifying Deception

- What are some ways secret societies present themselves as harmless or beneficial in the eyes of the world?
- How can Christians discern whether an organization or group compromises their faith, even if it appears charitable or virtuous?

4. Spiritual Consequences

- What are the dangers of swearing secret oaths or participating in spiritual rituals outside of biblical Christianity?

- How might involvement in these groups affect a believer's spiritual authority, witness, and relationship with God?

5. Personal Application

- Have you (or someone you know) ever had to walk away from an organization or relationship that conflicted with your loyalty to Christ? What was the experience like?
- What steps can a believer take to disentangle themselves from secret allegiances and restore full devotion to Jesus?

6. Corporate Discernment

- How can the church better educate and protect believers from being drawn into organizations that conflict with biblical truth?
- What role should spiritual accountability play when a Christian is involved in questionable affiliations?

7. Prayer and Repentance

- Spend time as a group praying for those who may be unknowingly trapped by secret societies.
- Ask God for spiritual discernment, courage to confront deception, and the grace to walk in the light.

Recommended resources:

(The information provided in this chapter can primarily be found in the following resources. We recommend them for additional information and clarity)

"The True Alpha and Omega," by Minister Jerrod Smith & Brother Clifton Lucas
"Coming Apart at the Seams," by Minister Fred Hatchett (This book can be downloaded @ DontGoGreek.com)
"College Fraternities," by David & Donna Carrico
"Freemasonry," by Jack Harris
"Free From Freemasonry," by Ron G. Campbell

Chapter 10

Trapped by the Evilness of Racism

The Roots of Racism

Racism stems from pride, fear, ignorance, and the sinful desire to dominate or exclude others based on ethnic, cultural, or physical differences. Its roots go as far back as human history: Cain's jealousy of Abel was not racially motivated, but it marked the first act of hatred against a fellow human being. Racism is a form of partiality and prejudice that contradicts God's design of humanity: that we are all made in His image (Genesis 1:26–27).

From a biblical perspective, racism is not merely a social or political issue; it is a spiritual evil born out of humanity's fallen nature. The sin of pride manifests itself when one group believes it is inherently superior to another, forgetting that "God shows no partiality" (Acts 10:34, ESV).

The Origin of Racism in America

In the United States, racism became institutionalized through slavery, beginning in the early 1600s. African people were kidnapped, dehumanized, and forced into slavery under the guise of economic necessity and racial inferiority. The myth of racial superiority was systemically crafted to justify exploitation. This evil was later codified in laws, supported by non-scientific theories, and enforced through brutal violence.

The American narrative of liberty and justice for all has been tainted by centuries of racial injustice. Even after the abolition of slavery, Jim Crow laws, redlining, segregated schooling, and mass incarceration continued the legacy of racial oppression. These systems affected not just civil society, but also the Church. (Reference *"Justice: The Deception of Christianity in America"* by this same writer for more information.)

The Origin of Racism in the Church

The Church in America has a tragic history of racial complicity. Many white Christians, especially in the 18th and 19th centuries, used Scripture out of context to justify slavery. Passages such as Ephesians 6:5 *("Slaves, obey your earthly masters...")* were misused to maintain power rather than to understand the heart of the Gospel, which brings freedom to all people (Galatians 5:1).

Instead of being a prophetic voice for justice, large portions of the Church became silent—or worse, supportive—of racial injustice. This sin continues to haunt many denominations today.

The History of the White Racially-Segregated Church

White racially-segregated churches became the norm in America, not the exception. In fact, some denominations formed *because* of their desire to uphold slavery and white supremacy. For example, the Southern Baptist Convention was established in 1845 by Baptists in the South who supported the right to own slaves.

Even after the Civil Rights Movement, many white churches remained segregated, either explicitly or by virtue of culture, music, neighborhood lines, and comfort zones. This segregation was not merely incidental; it was nurtured by years of social conditioning and theological negligence.

Christians Living in Racially Segregated Communities

Many Christians live in segregated neighborhoods, not always by choice but often by comfort. However, segregation becomes sinful when it fosters ignorance, fear, and indifference. Christians are called to cross boundaries, break down walls, and engage in peacemaking.

Intentional relationships across racial lines reflect the Gospel of reconciliation. We must examine whether our communities reflect convenience or conviction.

The Dilemma of Pastors Who Choose Not to Address Racism

Many pastors avoid addressing racism because they fear division, backlash, or loss of membership. Yet silence in the face of sin is itself sinful. As James 4:17 states, *"So whoever knows the right thing to do and fails to do it, for him it is sin."*

Pastors are called to preach the *whole counsel of God* (Acts 20:27), and that includes justice, repentance, reconciliation, and love. Avoiding racism to preserve comfort or unity is a false peace built on denial. Jesus confronted both individual and societal sin. So must His shepherds.

Why Racism Persists

Racism persists because it remains unchecked in the human heart. It is reinforced by social structures, inherited attitudes, and silent complicity. It is nurtured by stereotypes, cultural fears, and unbiblical worldviews. More dangerously, it thrives when Christians separate their faith from their social behavior.

As long as Christians remain passive or defensive about racism, it will continue to fester in the pews and pulpits. When sin is tolerated, it spreads.

Most Racists Don't Realize They Are Racists

Many who harbor racial prejudice would never label themselves as racist. But racism is not just about overt slurs or acts of violence. It can be found in silence, avoidance, assumptions, and unchecked privilege. It is possible to benefit from systemic racism and still be unaware. Many unsuspecting souls are generational beneficiaries of African slavery.

This is why David prayed, "Search me, O God… and see if there be any grievous way in me" (Psalm 139:23–24). Self-examination is essential to rooting out hidden sin.

Those Who Say, "I'm Not a Racist," But Really Are

Often, those who deny being racist become defensive when challenged. They may say, "I have Black friends," or "I don't see color." But racism is more than personal behavior, it's about beliefs, systems, and attitudes.

The Pharisees didn't believe they were sinful either, but Jesus rebuked them for their hypocrisy. Racism hides behind good intentions. Only God's Word can reveal what's truly in the heart (Hebrews 4:12).

Why Professing Christians Struggle to Love All Humanity as Jesus Did

Jesus Christ modeled a radical, all-encompassing love that transcended ethnicity, culture, and social boundaries. He spoke with the Samaritan woman (John 4), healed the servant of a Roman centurion (Matthew 8:5–13), praised the faith of Gentiles, and gave the parable of the Good Samaritan (Luke 10:25–37) to shatter the boundaries of ethnic hatred. His life and teachings command His followers to do the same. Yet, many Christians throughout history—and still today—have found it difficult to fully embrace this Christlike love for all humanity. The lingering evil of racism, both overt and subtle, continues to trap believers in mindsets and behaviors that contradict the very essence of the gospel.

1. Cultural Conditioning and Unchallenged Prejudices

One primary reason Christians struggle to love all people as Jesus did is that many have been deeply shaped by the culture around them rather than the Kingdom of God. Racism is not always learned through hatred; it is often absorbed quietly through silence, segregation, and social norms. From an early age, people are exposed to stereotypes, assumptions, and cultural hierarchies that elevate certain groups while devaluing others.

These biases—whether toward skin color, ethnicity, language, or nationality—can become so embedded in the Christian's worldview that they seem "normal" or "just the way things are." When such prejudices go unchallenged by biblical truth, believers may unconsciously carry racial superiority or apathy into their faith, allowing cultural comfort to overrule Christ's command to love.

2. Misapplication of Scripture

Another barrier is the misuse of biblical scripture to justify division rather than unity. Some have twisted biblical narratives, such as the curse of Ham in Genesis or God's separation of nations at Babel, to support racist ideologies. Others confuse Old Testament ethnic distinctions with New Testament realities, ignoring that Jesus tore down the wall of hostility (Ephesians 2:14) and made one new humanity in Himself.

Rather than reading Scripture through the lens of Christ's love and the gospel's inclusive power, some Christians read it through the lens of nationalism, tribalism, or denominational pride. This leads to distorted theology that separates rather than unites, and defends exclusion rather than embraces reconciliation.

3. Comfort Over Conviction

True love, especially love for those who are different, is often uncomfortable. It requires humility, repentance, listening, and sometimes the dismantling of long-held views. Many Christians struggle with racism not because they openly hate others, but because they fear the discomfort that comes with change. It's easier to stay within racially or culturally equivalen churches, communities, and friend groups than to reach across divides and cultivate relationships with those from different backgrounds.

Christ-like love is sacrificial. Jesus left the perfection of heaven to walk among the broken. He touched the untouchable, ate with the outcasts, and died for His enemies. Yet some Christians today resist even having a conversation about racial injustice or diversity in the Church because it threatens their comfort. The gospel calls us to a higher standard—one where love requires action, even when it costs us something.

4. The Sin of Pride and Superiority

Racism is ultimately rooted in pride, the belief that one's group is better, more worthy, or more chosen than others. This pride can be cloaked in religious language, patriotism, or even theological superiority. But pride of this kind blinds Christians to the imago Dei, the image of God, in every person, regardless of background or skin tone.

Jesus humbled Himself. He washed the feet of sinners and welcomed the marginalized. The love He modeled was free from superiority. When Christians hold on to racial pride or remain silent about inequality, they violate the very heart of the gospel, which is grounded in humility, unconditional sacrificial love, and reconciliation.

5. Historical Complicity and Collective Amnesia

The Church's historical complicity in racism, through slavery, segregation, colonialism, and systemic injustice, has left a deep wound. Instead of confessing and repenting of these sins, many believers prefer to forget or minimize them. This selective memory fosters a shallow understanding of love. It avoids the hard work of reconciliation, which requires truth-telling, accountability, and restoration.

Jesus never ignored sin. He exposed it, confronted it, and forgave it. Christians cannot truly love all humanity while ignoring or rewriting history. Only by facing the past with honesty and humility can we move toward a future shaped by gospel healing.

6. Failure to Understand the Global Body of Christ

Christianity is not a Western religion or the possession of any one race or nationality. It is a global, multiethnic movement under the lordship of Christ. Yet many Christians still view the faith through a narrow lens, often prioritizing their national identity or cultural expression over the unity of the body.

The Apostle Paul said, *"There is neither Jew nor Gentile... for you are all one in Christ Jesus"* (Galatians 3:28). This does not erase our cultural distinctions, it celebrates them under a greater identity. When Christians fail to grasp this truth, they limit their love to those who look, vote, speak, or worship like them. But Jesus calls us to something greater: to love as He loved, without borders or bias. This remains the foundation for Christianity.

The Spiritual Implications of Racism

Racism is not only a moral evil; it is a spiritual stronghold. It distorts the image of God in others, mocks the unity Christ prayed for (John 17:21), and grieves the Holy Spirit. It is the converse of love, which is the defining mark of a true believer (John 13:35).

Racism alienates Christians from one another, hinders prayer (1 Peter 3:7), and erodes the credibility of the Church's witness. The cross of Christ was meant to reconcile "Jew and Gentile" into "one new humanity" (Ephesians 2:14–16). To embrace racism is to reject the reconciling power of the cross.

The Deception of Racism and Eternal Salvation

One of the most dangerous lies is that a person can harbor racism and still inherit eternal life without repentance. Scripture teaches that no one who "hates his brother" can claim to love God (1

John 4:20). Racism, if unrepented, is a soul-damning sin that will result in eternal separation from God.

Jesus said, *"By their fruit you will recognize them"* (Matthew 7:20). Racist attitudes, when left unchallenged, bear rotten fruit and signify a heart that may not truly know Christ.

What the Bible Says About Racism

- **Genesis 1:27** – All humans are made in God's image.
- **Acts 17:26** – *"From one man he made all the nations."*
- **Galatians 3:28** – *"There is neither Jew nor Greek... for you are all one in Christ Jesus."*
- **James 2:1, 8–9** – Warns against partiality and discrimination in the Church.
- **Revelation 7:9** – Heaven will include a *"great multitude... from every nation, tribe, people, and language."*

Scripture is clear: Racism has no place in the kingdom of God.

What Should Christians Do About Racism in the Church?

1. **Repent**: Individually and corporately for the sin of racism.
2. **Teach truth**: Pastors must preach boldly on unity, justice, and reconciliation.
3. **Build relationships**: Pursue cross-cultural friendships and accountability.
4. **Confront injustice**: Use influence to speak against discriminatory practices.
5. **Disciple wisely**: Train members to think biblically about race and justice.
6. **Pray deeply**: Ask God for healing, wisdom, and transformation.

Deliverance from Racism

The Gospel of Jesus Christ offers true freedom from racism. The cross reconciles us to God **and** to one another (Ephesians 2:13–16). In Christ:

- We are given **a new heart** (Ezekiel 36:26)
- We are made **one body** (1 Corinthians 12:13)

- We are called to **bear one another's burdens** (Galatians 6:2)
- We are empowered to **walk in love** (Ephesians 5:2)
- We are commanded to **do justice and love mercy** (Micah 6:8)

Deliverance begins with humility and submission to the Holy Spirit, who renews our minds (Romans 12:2) and transforms our hearts.

Final Reflection

Racism is a sin that deceives many, yet it is one of the clearest signs of worldliness in the Church today. To be trapped by racism is to be spiritually blind. Christ came to set captives free—not just from personal sin, but from social bondage, hate, and division.

Let the Church be the light of reconciliation in a dark and divided world. Let us be known not for segregation, but for unconditional sacrificial love for all humanity, loving others more than we love ourselves (John 13:34).

Before we conclude this chapter, we will give the examples of Mrs. Karen Riley, Pastor Edwin Snow, and Mrs. Marilyn Sykes for the edification of the body of Christ.

The Story of Mrs. Karen Riley: A Life of Quiet Hatred

Mrs. Karen Riley, a 73-year-old white woman, has been a professing Christian for as long as she can remember. Raised in a segregated, all-white church in a rural farming community outside Opelousas, Louisiana her spiritual formation was shaped by the warm glow of Sunday morning hymns, church picnics, and an unspoken but deeply ingrained social order. She learned the Bible from group study and fire-and-brimstone preachers, but no one ever challenged the racial assumptions that permeated her environment.

Karen had little meaningful contact with Hispanics and Latinos during her formative years. Her perceptions of them were shaped largely by portrayals on television, depictions that emphasized stereotypes, or by local news stories that associated Hispanics and Latinos with laziness, crime, poverty, and unrest. These impressions settled into her heart like sediment, forming what she did not recognize as racism, but what Scripture would call sin.

Throughout her life, Karen remained an active member of her church and a respected leader in the women's ministry. She taught Sunday school, organized charity drives, and even mentored younger women in the faith. Outwardly, she was a model Christian. But hidden beneath her polite Southern demeanor was a deep and persistent disdain for Hispanics and Latinos, a contempt she never admitted, never confessed, and never thought of as incompatible with her faith.

She avoided racially diverse churches. When the women's group suggested inviting a guest speaker from a predominantly Hispanic congregation in the nearby city of Lafayette, Karen subtly steered the group in another direction. She often rationalized her discomfort: "It's not about race; it's about cultural differences." But the truth was uglier. Her heart was hardened by a life-long prejudice that she had sanctified with tradition and familiarity.

Karen's racism created an invisible but real barrier in her congregation. Even though the church rarely spoke about race, her attitudes helped maintain an unwelcoming atmosphere for believers of color. Her silent resistance to diversity ensured the church remained homogenous, contrary to the biblical image of the Church as one body with many members (1 Corinthians 12:12–13).

Her presence reinforced the idea that one could love God without loving *all* of God's people. In truth, Scripture strongly refutes this:

"If someone says, 'I love God,' and hates his brother, he is a liar; for the one who does not love his brother whom he has seen, cannot love God whom he has not seen." - 1 John 4:20

Karen's leadership subtly but powerfully shaped the attitudes of other women. Her unspoken prejudice filtered into group decisions, outreach events, and spiritual discussions. The group never grappled with issues of racial reconciliation or justice, and opportunities for growth and repentance were lost. In ignoring the sin of racism, Karen led others into passive complicity, and her influence became a spiritual stumbling block (Romans 14:13) for the church and entire community.

Though she spoke often of Jesus, Karen's life presented a distorted witness. Her failure to love across racial lines contradicted the message of the gospel, which calls all people to unity in Christ:

"There is neither Jew nor Greek, slave nor free, male nor female, for you are all one in Christ Jesus." — Galatians 3:28

Unbeknownst to her, Karen's racism made her testimony ring hollow to those listening and watching. Nonbelievers saw her hypocrisy. The gospel she preached was discredited by the hatred she harbored.

The most sobering truth is this: racism is not merely a social flaw, it is a spiritual sin. Jesus taught that the two greatest commandments are to love God and love one's neighbor (Matthew 22:37–39). Karen may have believed she kept the first, but she utterly failed the second.

If Karen never repented of her hatred, it is entirely possible that her salvation was self-deceived.

"Not everyone who says to me, 'Lord, Lord,' will enter the kingdom of heaven, but only the one who does the will of my Father who is in heaven." - Matthew 7:21

Jesus warns that many will be shocked at the judgment seat, having claimed His name but not His heart. Hatred is incompatible with the new life in Christ:

"Everyone who hates his brother is a murderer, and you know that no murderer has eternal life abiding in him." - 1 John 3:15

Redemptive Possibility

Karen's story doesn't have to end in judgment. Had she been willing to confront the sin embedded in her heart, the gospel would have offered cleansing, transformation, and reconciliation. Christ came to break every dividing wall of hostility (Ephesians 2:14). But for that to happen, Karen would have needed to humble herself, confess her sin, and allow God to remake her heart.

Closing Thought

Mrs. Karen Riley's life serves as a tragic picture of how cultural sin, if unexamined, can burrow deep into a soul and corrupt a Christian's witness, community, and possibly their very salvation. The church must not ignore racism as a peripheral issue. It is a gospel issue. And it must be dealt with as seriously as any other sin that threatens to separate a person from God.

The Story of Pastor Edwin Snow

Pastor Edwin Snow, age 58, was born and raised in a predominantly white suburb just outside Kansas City, Kansas. Raised in a conservative evangelical household, Edwin was taught the value of faith, hard work, and moral living. His parents, though cordial toward people of different races, rarely discussed race beyond vague generalizations or outdated stereotypes.

Edwin attended an integrated public high school from 9th through 12th grade. It was during his junior year that a defining moment occurred. Hoping to find camaraderie and confidence, Edwin tried out for the varsity basketball team. Though he had practiced long hours and was especially skilled at free throws, he was cut from the team during the final round. Most of the players who made the team were black students, athletic, fast, and naturally gifted in ways he felt he could never match.

That rejection planted a seed of quiet bitterness in Edwin's heart. Though he never vocalized his resentment, he began associating black males with his personal feelings of failure and inadequacy. He rationalized it over the years: *"They always get picked,"* or *"They're flashy, not disciplined."* These attitudes hardened into subtle, unspoken prejudices that would go unchecked.

After college, Edwin accepted a call into the ministry. His theological education was sound, his preaching passionate, and his leadership respected. Eventually, he was appointed senior pastor of a traditional, mostly white congregation in Topeka, Kansas. The church had minimal diversity, and its outreach efforts reflected that. Over the years, Edwin's ministry subtly reinforced his unrecognized bias. He connected more authentically with white men, mentored them intentionally, and often overlooked or behind closed doors, was overly critical of African American men in his church, of those who visited, or those who tried to get involved.

To Edwin, this discrepancy seemed normal, perhaps even spiritually discerned. But those close to the church could feel it. African American members and visitors often felt unseen or subtly dismissed. While Edwin spoke of unity in Christ, his actions told a different story.

The Effects of Pastor Snow's Bias

On His Ministry:

1. **Stunted Growth of a Multicultural Church:**
   Edwin's unaddressed bias becomes a spiritual barrier, preventing the church from embracing the full unity and diversity of the body of Christ (Revelation 7:9). His inability to shepherd all people equally compromises the mission of the gospel.
2. **Damaged Witness:**
   His favoritism undermines his credibility. James 2:1–4 warns against showing partiality:

   "My brothers, show no partiality as you hold the faith in our Lord Jesus Christ, the Lord of glory."

3. **Missed Discipleship Opportunities:**
   Potential leaders of color are overlooked. His implicit bias prevents him from recognizing the spiritual gifts of those unlike himself (1 Corinthians 12:21–26).

On His Personal Life:

1. **Spiritual Blindness and Hardened Heart:**
   Edwin lives with a sin he refuses to see, which grieves the Holy Spirit (Ephesians 4:30–32). Over time, bitterness defiles not only his heart but his joy and peace.
2. **Isolation from the Full Body of Christ:**
   By limiting his relational circle, he forfeits the richness of relationships across cultures, backgrounds, and perspectives, which the gospel invites.
3. **False Righteousness:**
   Edwin may feel morally upright while walking in darkness (1 John 2:9–11).

"Whoever says he is in the light and hates his brother is still in darkness."

What Should Pastor Snow Do About His Racism?

1. **Confess and Repent:**
   He must begin with honest confession before God (Psalm 139:23–24) and true repentance.
   "If we confess our sins, he is faithful and just to forgive us..." (1 John 1:9)
2. **Seek Accountability and Racial Reconciliation Training:**
   Edwin should engage in soul-searching conversations, seek mentorship from diverse leaders, and participate in anti-racism discipleship that is rooted in Scripture.
3. **Apologize and Make Amends:**
   Public or private apology to those he has hurt or excluded, and concrete steps to make amends, are necessary (Luke 19:8).
4. **Pursue Sanctification in This Area:**
   Like all sin, racism must be actively put to death (Colossians 3:5–11).
   "Here there is not Greek and Jew...but Christ is all, and in all." (v.11)

What Should the Church Do?

1. **Confront Sin Honestly:**
   The elders or church leadership must lovingly confront Pastor Snow (Galatians 6:1) and offer support for repentance and restoration.
2. **Promote a Culture of Gospel Unity:**
   The church should intentionally disciple its members to reflect Christ-centered unity across racial and ethnic lines (Ephesians 2:14–22).
3. **Create Space for Diverse Leadership:**
   The church should identify and empower believers of different backgrounds to lead and shape the church's mission and culture.

Biblical Solution and Framework
Key Scriptures:

- **Micah 6:8** – *"What does the Lord require of you? To act justly, to love mercy, and to walk humbly with your God."*
- **Ephesians 2:14–16** – *"For he himself is our peace, who has made the two groups one and has destroyed the barrier... making peace."*
- **Romans 12:2** – *"Do not conform to the pattern of this world, but be transformed by the renewing of your mind."*
- **James 2:8–9** – *"If you really fulfill the royal law according to the Scripture, 'You shall love your neighbor as yourself,' you are doing well. But if you show partiality, you are committing sin..."*
- **Galatians 3:28** – *"There is neither Jew nor Greek... for you are all one in Christ Jesus."*

The Story of Marilyn Sykes: A Secret Burden and the Strain of Racial Idolatry

Marilyn Sykes grew up in the heart of the Deep South, in a conservative white neighborhood of Mobile, Alabama. Her childhood was, in her own words, "uneventful." Her family attended church regularly, upheld traditional values, and lived a life that seemed respectable and morally upright. Marilyn attended a predominantly white high school where she found friendship with another quiet and thoughtful girl named Joyce Singleton. The two were inseparable. Reserved and modest, they found comfort in each other's silence and security in their sameness.

Marilyn had no interest in sports, but one Friday night, Joyce convinced her to attend their school's homecoming football game. It was there, amidst the roar of the crowd and the bright lights of the stadium, that Marilyn encountered a moment that would quietly, but powerfully, alter the course of her inner world.

Seated near the sidelines, she caught sight of several black players warming up - strong, focused, athletic young men. Their physicality, their presence, their very difference from the world she had known up to that point mesmerized her. For the first time in her life, Marilyn's mind was flooded with unfamiliar, even forbidden, thoughts. She became obsessed, not with individuals, but with the idea, the image, the mystery she had been shielded from her entire life. It was a secret attraction, shaped more by cultural repression and fantasy than reality. Still, it planted seeds that would never quite die.

She never spoke of it, not to Joyce, not to her parents, not to any pastor or counselor.

Years later, Marilyn married James Wittington, a kind, respectable white Christian man she met after college. He was everything a Southern Christian family would hope for, stable, hardworking, and active in their church. They had three children and raised them with prayer, discipline, and Sunday School lessons. From the outside, theirs was the picture of a good Christian home.

But Marilyn carried a dark secret. The thoughts that had begun years ago still haunted her dreams. Her mind would drift to the images and fantasies she had suppressed for decades. She hated herself for it. She prayed, she wept, but she never told a soul. Until one day, broken by the weight of her inner turmoil, she called the one person she believed she could trust, her lifelong friend Joyce.

Unbeknown to Marilyn, that very afternoon, James had left work early to surprise her with a dinner date. Entering the house quietly, he overheard Marilyn speaking on the phone to Joyce. The words stunned him. His wife, the woman he had trusted and built a life with, was pouring out her heart about her racialized sexual fantasies, fantasies that excluded him and betrayed the ideals he believed they shared.

James didn't confront her. He walked out of the house silently, shattered, disillusioned, and confused. But something changed. Over the following months, his behavior darkened. He became distant and short-tempered. His anger over spilled milk or forgotten errands turned into outbursts of rage. The children noticed. Marilyn noticed. But no one spoke the truth.

They still attended church as a family. They still sat in the same pew and sang the same hymns. But their worship was empty and hollow. Both were drowning in isolation, Marilyn in shame, James in betrayal.

Reflection Questions: (Take a pause to ponder the following questions.)
- What should Marilyn do?
- What should James do?
- What should Joyce do?
- How should the church respond?
- What does this reveal about how racism and suppressed sin can poison even "good" Christian homes?

Spiritual and Scriptural Analysis

Marilyn and James's story is a tragic window into how deeply racism and worldly lust can entangle even those who claim Christ. Marilyn's fantasies were not merely about attraction, they were shaped by racial curiosity and degrading a race to a status of mere objects, a product of a segregated, idol-driven culture that sexualized what it suppressed. James's anger, though rooted in betrayal, was inflamed by racial pride, identity, and fear of inadequacy.

Marilyn's Heart: The Call to Confession and Renewal

"Therefore confess your sins to one another and pray for one another, that you may be healed." - James 5:16 (ESV)

Marilyn needs grace, but grace requires truth. She must confess, not only her thoughts, but the deeper prejudice and fantasy that became idols in her heart. Her issue is not merely one of desire, but of unhealed wounds shaped by a racialized culture that she never confronted.

"Flee from sexual immorality... You are not your own, for you were bought with a price." - 1 Corinthians 6:18-20

Marilyn's thoughts violated the spiritual purity God calls His children to uphold. Healing begins with repentance and renewal through God's Word.

James's Heart: Confronting Rage and Seeking Redemption

"Be angry and do not sin; do not let the sun go down on your anger... and give no opportunity to the devil." - Ephesians 4:26–27

James must not allow betrayal to turn to bitterness. His pain is real, but rage is not the answer. Silence will not heal wounds. He must seek counsel, even confront Marilyn with grace, and invite God to bring peace to his soul.

Joyce's Role: A True Friend and Wise Counselor

"Faithful are the wounds of a friend; profuse are the kisses of an enemy." - Proverbs 27:6

Joyce must speak the truth in love. She cannot be a passive listener. She must encourage Marilyn to bring her secret into the light and seek spiritual help. A friend who stays silent in the face of sin is not a true friend.

The Church's Role: A Place for Truth and Healing

"Brothers, if anyone is caught in any transgression, you who are spiritual should restore him in a spirit of gentleness." - Galatians 6:1

Too many churches ignore the intersection of racial idolatry and spiritual bondage. This is a chance for the church to minister through biblical counseling, discipleship, and racial reconciliation, not just for Marilyn and James, but for all families secretly suffering under the weight of shame, fantasy, and cultural sin.

Path to Spiritual Wholeness

- **Confession:** Both Marilyn and James need to acknowledge their sin, Marilyn for her secret indulgence; James for his silent rage.
- **Repentance:** True change requires turning from fantasy, anger, and prejudice, and turning to Christ.
- **Forgiveness:** They must forgive one another, not because they "feel" like it, but because Christ has forgiven them.
- **Counseling:** With the help of trained biblical counselors, they must process not just the hurt, but the deeper issues of identity, race, intimacy, and faith.
- **Community:** They must not isolate. Healing requires community. The church must provide a safe space for truth, confession, and restoration.

This is not merely a story of private struggle. It is a spiritual tragedy born from racial myths, cultural silence, and unspoken shame. Yet it is not beyond redemption. God can take brokenness

- racial, marital, emotional - and turn it into something whole. But only if His people are willing to confront the truth, forsake the world's lies, and walk in the light.

"But if we walk in the light, as he is in the light, we have fellowship with one another, and the blood of Jesus his Son cleanses us from all sin." - 1 John 1:7

Gospel Response:

The gospel of Jesus Christ tears down every dividing wall and unites all believers into one body. Racism, whether explicit or subtle, has no place in the life of a Christ-follower.

The cross brings reconciliation, not only between God and humanity but between people groups (2 Corinthians 5:17–19). The solution is not worldly diversity for its own sake, but Spirit-led reconciliation rooted in the blood of Christ.

Conclusion: Christ's Love Knows No Color Line

Christians are called to a love that breaks barriers, builds bridges, and reflects the boundless grace of God. Racism is contrary to the gospel, yet many remain trapped by it because of fear, pride, ignorance, or indifference.

To love like Jesus means to see every person as a divine image-bearer, to listen to the cries of the oppressed, and to pursue justice and unity with courage.

The Church must no longer remain a mirror of the world's divisions. It must become the radiant example of Christ's love in action. This love does not stay silent in the face of injustice. It does not retreat to comfort. It stretches wide, as Jesus did on the cross, to embrace all of humanity, every tribe, tongue, and nation.

<u>Personal Reflection Questions</u>

1. Have I ever silently tolerated racist comments or attitudes among friends, family, or fellow Christians?
2. Do I harbor any unspoken biases or assumptions about people of a different race or ethnicity?

3. How has my upbringing or environment influenced my view of other races?
4. Have I confused cultural comfort with spiritual righteousness in my church or community?
5. Do I genuinely seek relationships with people of different racial or ethnic backgrounds?
6. Have I ever justified racism using Scripture or remained silent when it was misused?
7. Do I reflect Christ's reconciling love in the way I treat and speak about people who are different from me?
8. Have I repented of any racist attitudes, behaviors, or passivity in confronting racism?
9. Do I pray regularly for racial unity in the Church and for God to expose any hidden prejudice in me?
10. Am I willing to take steps toward reconciliation and justice, even if it costs me comfort, approval or restitution (Luke 19:1-10)?
11. Can I truly love someone of another race as much as I love myself? More than myself? (John 13:34, the foundation for Christianity.)
12. Am I harboring any dark secrets about race relations that I should confess and perhaps seek counseling?

Group Discussion Questions

1. Why is racism a spiritual issue and not just a social or political one?
2. How has the Church historically failed to address racism, and what are the consequences of that failure?
3. In what ways can modern churches move from racial tolerance to genuine reconciliation and unity?
4. What role should pastors and church leaders play in confronting racism within their congregations?
5. How can Christians identify and confront subtle forms of racism in their own hearts and communities?
6. What does true biblical repentance look like in the context of racism?
7. How can the Gospel reshape the way we understand race, ethnicity, and justice?
8. How should Christians respond when fellow believers deny the existence of institutional racism?

9. What does Revelation 7:9 teach us about God's vision for the diversity of His kingdom?
10. What practical steps can your church take to embody racial unity and justice?

Prayer of Repentance and Deliverance

Heavenly Father,

I come before You with a humble and contrite heart. I acknowledge that racism is a sin, one that grieves Your heart and distorts Your image in humanity. Lord, if there is any prejudice, hatred, or pride in my heart, I ask You to expose it by the light of Your Holy Spirit.

Forgive me, O God, for any ways I have participated in, ignored, or justified racism. Forgive me for my silence when I should have spoken, for my indifference when I should have cared, my selfishness when I should have given, and for my complacency when I should have acted.

I renounce every lie that says one race is superior to another. I declare that every person is made in Your image and is deeply loved by You. I ask You to deliver me from the grip of any sinful mindset that separates or exalts.

Give me a new heart, Lord. Fill me with compassion, courage, and conviction to live out the unity of the Gospel. Let me be a vessel of Your justice, mercy, and reconciliation. Help me to speak truth in love, to build bridges, and to tear down walls.

Cleanse me, renew me, and use me to bring healing to a divided world. May the Church rise up as a light of unity, love, and truth, reflecting Your glory in every tribe, tongue, and nation.

In Jesus' name I pray,

Amen.

Chapter 11

Honoring and Celebrating Pagan Holidays and Events

One of the most subtle and destructive forms of worldliness infiltrating the Church today is the honoring and celebration of pagan-rooted holidays and celebrations—cloaked in Christian language but filled with traditions and practices that have no foundation in the Word of God. Chief among these are **Christmas** and **Easter**, the two main events of the Christian calendar. They are widely embraced by the professing Christian world yet deeply rooted in pagan worship and mythology.

The **1st-century Christian Church** did **not celebrate Christmas or Easter** because these holidays—**as we know them today**—did **not exist** and had **no basis in the teachings or practices of the Apostles or early believers. Here's why:**

---

1. The Focus of the Early Church Was Obedience and Spiritual Purity

The early Church, established by the Apostles and empowered by the Holy Spirit, was deeply committed to preserving the **purity of the gospel** and avoiding anything that even resembled **idolatry** or **paganism**. Their worship was simple, Spirit-led, and centered on:

- The **resurrection** of Jesus, celebrated **weekly on the first day (Sunday),** not annually (Acts 20:7; 1 Corinthians 16:2).
- The **Lord's Supper**, commemorating Christ's death (1 Corinthians 11:23–26).
- Prayer, teaching, and fellowship (Acts 2:42).

They **did not create man-made holidays** to commemorate events like Christ's birth or resurrection. Their daily lives were lived in the **reality of those truths**, not in ceremonial observances borrowed from pagan cultures.

2. Christmas Was Not Instituted Until Centuries Later

There is **no biblical record or apostolic teaching** that suggests the early Christians ever celebrated the birth of Jesus.

- The New Testament is **silent** on celebrating Jesus' birth.
- The **birth date of Jesus was unknown**, and early Church leaders like **Origen (3rd century)** explicitly **opposed celebrating birthdays**, considering it a **pagan practice**.
- It wasn't until the **4th century—hundreds of years after Christ**—that December 25th was officially recognized as the date to celebrate Jesus' birth, chosen **not based on Scripture** but to **absorb the pagan Roman festival of Saturnalia and Sol Invictus.**

3. "Easter" Was Not Celebrated as It Is Today

The early Christians did **remember and honor the resurrection of Jesus**—but not with pagan symbols like eggs, bunnies, or spring festivals which are an abomination in God's Kingdom.

- The resurrection was **remembered every Sunday**, not once a year.
- The word "**Easter**" doesn't appear in the Bible in its true form. The King James Version mistranslates **Pascha** (Greek for Passover) as "Easter" in Acts 12:4, but the correct reference is to the **Jewish Passover**, not a spring festival.
- The early Church **connected Christ's death and resurrection with Passover**, not with a new holiday.
- Pagan customs (like fertility goddesses, eggs, and rabbits) were **later merged** with Christian observances during **the Roman Catholic syncretism of the 4th–6th centuries.**

4. Early Christians Avoided Pagan Influences

The early believers were surrounded by Roman and Greek paganism—idols, temples, festivals, and rituals. They were under constant pressure to conform, but they resisted strongly:

"You turned to God from idols to serve the living and true God."— 1 Thessalonians 1:9

"Do not be conformed to this world, but be transformed by the renewal of your mind…"— Romans 12:2

They saw the world's customs as **dangerous** and spiritually **corrupt**, often tied to **demonic practices** (1 Corinthians 10:20). Introducing even seemingly harmless traditions from the world was considered a **threat to their spiritual purity**.

Facts, Warnings, and Recommendation

1. The Pagan Origin of Christmas

Though Christians are taught that Christmas is the celebration of the birth of Jesus Christ, historical evidence reveals that **December 25th** has no biblical connection to the actual birth of Christ. Instead, it was originally a pagan festival.

- **Saturnalia**: In ancient Rome, December 17–25 marked **Saturnalia**, a festival in honor of **Saturn**, the god of agriculture. This time was filled with gift-giving, feasting, drunkenness, and role reversals.
- **Sol Invictus**: December 25th was celebrated as the birthday of the **sun god**, **Sol Invictus**—"the unconquered sun"—as the days began to grow longer after the winter solstice.
- When Christianity spread through the Roman Empire, church leaders—desiring to convert pagans—**adopted and Christianized** these festivals, merging the pagan celebration of the sun god with the story of the **Son of God**.

Christmas customs such as the **Yule log**, **decorated trees**, **mistletoe**, and **Santa Claus** are all rooted in **pagan Norse**, **Druid**, and **Roman** traditions.

2. The Pagan Origin of Easter

Easter, often associated with the resurrection of Jesus, is another holiday layered with paganism.

- The very name "**Easter**" is believed to be derived from **Ēostre (or Ostara)**, a fertility goddess in Anglo-Saxon paganism.
- The **egg** and **rabbit**, prominent symbols of Easter, were symbols of fertility and new life long before Christ's resurrection. Pagans used these in springtime festivals celebrating the **rebirth of nature**, not the resurrection of the Savior.
- The timing of Easter is determined by the **spring equinox and the full moon**—a practice rooted in ancient lunar and solar worship.

The resurrection of Jesus Christ, a cornerstone of the Christian faith, is not honored through biblical instruction with eggs, rabbits, or sunrise services—but rather through **daily holy living** and remembering His death and resurrection during the **Lord's Supper (1 Corinthians 11:23–26)**.

3. Why Christians Should Not Celebrate These Holidays – A Biblical Warning

God has always commanded His people to **separate themselves** from the customs of the ungodly:

"Thus says the Lord: Do not learn the way of the nations..." — Jeremiah 10:2 (ESV)

This is immediately followed by a description of what sounds eerily similar to decorating a Christmas tree:

"...for the customs of the peoples are vanity. A tree from the forest is cut down and worked with an axe by the hands of a craftsman. They decorate it with silver and gold..." — Jeremiah 10:3–4 (ESV)

God is clear that He detests syncretism—the blending of His truth with pagan practice.

"What fellowship has light with darkness? What accord has Christ with Belial?" — 2 Corinthians 6:14–15

"You cannot drink the cup of the Lord and the cup of demons. You cannot partake of the table of the Lord and the table of demons." — 1 Corinthians 10:21

When Christians engage in pagan-rooted celebrations—even with good intentions—they open the door to **spiritual strongholds**, confusion, and compromise. These celebrations often become **idolatrous**, exalting tradition, materialism, and worldly fun above the holiness and truth of God.

4. Evil Strongholds Through Pagan Celebrations

Participating in and honoring worldly holidays is spiritually damaging. Over time, it leads to:

- **Spiritual dullness**: Replacing biblical truth with emotional traditions.
- **Idolatry**: Elevating man-made customs and symbols.
- **Demonic influence**: Pagan rituals were often tied to idol worship and demonic powers. Reviving these rituals invites spiritual bondage.
- **Corrupted witness**: When Christians celebrate what the world celebrates, they lose their distinction and compromise their testimony as witnessed in today's church.

Many Christians report feelings of emptiness, stress, or depression during these holidays—a spiritual backlash of participating in something that dishonors God.

5. The Church's Role in Promoting Pagan Holidays

The institutional Church has played a significant role in this deception. From the **Roman Catholic Church** to many **modern Protestant denominations**, there has been a systematic promotion of these festivals:

- In the **4th century**, the Roman Catholic Church **officially adopted December 25th** as Christ's birthday—despite no biblical basis—to make Christianity more palatable to pagans in the Roman society.
- The **Council of Nicaea (325 A.D.)** helped set the date for **Easter**, aligning it with pagan lunar cycles.

- Church leaders allowed **syncretism**—the blending of Christian and pagan elements—to **attract converts**, not realizing the long-term consequences of such compromise.

Today, many churches **host Easter egg hunts, decorate trees**, and preach "holiday sermons" that **ignore the origins** of these practices rather than use these holidays as opportunities for warning the body of Christ regarding their embedded evilness. Instead of calling the body to holiness and separation, many churches have become promoters of **worldly traditions** disguised as worship.

6. A Call to Return to Biblical Faithfulness

God is calling His people to come out from Babylon and reject every form of compromise:

"Come out of her, my people, lest you take part in her sins, lest you share in her plagues."— Revelation 18:4

True worship is **in spirit and in truth (John 4:24)**—not in rituals borrowed from paganism. Christ is not honored by trees, ornaments, rabbits, or eggs. He is honored when we obey His Word, walk in holiness, and reject the ways of the world.

Christians must **discern the spiritual danger** in adopting and celebrating holidays with roots in darkness. Just because a tradition is widely accepted—even by churches—doesn't make it pleasing to God. **Satan has effectively used institutional religion as his primary tool for deception.**

Eternal Warnings

1. **God does not accept worship that is blended with paganism.**

    "In vain do they worship me, teaching as doctrines the commandments of men."— Mark 7:7

2. **Compromise leads to spiritual deception.**
    "For the time will come when people will not endure sound teaching... and will turn away from listening to the truth and wander off into myths."— 2 Timothy 4:3–4

3. **Participating in worldly practices can open doors to demonic strongholds.**

   "They sacrificed to demons that were no gods... they stirred him to jealousy with strange gods. -Deuteronomy 32:17, 16

4. **God will judge those who refuse to separate from Babylon.**

   "Come out of her, my people... for her sins are heaped high as heaven, and God has remembered her iniquities."— Revelation 18:4–5

5. **The broad path of tradition leads to destruction.**
   "Enter by the narrow gate... For the gate is wide and the way is easy that leads to destruction, and those who enter by it are many."— Matthew 7:13

Summary: Why the Early Church Rejected These Holidays

Holiday	Not Celebrated in 1st Century Because...
Christmas	No biblical command; Jesus' birth date unknown; birthdays were pagan customs; festival introduced centuries later to replace pagan sun-god celebrations.
Easter	Name and symbols derived from pagan spring goddess worship; early Christians remembered the resurrection during weekly worship and Passover—not with a paganized festival.

The Early Church's Model: A Warning for Today

The **1st-century Church** is our **biblical model**. They walked in **power, purity, and separation from the world**. They did not

~ 141 ~

need seasonal traditions to feel close to Christ—they lived in continual fellowship with Him.

When modern Christians adopt holidays that the early Church avoided, they **depart from the apostolic foundation** and **open themselves to deception**, worldliness, and spiritual compromise.

CHRISTMAS – Timeline of Introduction

Date	Event	Details
1st–2nd Century	No celebration of Jesus' birth	Early Christians focused on the resurrection and avoided birthday celebrations, viewing them as **pagan and worldly**.
ca. 200 A.D.	Some begin speculating about Jesus' birth date	A few early writers like Clement of Alexandria mention theories, but no official holiday exists.
ca. 245 A.D.	Origen condemns birthday celebrations	Church Father Origen writes that celebrating birthdays is **a pagan custom**, not fitting for saints.
274 A.D.	Roman Emperor Aurelian institutes "Dies Natalis Solis Invicti"	December 25th is declared the **"Birthday of the Unconquered Sun"**, honoring the **sun god Sol Invictus**.
336 A.D.	First recorded Roman celebration of Jesus' birth on December 25th	Church leaders begin merging **sun-god worship** with Christianity, **Christianizing** pagan festivals to ease the empire's transition to the faith.
350 A.D.	Pope Julius I officially declares December 25th as Jesus' birthday	This institutionalizes the **compromise**, despite no scriptural basis.
4th–6th	Pagan symbols and	Many **northern European**

~ 142 ~

Date	Event	Details
Centuries	customs added (e.g., Yule logs, holly, trees)	**traditions** were baptized into "Christian" practice.
Middle Ages	Christmas becomes a public festival with drunkenness and revelry	Often marked by **wild behavior**, far from honoring Christ.
17th Century	Puritans in England and America **ban Christmas**	Considered a **pagan and sinful holiday**, outlawed in places like **Massachusetts** (1659–1681).
19th Century	Christmas revived as a sentimental holiday	Authors like **Charles Dickens** and poets reshape it as a family-centered, gift-giving celebration.
20th–21st Centuries	Christmas becomes highly commercialized	The modern focus is on **Santa Claus, gifts, lights, and consumerism**, with **little to no biblical foundation** remaining.

EASTER – Timeline of Introduction

Date	Event	Details
1st Century	Christians remember Jesus' resurrection weekly	Early believers gathered **every Sunday** to commemorate the resurrection (Acts 20:7).
2nd Century	Disputes arise over **when to celebrate the resurrection**	Some commemorate it during **Passover (Nisan 14)**; others on the **Sunday after Passover**. This is called the **Quartodeciman controversy**.
325 A.D.	**Council of Nicaea** sets the official date for "Easter"	Under Emperor Constantine, the Church breaks ties with **Jewish Passover** and **aligns**

~ 143 ~

Date	Event	Details
		with pagan solar calendar (Sunday after the full moon following the spring equinox).
4th Century	Name "Easter" introduced (in English/Germanic regions)	Derived from **Eostre**, an Anglo-Saxon **fertility goddess** worshipped in spring.
4th–6th Centuries	Pagan fertility symbols added: eggs, rabbits, sunrise	These ancient symbols of fertility and rebirth were blended into the celebration of Christ's resurrection.
Middle Ages	Church services include sunrise rituals and blessing of eggs	Further pagan elements are integrated under the appearance of Christian symbolism.
16th Century	Protestant Reformers challenge some Easter customs	Reformers like Zwingli and Calvin opposed many traditions, yet the name and symbols persisted.
19th–20th Centuries	Easter bunny, candy, and egg hunts emerge	Commercialism and secular customs now dominate the celebration in the West.

Summary of Pagan Influences & Church Compromise

Holiday	Pagan Origin	Christian Adoption	Compromises Introduced
Christmas	Roman Saturnalia & Sol Invictus (sun worship)	336 A.D. (first recorded observance); 350 A.D. (official)	Yule logs, evergreen trees, gift-giving, Santa Claus
Easter	Spring fertility	Post-Nicaea	Easter eggs,

Holiday	Pagan Origin	Christian Adoption	Compromises Introduced
	festivals honoring **Eostre/Ishtar**	(325 A.D.)	rabbits, sunrise services, pagan dating system

Final Thoughts

These holidays **were not instituted by Jesus or the Apostles**, nor were they practiced by the **1st-century Church**. Instead, they were **gradually introduced over centuries** as part of a larger effort to **blend Christianity with the Roman Empire's pagan religions**.

Rather than rejecting false worship, the institutional church **baptized pagan rituals** to make Christianity more appealing to the masses. This compromise has led generations into **spiritual confusion**, idolatry, and worldliness disguised as Christian tradition.

"You have let go of the commands of God and are holding on to human traditions." — Mark 7:8

We will conclude this chapter with the story of Sister Mattie Crockett. We will purposely detail her experience for the edification of the remnant of believers who are frustrated with the status quo and truly feel in their hearts that God is leading them to a higher calling for a greater purpose in His Kingdom.

Sister Crockett's Awakening: From Festivities and Religiosity to Faithfulness

Sister Mattie Crockett was a pillar in her local church. She was a respected, gentle-spirited woman known for her faithfulness, hospitality, and radiant smile. At 63 years old, she served as church secretary in one of the city's largest denominational churches. She had been a part of that congregation for decades and rarely missed a service, meeting, Bible study, or prayer breakfast. Raised in a devout Christian home, Sister Crockett had lived her entire life immersed in the church and its traditions.

Christmas was always her favorite time of year. Her eyes would light up every December as the sanctuary was draped in garlands and twinkling lights. Her heart would warm as she remembered her childhood role as Mary in the church's annual nativity play. She could still recall the laughter of children as they helped decorate the fellowship hall Christmas tree and the aroma of spiced apple cider coming from the church's kitchen.

But everything changed one quiet evening.

As she sat on her couch folding bulletins and half-watching a late-night Christian broadcast, a statement from a televangelist pierced her like a sword.

"Christians," he said firmly, "have no business celebrating Christmas. It is a pagan holiday cloaked in religious deception."

The words stunned her. For days she couldn't shake them. At first, she dismissed it as extreme rhetoric. But the seed of curiosity had been planted. She had to know the truth.

Armed with her Bible and the internet, Sister Crockett began to study. What she uncovered shocked her. The origin of Christmas was tied to ancient Roman festivals and the worship of false gods. The use of evergreen trees and Yule logs was rooted in pagan winter solstice rituals. Even the date of December 25th had no biblical basis for the birth of Christ. She discovered that the date of Christ's birth was unknown and was most likely to have been in the fall season of the year when shepherds would be in the fields keeping watch over their flocks (Lk. 2:8), not winter.

The more she learned, the more disturbed she became. *How could something so beloved, so cherished in her Christian journey, be so deeply rooted in deception?* She sat in silence, questioning all she had been taught.

Her thoughts then turned to her former pastors, four men of God she had trusted through the decades. *Why didn't any of them ever mention this?* Why had they all faithfully overseen nativity plays, Christmas musicals, and holiday offerings without a single word about the truth?

What began as curiosity soon turned to righteous indignation.

Determined to dig deeper, she researched other celebrated holidays. The results contradicted her lifelong understandings and Christian beliefs. Easter with its fertility symbols of eggs and rabbits, Valentine's Day tied to Roman gods and mythologies, Halloween and Mardi Gras, drenched in the occult and unbridled fleshly indulgence were all deeply disturbing to her. Each discovery made her heart grieve more deeply. These were not harmless traditions—they were spiritual traps.

Her study didn't stop there. She began to examine church practices she had accepted over her lifetime.

One evening, while studying biblical giving, she was confronted with yet another startling revelation: the modern-day teaching on tithing, binding Christians to a rigid 10% requirement of their income, was not supported by New Testament nor Old Testament Scriptures. She began to realize that her pastors had been using Biblical scriptures out of context to make their argument for the Biblical basis for paying 10% of her income for church support. She began to see tithing as a stumbling block that distorted the heart of Christian discipleship, which calls for complete surrender as implied in God's "Great Commandment" of love. She came to the realization that Christian Discipleship necessitated a dedication of all of her resources to the glory of God, not paying 10% of her income to a religious institution (Reference *"The Fanaticism of Christian Discipleship for more information).*

The institutional church, the very place she once found comfort and community, now felt foreign. After much prayer and fasting, Sister Crockett made the hardest decision of her life: she left her church, not in bitterness, but in obedience. She still loved her former church family, but she could not ignore the truth. She knew God was calling her to something deeper.

Lonely yet determined, she cried out to God for direction. And slowly, He began to lead her. What started as a simple Friday night Bible study in her home, just her, two cousins, and a neighbor, soon grew. Others, many from her former church, came, hungry for the truth, weary of religious showmanship disguising deception. Sister Crockett taught with grace and boldness, uncompromising in her stand against spiritual deception.

In less than a year, they outgrew her living room and relocated to a small rented facility. Today, that Friday night Bible study has blossomed into a thriving gathering of believers committed to living by the Word of God and walking in spiritual truth.

Sister Crockett never imagined her golden years would look like this. She thought she'd live out her days printing bulletins and decorating Christmas trees. But God had other plans.

She is no longer decorating the sanctuary with holiday tinsel—she is adorning souls with truth.

What once deceived her now fuels her mission. And through her obedience, many are being set free from the grip of worldly traditions disguised as Christian celebrations.

Sister Crockett's experience reveals the tragic reality that many well-meaning Christians are unknowingly trapped in traditions and practices that are not rooted in Scripture but in paganism. The blending of pagan customs with Christian worship pollutes the holiness of God's people and invites spiritual confusion.

"My people are destroyed for lack of knowledge..."
— Hosea 4:6

Celebrating holidays like Christmas, Easter, and Halloween that have origins in idol worship is a form of **syncretism**, the mixing of truth with error. God repeatedly warns His people not to adopt the customs of pagan nations, especially in worship.

"Take heed to yourself that you are not ensnared to follow them...and that you do not inquire after their gods, saying, 'How did these nations serve their gods? I also will do likewise.' You shall not worship the Lord your God in that way..."— Deuteronomy 12:30–31

Sister Crockett's long-time participation in these traditions dulled her discernment and kept her in spiritual bondage for years. This shows how cultural and religious compromise can blind Christians from recognizing error, even when it surrounds them.

"Having a form of godliness, but denying the power thereof: from such turn away."— 2 Timothy 3:5

Once she began to seek truth and examine Scripture for herself, the Holy Spirit opened her eyes. This affirms that God will guide those who diligently seek Him, even if it means stepping away from traditional religious structures.

"You will seek Me and find Me, when you search for Me with all your heart."— Jeremiah 29:13

Celebrating pagan-rooted holidays, even under a Christian label, is still **idolatry** in God's eyes. God does not accept worship that is mingled with the traditions of false gods. Unrepentant idolatry has eternal consequences.

"But the cowardly, unbelieving, abominable, murderers, sexually immoral, sorcerers, idolaters, and all liars shall have their part in the lake which burns with fire and brimstone..." - Revelation 21:8

Sister Crockett's discovery that none of her pastors warned her of these truths reveals a sobering reality: spiritual leaders will be held accountable for what they teach, or fail to teach, the flock.

"His watchmen are blind... they are shepherds who cannot understand... they all look to their own way..."- Isaiah 56:10–11

"Son of man, I have made you a watchman... if you do not speak to warn the wicked... his blood I will require at your hand."— Ezekiel 3:17–18

Sister Crockett had lived her life assuming that her participation in church traditions made her spiritually safe. Her awakening underscores that religious tradition cannot substitute for truth. Many will stand before God thinking they served Him, only to discover that they were never aligned with His will.

"Not everyone who says to Me, 'Lord, Lord,' shall enter the kingdom of heaven... Many will say to Me in that day, 'Lord, Lord, have we not prophesied in Your name...? And then I will declare to them, 'I never knew you; depart from Me, you who practice lawlessness!'"— Matthew 7:21–23

Sister Crockett's story is not just a personal awakening—it is a clarion call to the Church. Her courage to step away from man-made traditions and seek biblical truth demonstrates what it means to **worship God in spirit and in truth**. The spiritual ramifications of celebrating pagan holidays extend beyond harmless tradition. They risk cultivating false worship, dulling spiritual discernment, and leading souls away from the holiness God requires.

Her life is now a testimony that obedience to God's Word, even when it is uncomfortable, leads to spiritual freedom and eternal reward.

Scriptural References Supporting Her Journey

- **Romans 12:2** – *"Do not be conformed to this world, but be transformed by the renewing of your mind…"*
- **2 Corinthians 6:14–17** – *"What fellowship has righteousness with lawlessness?… Come out from among them and be separate, says the Lord."*
- **Ephesians 5:11** – *"And have no fellowship with the unfruitful works of darkness, but rather expose them."*
- **Acts 17:30** – *"Truly, these times of ignorance God overlooked, but now commands all men everywhere to repent…"*
- **John 4:23–24** – *"True worshipers will worship the Father in spirit and truth…"*

Conclusion

The deception of celebrating pagan holidays like Christmas and Easter is one of the most widespread traps of worldliness affecting the Church today.

Though often embraced with good intentions, these celebrations **open the door to evil strongholds**, **blur the lines between holy and profane**, and **hinder spiritual growth**.

The Church must repent of promoting such customs and return to **radical obedience** and **pure biblical worship** based on Scriptural integrity that is untainted by the world.

Only then can the light of Christ truly shine through His people.

Group Discussion Questions

1. What are some popular holidays celebrated by Christians that have questionable or known pagan roots?
2. How has the church historically justified the adoption of pagan traditions into Christian worship?
3. Read Jeremiah 10:1–4 and 2 Corinthians 6:14–17. What do these scriptures reveal about God's stance on mixing pagan customs with worship?
4. Why do many believers continue to celebrate holidays like Christmas and Easter, even after learning about their origins?
5. What dangers (spiritually or emotionally) have you personally witnessed or experienced during the celebration of worldly holidays?
6. What would true biblical separation from pagan customs look like in a believer's life today?
7. How can we graciously explain our convictions to family, friends, or churches without causing unnecessary division?
8. How might celebrating worldly holidays affect the next generation's understanding of God's holiness?
9. What are some biblical alternatives to honoring Christ without participating in these worldly traditions?
10. Is it possible that honoring these holidays could become a spiritual stronghold in a believer's life? Why or why not?

Prayer of Repentance and Correction

Heavenly Father,

I come before You in humility and truth. I acknowledge that I have participated in traditions and celebrations that were not birthed in Your Word but rooted in the world and in idolatry. Forgive me, Lord, for honoring what You have not commanded and for giving place to rituals that dishonor Your holiness.

Open my eyes to see the truth. Cleanse me from the influence of pagan practices, no matter how accepted they may be in society or even in the church. I repent of following the traditions of men over the commands of God. I renounce any spiritual strongholds that have formed in my life or within my family through these ungodly celebrations.

Lead me in the way of righteousness. Help me to walk in holiness, to worship You in spirit and in truth, and to separate myself from the patterns of this world. Strengthen me to take a bold stand in love and truth, even when it is unpopular or misunderstood.

Lord, purify Your Church. Expose the deceptions that have crept in and call us back to pure, undefiled worship as experienced in Your first-century church. May we be a people set apart for You alone. I surrender my traditions, my comforts, and my habits to You.

Replace them with obedience, reverence, and truth.
In the name of Jesus Christ, the only true Savior and King, I pray.
Amen.

(The information in this chapter can be found in the following resources. We recommend them for additional information and clarification: www.eternalcog.org, TomorrowsWorld.org, fwa@faithfulword.com, and radiomissions.org.)

Chapter 12

False Teachers and Celebrity Preachers

The Bible repeatedly warns of a sobering reality: not everyone who preaches in the name of Jesus is sent by Him. In fact, some are wolves in sheep's clothing (Matthew 7:15), hired hands who care more about applause than accountability, and shepherds who feed themselves instead of the flock.

False teachers aren't always easy to spot. They often use Scripture. They sound convincing. They wear suits, have degrees, and fill stadiums. But their messages are hollow. Their gospel is another gospel, a watered-down, self-help version that emphasizes blessing without obedience, purpose without repentance, and grace without truth. False teachers often come packaged with smiles, eloquence, and popularity. They use Christian phrases, but twist their meaning. They build large audiences, but lead them away from truth.

Not every voice behind a pulpit is speaking truth. In an age of media saturation and global platforms, anyone with charisma and influence can rise to prominence, even if their message contradicts the Word of God. The Church today faces a dangerous trend: the rise of celebrity preachers and the spread of false teaching cloaked in Christian language.

Jesus warned us:

"For false Christs and false prophets will appear and perform great signs and wonders to deceive, if possible, even the elect." — Matthew 24:24

The presence of false teachers within Christianity is not a modern phenomenon. It is a timeless threat that has existed since the earliest days of the church and continues to this day, more subtle and more dangerous than ever. These individuals do not always appear as wolves, they often come cloaked in sheep's clothing (Matthew 7:15), using the language of the church, citing Scripture, and appealing to emotions while subtly diverting believers from the truth of God's Word.

In this chapter, we expose the growing danger of false teaching in the Church and how it contributes to the trap of worldliness.

The Scripture's Warnings About False Teachers

The Bible issues stern and repeated warnings against false teachers. These are not optional warnings, they are essential for the survival of the faithful.

1. Jesus' Warning

Jesus Himself warned His followers, ***"Beware of false prophets, who come to you in sheep's clothing but inwardly are ravenous wolves"*** (Matthew 7:15). He emphasized that the fruit of their lives - their character, conduct, and doctrine - will reveal them.

2. Paul's Exhortation to the Elders

In Acts 20:29–30, Paul gave a tearful warning to the elders of the Ephesian church:

"I know that after I leave, savage wolves will come in among you and will not spare the flock. Even from your own number, men will arise and distort the truth in order to draw away disciples after them."

This reveals that false teachers may arise not just from outside the church but even from within leadership itself.

3. Peter's Sobering Prediction

Peter warned that just as there were false prophets in Israel, there would be false teachers among Christians:

"They will secretly introduce destructive heresies, even denying the sovereign Lord who bought them, bringing swift destruction on themselves. Many will follow their depraved conduct and will bring the way of truth into disrepute." (2 Peter 2:1–2).

Peter exposes their motivation: greed, lust, and pride.

4. Jude's Description of Apostates

The book of Jude is a short but urgent letter entirely dedicated to contending for the faith. Jude writes:

"For certain individuals whose condemnation was written about long ago have secretly slipped in among you. They are

ungodly people, who pervert the grace of our God into a license for immorality and deny Jesus Christ our only Sovereign and Lord." (Jude 4)

The Rise of Celebrity Christianity

Social media has birthed a new kind of preacher, one whose image is coordinated, whose sermons are crafted for clicks, and whose success is measured in followers rather than fruit. These celebrity preachers may be gifted communicators, but gifting is not the same as anointing.

- They often avoid controversial truths.
- They preach self-help instead of self-denial.
- They prioritize branding over biblical depth.

In this culture, the Church can become more like a fan base than a family. People quote pastors more than Scripture. Loyalty is to personalities rather than to Christ.

The Danger of a Crowd-Pleasing Gospel

A gospel that never offends is not the gospel of Jesus Christ. Jesus didn't come to make people feel good. He came to make them new. His message included:

- Deny yourself.
- Take up your cross.
- Follow Me.

True preaching comforts the broken, yes, but it also confronts sin. It calls for surrender. It doesn't just inspire, it transforms.
Celebrity culture makes it easy to elevate the messenger over the message. **But we must remember: any preacher who refuses to preach the cross is not preaching Christ.**

False teaching often hides beneath motivational slogans and emotional highs. It offers temporary encouragement with no eternal foundation:

- "Live your best life now."
- "You are enough."
- "Just believe in yourself."

These messages sound good, but they leave out the cross. They remove sin, repentance, sanctification, and spiritual warfare, the very core of the gospel. They promise heaven on earth but fail to prepare people for eternity.

A gospel that never offends the flesh will never crucify it.
Many modern messages feed the ego, not the soul. They cater to our desires:

- Success
- Prosperity
- Favor
- Destiny

These are biblical concepts when rightly understood, but false teachers twist them into idols. Instead of exalting Christ, they elevate man. Instead of calling us to die to self, they teach us to serve self, and dress it up in Christian language.

As a result, churches become platforms for performance rather than altars of sacrifice. The sheep are entertained, not equipped.

The Marks of False Teachers

The Apostle Peter, in 2 Peter 2, describes false teachers as:

- Exploiters of people through deceptive words (v. 3)
- Those who despise authority and speak evil of truth (v. 10–12)
- Lovers of gain more than lovers of God (v. 15)

Today, people seek preachers who validate their lifestyles, not challenge them. And many preachers, desiring influence more than impact, gladly oblige.

False teachers are not always easy to identify. They often blend into the community of faith, appearing sincere, passionate, and even successful. The Apostle Paul warned the Corinthians that

"Satan himself masquerades as an angel of light. It is not surprising, then, if his servants also masquerade as servants of righteousness" (2 Corinthians 11:14–15).

Their deception lies not in blatant heresy but in distortion. They preach a *partial gospel*, or worse, a *different gospel altogether* (Galatians 1:6–9). How do we recognize false teaching? Scripture gives us clear signs:

- **Minimizing sin:** Messages that make sin sound like weakness rather than rebellion.

- **Rejecting repentance:** Teaching that says you don't need to change because "God loves you as you are."
- **Prosperity gospel:** Promising wealth and health as a guaranteed right of faith.
- **Universalism:** Claiming that everyone will be saved, regardless of faith in Christ.
- **Twisting Scripture:** Using isolated verses out of context to support personal agendas.
- **Appealing to itching ears,** saying what people want to hear rather than what they need to hear.
- **Promoting self over Christ,** subtly shifting focus from God's glory to personal empowerment and ambition.
- **Disguising truth with flattery, mysticism, or emotionalism,** leading believers away from sound doctrine.

Paul warned Timothy:

"For the time will come when people will not put up with sound doctrine... they will gather around them a great number of teachers to say what their itching ears want to hear." - 2 Timothy 4:3

That time is now.

The Consequences of Following False Teachers

The danger of false teachers is not merely academic, it has eternal consequences. They lead people away from Christ and toward destruction. Jesus said of the Pharisees, ***"Leave them; they are blind guides. If the blind lead the blind, both will fall into a pit"*** (Matthew 15:14).

- **They distort the character of God**, presenting Him as a genie or a vending machine for blessings.
- **They weaken the believer's ability to endure suffering**, teaching that hardship is always a sign of weak faith or sin.
- **They turn grace into license**, encouraging sin by denying the call to holiness and repentance.
- **They create false conversions**, where people respond emotionally but not spiritually, falsely assured of salvation without fruit or transformation.

Why People Prefer False Teaching

There are many reasons why false teachers gain large followings:

1. **They confirm what the flesh wants to hear.**
2. **They provide a form of godliness without the power (or cost).**
3. **They help people feel better without truly changing.**
4. **They appeal to emotion more than truth.**

When people are spiritually malnourished, even junk food tastes good. But over time, the damage becomes evident: weak faith, shallow roots, and lives conformed to the world instead of transformed by the Word.

Signs of a Sound Teacher

Not all who speak powerfully are false. God still raises up anointed, faithful voices who preach truth. Here's how to recognize them:

- They preach **the full counsel of God**, not just the comfortable parts.
- They point to **Christ**, not themselves.
- They call for **repentance**, not just inspiration.
- They emphasize **holiness**, not just happiness.
- They are **accountable**, not isolated or self-appointed.

A sound teacher prepares the Church for eternity, not just for tomorrow.

False Signs and Wonders

In a time when experience is often valued over truth and emotionalism is mistaken for spiritual vitality, the modern church has become vulnerable to deception, particularly through **false signs and wonders** performed by **false preachers**. These deceptive displays, though appearing supernatural, are not of God but serve to distract, mislead, and enslave people under a counterfeit gospel. These signs, performed by deceiving preachers and self-appointed "prophets," are **designed to mimic**

the work of the Holy Spirit while leading people away from the truth of the gospel.

These signs are not mere parlor tricks. They can be powerful and convincing, often mimicking true miracles to create a sense of awe and credibility. But they are detached from the foundation of **biblical truth**, which is the test of any authentic work of God.

A true miracle points to Christ, confirms His Word, and leads to repentance and holiness. False miracles, however, often serve to **elevate the preacher**, accumulate wealth, or perpetuate spiritual manipulation.

Emotional Manipulation Masquerading as Power

In many congregations today, preachers orchestrate emotional atmospheres using lighting, music, and choreography designed to produce a **manufactured sense of the "Spirit."** The line between genuine worship and theatrical production becomes increasingly blurred. Audiences are primed to respond with tears, laughter, or falling to the ground, believing that these reactions indicate the presence of God.

However, Scripture teaches us to **test the spirits** (1 John 4:1), for not every supernatural experience is from the Holy Spirit. False teachers exploit people's desire for an encounter with God and turn it into **a performance filled with hype, not holiness**.

False signs are often connected to the **prosperity gospel**, which promises healing, wealth, and breakthrough in exchange for "seed offerings." Faith is redefined not as trust in Christ's finished work, but as a currency used to "activate" miracles. This theology is not only unbiblical, it is dangerous. It reduces God to a spiritual vending machine and conditions people to chase **results rather than righteousness**.

This is not new. Paul warned the Corinthians that **Satan masquerades as an angel of light** and that his servants do the same (2 Corinthians 11:13–15). These individuals may sound convincing, appear godly, and even produce results, but their **motives are rooted in self-promotion, not Christ-exaltation**.

Warning Signs of False Signs and Wonders

1. **The "sign" glorifies the preacher, not Christ.**
   If the result of a miracle is more attention, wealth, or praise going to the preacher rather than to Jesus, it is a red flag. True miracles always exalt Christ, not men (John 16:14).
2. **It contradicts or sidelines Scripture.**
   No true work of the Holy Spirit will ever contradict God's Word. If someone claims a "revelation" or miracle that undermines biblical truth, it is false (Galatians 1:8).
3. **There is a demand for money to access the "power."**
   The gospel is not for sale. Promises of healing or breakthrough in exchange for money are manipulative and demonic (2 Peter 2:1–3).
4. **Emotionalism replaces sound doctrine.**
   If a church relies on hype, mood lighting, and manipulated emotions rather than the clear teaching of God's Word, the environment is ripe for deception.
5. **Signs are used to validate a false gospel.**
   When signs are used to support prosperity theology, self-help messages, or motivational speeches instead of repentance, faith, and the cross, they are counterfeit.

Why This Deception Is So Destructive

False signs and wonders **lead people away from saving truth** and into a false sense of spiritual security. Rather than leading to repentance and holiness, they lead to:

- **Spiritual confusion:** People begin to trust experiences over the authority of Scripture.
- **Idolatry:** Preachers become the object of faith rather than Christ.
- **Doctrinal drift:** The core message of the gospel is replaced by promises of health, wealth, and personal success.
- **Hardness of heart:** Over time, exposure to spiritual manipulation can make people cynical or spiritually numb.

Worst of all, this deception **can keep people from genuine salvation**, as they are entertained into hell rather than convicted into repentance.

Jesus warned plainly in Matthew 24:24:

"For false christs and false prophets will appear and perform great signs and wonders to deceive, if possible, even the elect."

The fact that these signs can be so convincing that even sincere believers might be drawn in highlights the severity of the danger. These are not mere exaggerations or harmless spiritual theatrics. They are tools of **Satanic deception**, rooted in pride, greed, and rebellion against God's truth.

How to Protect Yourself from Deception

1. **Know the Word of God.**
   The best defense against lies is to know the truth. Regular, prayerful study of the Bible is essential (2 Timothy 2:15).
2. **Test every spirit.**
   1 John 4:1 says: *"Beloved, do not believe every spirit, but test the spirits to see whether they are from God..."* Don't accept everything just because it's done in the name of Jesus.
3. **Watch for fruit, not just fireworks.**
   Jesus said, *"You will know them by their fruits"* (Matthew 7:16). Is the preacher living a life of humility, holiness, and integrity? Or is it all show?
4. **Stay in a biblically sound church.**
   Find a fellowship that values expositional preaching, theological depth, and the lordship of Christ - not hype, celebrity pastors, or unbiblical manifestations.
5. **Pray for discernment.**
   Discernment is a spiritual gift that God gives to those who seek it (Philippians 1:9–10). Ask God to help you recognize what is true and what is counterfeit.

The Eternal Consequences for Deceivers

Scripture is clear that those who lead others astray will face **severe judgment**.

"Not everyone who says to me, 'Lord, Lord,' will enter the kingdom of heaven... Many will say to me on that day, 'Lord, Lord, did we not prophesy in your name... and perform many miracles?' Then I will tell them plainly, 'I never knew you. Depart from me, you workers of lawlessness.'
--Matthew 7:21–23

False teachers and miracle workers may gain fame on earth, but unless they repent, they will suffer **eternal separation from God**. Jude 13 calls them *"wandering stars, for whom the blackest darkness has been reserved forever."*

They are not harmless. They are instruments of the enemy, dragging souls away from the truth and into destruction.

The True Work of the Spirit

It's important to note that **God still performs miracles**, heals, and moves in power today. But His works are always **aligned with His Word, glorify His Son**, and **produce the fruit of the Spirit** in the believer's life. Miracles are never an end in themselves. They are signs that point to **Jesus as Lord and Savior**.

Paul said in 2 Thessalonians 2:9-10 that the coming of the lawless one will be "**by the activity of Satan with all power and false signs and wonders, and with all wicked deception for those who are perishing, because they refused to love the truth and so be saved**." False signs thrive where the truth is neglected.

The Responsibility of Every Believer

Every believer is called to discernment. We are not to follow teachers based on charisma, popularity, or success, but on whether their lives and teachings align with Scripture. As Paul said, *"Test everything; hold fast what is good"* (1 Thessalonians 5:21).

The Bereans were commended because *"they received the word with all eagerness, examining the Scriptures daily to see if these things were so"* (Acts 17:11). That same diligence is required today.

Believers must:

- **Know the Word of God**: deep familiarity with Scripture protects us from deception.
- **Develop spiritual discernment**: ask the Holy Spirit for wisdom to detect subtle errors.
- **Submit to sound doctrine**: truth is not subjective or fashionable; it is eternal and unchanging.

- **Hold teachers accountable**: through Scripture, not preference or personality.
- **Refuse to tolerate error**: Paul urged Titus to *"rebuke them sharply, so that they may be sound in the faith"* (Titus 1:13).

Confronting false teaching is not easy. It often invites resistance, mockery, or even division. Yet silence is complicity. Paul instructed Timothy to *"preach the word; be ready in season and out of season; reprove, rebuke, and exhort, with complete patience and teaching"* (2 Timothy 4:2).

This requires courage. We must have courage to stand for truth when it's unpopular, to speak up when others remain silent, and the courage to lose favor, position, or relationships for the sake of Christ.

The Responsibility of the Church

It's not enough to point out error, we must also uphold truth. The Church must:

- Train believers in sound doctrine.
- Equip people to discern.
- Hold leaders accountable.
- Pray for purity in the pulpit.

Truth must matter more than talent. Holiness must matter more than hype. Faithfulness must matter more than fame.

The dilemma of false teachers is a real and present danger to the body of Christ. Yet it is not one without remedy. The solution is not fear but faithfulness. The church must return to its roots - Scripture, sound doctrine, holiness, and the centrality of Christ.

In a world filled with voices, the voice of the True Shepherd must be louder in the hearts of His people. Jesus said, *"My sheep hear my voice, and I know them, and they follow me"* (John 10:27). Let us, then, be those who listen, discern, and follow Him, no matter the cost.

Final Warning

Not every miracle is from heaven. Not every preacher is sent by God. **True Christianity is not built on sensationalism but on a crucified Savior.**

Let us not be dazzled by signs that have no roots in Scripture and no fruit of righteousness. Instead, let us walk in the truth of the gospel, grounded in Christ, filled with the Spirit, and discerning in a world of deception.

We must not be naive in these last days. Just because something looks spiritual does not mean it is from God. We must be **sober, watchful, and anchored in Scripture**, knowing that **truth is the measuring rod for all spiritual claims**.

Do not chase signs, chase **Christ**. Signs will fade. Emotional highs will pass. But the truth of God's Word endures forever.

Conclusion: Back to the Gospel

The gospel is not flashy. It's not always popular. It doesn't always fill seats or go viral. But it is *powerful*. It saves, it sanctifies, and it secures the soul.

We don't need clever communicators—we need broken vessels who will declare the truth without compromise.

Let us not be seduced by fleeting messages that tickle the ears. Let us return to the gospel that pierces the heart.

Jesus didn't come to entertain us. He came to rescue us.

Let's preach that gospel. Let's follow that Jesus. Let's reject falsehood and cling to truth.

For in the end, it's not the crowds we gather, but the Christ we follow that matters.

Celebrity preachers come and go. Trends rise and fall. But Jesus Christ is the same—yesterday, today, and forever.

Let us return to the simplicity and purity of the gospel. Let us hunger for truth, not theatrics. Let us follow Christ, not crowds.

- Exalt the message, not the messenger.
- Love the truth, even when it cuts.
- Guard your heart from deception.

For in the end, it's not the popularity of the preacher that saves—it's the power of the cross.

And that cross still calls us to deny ourselves, take it up daily, and follow Jesus—not a celebrity.

Reflection Questions

Use these personally or with a journal to examine your heart and convictions.

1. **Have I ever accepted a teaching without testing it against Scripture? If so, why?**
2. **Am I more drawn to speakers who comfort or those who confront with truth?**
3. **Do I know what the Bible says well enough to detect false teaching?**
4. **Have I ever prioritized charisma, popularity, or emotionalism over sound doctrine?**
5. **In what ways might I have unknowingly tolerated or promoted false teaching?**
6. **What steps can I take to grow in biblical discernment and spiritual maturity?**
7. **Do I encourage others to follow truth, even when it's uncomfortable?**
8. **What does it mean to "test the spirits" (1 John 4:1), and how do I do that practically?**

Small Group Study Guide

Topic: Guarding Against False Teachers

Opening Question:

What are some examples of teachings or trends you've seen in modern Christianity that raised questions for you?

Read Aloud:

- Matthew 7:15–20
- 2 Timothy 4:1–5
- 2 Peter 2:1–3
- Jude 3–4

Discussion Questions:

1. Understanding the Danger
- Why do you think false teachers are so persuasive?
- What are the subtle ways they gain influence in the church today?

2. Fruit Inspection
- Jesus said we would know false teachers "by their fruit." What kind of fruit should we be looking for?

3. Distorted Grace
- Read Jude 4 again. How is the grace of God distorted today? Why is this dangerous?

4. Church Accountability
- What responsibility do pastors and leaders have to guard against false teaching?
- What is the role of the average believer?

5. Truth in Love
- How can we confront error in a way that is both courageous and loving?

Reflection Questions:

1. **Why do you think false signs and wonders are so effective in deceiving people in today's churches?**
2. **What is the difference between a genuine miracle from God and a counterfeit sign?**
3. **Have you ever witnessed or encountered a questionable spiritual manifestation? How did you respond?**
4. **According to Scripture, what role should signs and wonders play in the life of a believer or a church?**
5. **What are some practical ways you can test the spirits and discern truth from deception?**
6. **How can a church guard itself from embracing emotionalism over sound doctrine?**
7. **Why is it important to evaluate the fruit of a ministry rather than its popularity or appearance of power?**
8. **What are the eternal consequences for those who perform or follow after false signs and wonders?**

9. How does the gospel of Christ contrast with the message of false miracle workers today?
10. What spiritual disciplines help strengthen your discernment and protect you from being led astray?

Application Challenge:

Identify one Christian teacher, influencer, or resource you follow. Research their doctrinal beliefs and compare them to Scripture. What did you learn?

"Every day I realize more and more that if the world is going to change at all, it is going to change through the healing of the victims. Abusers run the show. They insist on and instigate cover ups. They misuse their power and teach things falsely out of the desire to control. But as the victims heal and get stronger, the abusers will not be able to hide behind the fog that they create."

Darlene Ouimet

"It's been said that only the educated are free. But I contend, only those who are educated with TRUTH can be inherently free. Otherwise, you are simply indoctrinated with error.

J.E.B. Spredemann

Prayer for Discernment:

Heavenly Father,

I thank You for Your unchanging truth, revealed in Your Word. In a world full of voices, opinions, and spiritual confusion, I ask You to give me discernment. Help me to recognize truth from error, and to cling to the gospel of Jesus Christ without compromise.

Expose in me any hidden pride that might make me vulnerable to false teaching. Root me in the Scriptures. Give me ears to hear Your voice and eyes to see clearly in a time of deception. Fill me with the wisdom of Your Holy Spirit, so I may not be swayed by eloquence or popularity, but guided by righteousness and sound doctrine.

Strengthen me to stand for truth, even when it costs me comfort or approval. Give me love for those who are led astray, and courage to speak truth in love when it's needed.

Lord, open our eyes to discern what is truly from You and what is counterfeit. Guard our hearts against chasing experiences over intimacy with Christ. Strengthen our love for Your Word and keep us anchored in sound doctrine.

Forgive us for any time we have been drawn to signs without seeking Your heart. Expose every lie and falsehood that seeks to exalt man rather than You. Raise up bold and faithful believers who will stand for truth, even when it is unpopular.

Let Your Holy Spirit give us wisdom and discernment. May we walk in truth, bear good fruit, and never be swayed by hype or false miracles. Keep our hearts fixed on Jesus, our Savior and Lord, until the day He returns in glory.

May I always seek You first. May I know You more deeply, and may my life reflect the true gospel of Jesus Christ.

In the name of Jesus, the Way, the Truth, and the Life,

Amen.

Chapter 13

The Deception of the Prosperity Gospel

One of the most deceptive forms of worldliness isn't overt rebellion—it's disguised devotion to self, cloaked in the language of blessing, purpose, and success. In our modern age, success has become a false gospel, and many Christians have unknowingly bowed to it.

We live in a culture that worships achievement. Social media showcases the highlight reels of influencers, preachers, and believers who appear to have it all: the platform, the following, the lifestyle. And slowly, we begin to measure our worth not by our obedience to God, but by how impressive our lives appear to others.

This is the snare of success, status, and self. It draws the heart away from surrender and toward self-promotion. It shifts our focus from pleasing God to building a brand. It whispers, "You can have Jesus—and still be the center of your story."

"For the time will come when they will not endure sound doctrine; but after their own lusts shall they heap to themselves teachers, having itching ears." 2 Timothy 4:3

We now have a generation of professing Christians chasing influence without character. But gifting without holiness is dangerous. Platform without integrity is a ticking time bomb.

- The world celebrates charisma. God looks for character.
- The world rewards success. God honors faithfulness.

Regretfully, when we pursue status without surrender, we may gain followers but lose our soul.

One of the most dangerous snares of modern-day Christianity is not always found outside the Church, but **within its pulpits**—the seductive and deceptive **Prosperity Gospel**. It is a doctrine that wraps worldliness in spiritual language, offering a message of wealth, success, and personal fulfillment, all under the banner of "faith."

But the truth is this: the Prosperity Gospel is a **distortion** of biblical Christianity. It is **not the Gospel of Jesus Christ**, but a counterfeit designed to trap hearts in the love of money, status, and comfort.

---

1. A Gospel of Greed Disguised as Faith

The Prosperity Gospel teaches that **God's will is for every believer to be rich, successful, and healthy**. It claims that if you have enough faith, speak the right words, and give the right offering, **you can command your blessing**.

But this message **twists Scripture** and **feeds the flesh**:

"Give, and it shall be given unto you..." - Luke 6:38
"Beloved, I wish above all things that thou mayest prosper and be in health..." — 3 John 1:2

These verses are ripped from context and turned into formulas for wealth, rather than truths about God's faithfulness in every season of life.

Instead of pointing people to **Christ crucified**, it points them to **cash, cars, and comfort**. It does not call for repentance or surrender—it promises **earthly gain in exchange for religious performance**.

---

2. A False View of Blessing

Many have redefined blessing to mean financial prosperity, public recognition, and worldly comfort. But the Bible gives a different picture:

"Blessed are the poor in spirit... Blessed are they that mourn... Blessed are they which are persecuted..."
— Matthew 5:3–11

Jesus didn't promise popularity or wealth—He promised suffering, sanctification, and eternal reward. Yet, in today's

Church, the one who suffers is often pitied, while the one who prospers financially is envied.

It's time to ask: Are we defining blessing the way Jesus does, or are we measuring success by worldly standards?

In Prosperity theology, **blessing is measured by material success**. If you're rich, you're "blessed." If you're poor, sick, or struggling, you must lack faith or favor.

The **true blessing of God** is not about **what you possess**, but **who possesses you**. The early Apostles were beaten, jailed, and martyred. Were they not blessed? The Apostle Paul stated,

"...I have learned, in whatsoever state I am, therewith to be content." - Philippians 4:11

Paul rejoiced in suffering. Jesus had **no home, no riches, and no reputation**, yet He was the **Son of God**. The Prosperity Gospel dares to call this kind of life a failure. That alone reveals its **worldly foundation**.

---

3. A Misrepresentation of Faith

The Prosperity Gospel teaches that **faith is a force**—a tool used to **get what you want** from God. If you don't receive your healing, your house, or your breakthrough, it's your fault. You didn't "sow enough" or "believe hard enough."

But true, biblical faith is **not about getting things from God— it's about serving Him and trusting Him no matter what**:

"Though He slay me, yet will I trust in Him..." - Job 13:15

"These all died in faith, not having received the promises..." - Hebrews 11:13

Faith is not a guarantee of ease—it is a call to endure trials, remain obedient, and glorify God whether in plenty or pain.

---

4. The Deception of Control

Another subtle aspect of this trap is the illusion of control. We think if we just work harder, network more, pray more strategically, we can make our lives turn out exactly as we envision.

But God is not obligated to fulfill our version of success. He calls us to die to our plans and trust His. Often, the life God blesses doesn't look like the one we planned.

Abraham was blessed—but he waited in barrenness. Joseph was blessed—but he was betrayed and imprisoned. Paul was blessed—but he was shipwrecked, stoned, and rejected.

True blessing doesn't always mean comfort. Sometimes it means being stripped of everything so that Christ can be everything.

---

5. A Trap of Worldliness

The greatest danger of the Prosperity Gospel is not merely doctrinal—it is **spiritual idolatry**. It **teaches believers to love the world** under the guise of loving God. It encourages:

- **Greed instead of contentment**
- **Pride instead of humility**
- **Self-focus instead of Christ-focus**

"For the love of money is the root of all evil..." - 1 Timothy 6:10

"Set your affection on things above, not on things on the earth." - Colossians 3:2

It leads professing Christians to believe they can **have the world and have Christ too**—but Jesus made it clear:

"If any man will come after Me, let him deny himself, and take up his cross daily, and follow Me." - Luke 9:23

The Prosperity Gospel offers **a crown without a cross**, but there is **no resurrection without crucifixion**.

At the heart of this deception is the idol of self. Self is the god of the age:

- Self-love over self-denial.
- Self-expression over self-control.
- Self-promotion over self-sacrifice.

The cross is not a symbol of personal breakthrough. It's a place of death—death to the flesh, to ego, to ambition. Yet many believers try to carry their cross without ever dying on it.

---

6. Christ Is Enough

The true Gospel is this: **Christ is the treasure**. He is more precious than silver or gold. To know Him is worth more than health, wealth, or worldly success. The Apostle Paul's testimony was,

"Yea doubtless... I count all things but loss for the excellency of the knowledge of Christ Jesus my Lord..."
— Philippians 3:8

Jesus did not come to make us millionaires. He came to make us holy.

He did not promise a life of ease, but **a life of purpose**.

He did not die to make us rich in things—but to make us rich in grace.

Social Media and the Self-Centered Gospel

As noted, we are living in the age of self. Platforms like Instagram, TikTok, and YouTube have made it easier than ever to build a brand, gain followers, and curate a life that is more admired than authentic. For many, even faith has become filtered—more about personal promotion than spiritual transformation.

Social media, when misused, can be a powerful tool in the enemy's hands to twist the gospel into something it was never meant to be: a message that revolves around *me*.

Also, as noted, the true gospel begins with a cross. It calls us to deny ourselves, die to our flesh, and follow Jesus. But the gospel portrayed online often begins with self.

- "God wants to make you successful."
- "God wants to elevate your platform."
- "God wants you to live your best life now."

The focus shifts from Christ to personal gain, from obedience to opportunity, from surrender to spotlight. The message becomes less about God's glory and more about self-fulfillment.

This is not the gospel. It's motivational speaking wrapped in spiritual language.

Spiritual influencers are prevalent throughout all of our social media platforms. There's nothing wrong with being influential. But influence without accountability can become idolatry.

- When the platform becomes the goal, the cross gets lost.
- When likes define identity, the fear of God is replaced by fear of man.
- When the message is shaped for engagement, truth is often diluted for approval.

Many Christian influencers begin with good intentions, but the temptation to compromise for popularity is real. If your faith must be edited to gain followers, it's not faithfulness—it's performance.

Social media fuels comparison. We measure our spiritual lives against curated images of others' highlight reels.

- "Their ministry is growing faster."
- "They're more anointed."
- "Why isn't God using me like that?"

But God never asked you to be like them—He asked you to be like Christ. Your calling is not to impress others online but to obey God in secret. What you do in the hidden place matters far more than what's seen on a screen.

The Illusion of Connection

Social media can give the illusion of spiritual community while leaving believers disconnected from real accountability and discipleship.

- Watching sermons online is not the same as being part of a local church.
- Sharing Bible verses is not the same as studying Scripture.
- Posting prayers is not the same as a private prayer life.

The early church grew not because of followers and shares, but because of fellowship, devotion, and Spirit-led obedience.

Redeeming the Platform

Social media isn't evil. It can be a tool for evangelism, encouragement, and truth. But it must be stewarded well:

- **Use your platform to glorify God, not yourself.**
- **Speak truth, even if it costs you likes.**
- **Encourage others to go deeper, not just trendier.**
- **Point to the cross—not your brand.**

God is not looking for influencers—He's looking for intercessors.

Re-Centering the Gospel on Christ

The gospel is not about self-expression—it's about self-denial. Jesus didn't die to boost your platform—He died to save your soul.

"He must increase, but I must decrease." — John 3:30

This is the heart of the true gospel. It's not about you. It's about Him. His glory. His kingdom. His will.

Social Media in Its Proper Place

Social media can either be a stage for self or a platform for truth. It can feed our pride or fuel our purpose. The difference lies in who it's ultimately about.

Let us not trade authentic Christianity for online spirituality. Let us not confuse digital influence with divine calling. Let us not build followers at the expense of faithfulness.

The gospel calls us to come and die—not come and post. May we use every tool, including social media, to lift high the name of Jesus—not ourselves.

In the end, when we stand before God, He won't ask how many followers we had. He'll ask if we followed Him.

An anonymous Personal Testimony: From Greed to Grace

I remember a time in my own life when I was **enticed by the Prosperity Gospel**. I didn't call it that, of course, not at first. I called it "walking in victory," "claiming God's promises," and "believing for abundance." I was taught that if I gave more, I would get more. If I prayed longer, confessed louder, and sowed bigger financial seeds, God was obligated to bless me with material success.

I began measuring God's favor by my bank account, my job promotions, and the size of my house. I'd look at others who were struggling and silently assume, "They must not have enough faith." I treated the Lord as a **divine business partner**, not a sovereign Savior. My prayers became transactions. My worship was conditional. My joy was fragile—entirely dependent on whether or not my life was going according to my desires.

But then everything I built came crashing down.

I lost my job. My finances dried up. I was passed over for every promotion I was "believing for." My health began to decline. I was devastated, not just because of the losses, but because my **faith didn't seem to work anymore**. I was angry at God, confused, and ashamed.

And that's when I encountered the real Gospel.

In the stillness of my brokenness, the Lord began to show me that I had placed my hope in the wrong gospel. I had worshiped the gifts and not the Giver. I had trusted in formulas instead of surrendering to His will. I had built a faith around **prosperity**, not around **the cross**.

Through the Word of God and the gentle correction of mature believers, I began to see the truth: **Christ is enough**. Whether I am in a palace or a prison, His grace is sufficient. Whether I have plenty or nothing at all, His presence is my portion. My faith is not a means to manipulate God—it is a posture of trust, even when the answers don't come.

Today, I no longer chase after material blessings. I chase after **Jesus**. I have found **peace in the storm, joy in sorrow, and purpose in the pain**. And now, I would rather have a simple life full of His presence than a rich life empty of Him.

The Prosperity Gospel nearly destroyed my relationship with God. But the true Gospel restored it—and in doing so, gave me everything I ever truly needed.

A Call Back to Humility

Philippians 2:5-8 reminds us:

"Let this mind be in you which was also in Christ Jesus... who made Himself of no reputation... and became obedient to the point of death, even the death of the cross."

This is the opposite of modern Christianity's obsession with image. Jesus had no brand, no publicist, and no mansion. Yet He changed the world.

We don't need more stars. We need more servants.

Afterthoughts

- The Prosperity Gospel distorts the character of God by portraying Him as a **cosmic vending machine**—serving the desires of man rather than being holy, sovereign, and worthy of worship.
- It places **material success** at the center of Christian faith rather than **spiritual transformation** and **obedient living**.
- This message **exploits the poor**, manipulates the desperate, and deceives millions by promising wealth instead of **pointing people to the cross**.
- Jesus did not promise His followers riches, fame, or ease—but **persecution, suffering, and reward in heaven** (John 16:33, Matthew 5:10–12).
- The true gospel is about **dying to self**, not exalting self. It is about **seeking God's kingdom**, not building our own.
- A gospel that doesn't require **repentance, surrender, or holiness** is no gospel at all. It may fill pews and bank accounts—but it **doesn't save souls**.

"**If anyone would come after me, let him deny himself and take up his cross daily and follow me.**"— Luke 9:23

Summary

The Prosperity Gospel presents a distorted version of Christianity—one that exchanges the cross for comfort, and Christ for cash. While it promises health, wealth, and success, it leads many into disillusionment, spiritual compromise, and even eternal loss.

Even spiritual language can become a mask for worldly ambition. It's possible to use ministry as a means of self-promotion:

- Posting Bible verses to build a following.
- Turning testimonies into marketing tools.
- Preaching messages that are designed to go viral, not to convict.

There's nothing wrong with platforms, technology, or influence. The issue is when our motives are rooted in self rather than in a desire to glorify Christ.

True faith is not measured by material abundance but by obedience, holiness, and trust in God's will—whether in abundance or in lack. The gospel of Jesus Christ is not about what we can get from God, but about surrendering everything to follow Him.

Conclusion

The deception of the Prosperity Gospel is one of the most dangerous traps facing the modern Church. It appeals to the flesh, manipulates Scripture, and reduces God to a servant of our desires. But Jesus did not die to make us rich, He died to make us holy. He did not call us to accumulate wealth, but to deny ourselves, take up our cross, and follow Him. We must return to the simplicity and power of the true gospel: one that calls for repentance, produces godliness, and leads to eternal life. Anything else is a counterfeit, no matter how popular or polished it may appear.

If success, status, and self have taken center stage in your walk with God, it's time to return to the altar. Lay down your dreams. Lay down your platform. Lay down your need to be seen, known, and applauded.

The only true success is faithfulness to Jesus.

You may never be famous, but you can be faithful. You may never be rich, but you can be righteous. You may never trend, but you can be trusted by God.

That is the life that pleases Him.

In the end, we won't hear, "Well done, good and successful servant." We'll hear, "Well done, good and faithful servant."

Let the Church arise in truth, and let every lie be exposed by the light of God's Word.

Let that be enough.

Reflection Questions

1. **Have you believed elements of the Prosperity Gospel?** How has it affected your view of God and suffering?
2. **Why do you think the message of wealth and comfort appeals so strongly to people—even in the Church?**
3. **What does the Bible say about true blessing?** How is it different from the world's definition?
4. **How can you guard your heart** from being drawn into a faith that is focused on material gain?
5. **Are you willing to follow Christ even if it costs you everything?**

Small Group Discussion Questions

1. **What is the Prosperity Gospel, and how does it differ from the true gospel of Jesus Christ?**
2. **How have you personally seen or experienced the influence of the prosperity message in churches or Christian media?**
3. **Read 1 Timothy 6:5–10. What does this passage say about the desire for wealth and its spiritual dangers?**
4. **Why do you think the Prosperity Gospel appeals to so many people—even sincere believers?**
5. **Can material blessing ever be a sign of God's favor? How do we discern when it becomes idolatry?**
6. **What are the eternal consequences of following a gospel centered on self, wealth, and success instead of Christ and the cross?**

7. How do Jesus' teachings about suffering, self-denial, and taking up the cross contradict the Prosperity Gospel?
8. In what ways can a focus on wealth hinder spiritual growth and distort a believer's view of God?
9. How should the Church respond to preachers or ministries promoting this deceptive teaching?
10. How can we return to a Christ-centered gospel that emphasizes contentment, faithfulness, and eternal reward over earthly gain?

"The greatest danger to the church today is not humanism, paganism, atheism, or agnosticism. The greatest danger is not increasing hostility against our faith from the culture. Our greatest danger is apostasy on the inside, arising from false teachers – theological liberals who deny and distort biblical doctrine and lead others down the same path."

Mark Hitchcock

"The gospel is not a message of health, wealth, and prosperity. It is a message of sin, redemption, and reconciliation."

Justin Peters

Prayer of Repentance and Redirection

Heavenly Father,

I come before You in humility and truth. I confess that at times I have been drawn to the message of prosperity, seeking blessing over obedience, gain over godliness, and comfort over the cross.

Forgive me, Lord, for putting material things above eternal things. Forgive the Church for exchanging the truth of the gospel for a lie that tickles ears and leads people away from Your heart.

Cleanse me from any greed, pride, or selfish ambition. Help me to be content in all circumstances and to treasure Christ above all. Teach me to pursue righteousness, godliness, faith, love, steadfastness, and humility.

Expose every false teaching and deliver Your people from deception. Strengthen the remnant that seeks holiness and truth. May we boldly proclaim the true gospel—one that is centered on Jesus, marked by sacrifice, and filled with eternal hope.

Help me to live with heaven in view, laying up treasures not on earth, but in Your kingdom.

In the name of Jesus, the only true Treasure, I pray. **Amen.**

"When you find that a theology has nothing more to offer than what the world already offers, then that theology as a theology is impractical, and therefore, useless."

Criss Jami

Chapter 14

The Spirit of Covetousness

Regretfully, the prosperity gospel can open the door for the spirit of covetousness. Covetousness is one of the most overlooked and under-preached sins in the church today. While the Bible is unrelenting in its condemnation of it, many believers have grown comfortable with its presence, cloaking it in terms like "ambition," "blessing," or "favor." In truth, covetousness is a sign that worldliness has deeply penetrated the church. It subtly shifts our affections from God to possessions, positioning worldly desires in the seat of worship that belongs to Christ alone.

Covetousness is a strong, inordinate desire to obtain more than one needs or deserves or to have what belongs to someone else, especially in relation to material possessions, material wealth, status, or power. It is rooted in discontentment with what God has provided and fueled by lust, comparison, envy, and pride.

The Bible emphasizes that God is a faithful provider, promising to meet the needs of those who trust in Him. This provision extends beyond material necessities, encompassing spiritual and emotional needs as well. Scripture encourages believers to trust in God's care, knowing He is aware of their needs and will provide for them in His perfect way and timing. Covetousness is a mindset that extends beyond needs to desires for more. The Apostle Paul assures us in Philippians 4:19,

"My God shall supply all your need according to his riches in glory by Christ Jesus."

The church is called to be a light in a dark world, but when covetousness is allowed to grow unchecked, the light becomes dimmed by greed, jealousy, and selfish pursuit.

This chapter will expose covetousness for what it is: a spiritual cancer that destroys our intimacy with God, undermines our witness, and threatens our eternal destiny if left unrepented.

Covetousness is a sin of the heart. As stated, it reveals that a person is not content with God's provision. When believers operate from a place of lust, greed, or envy, they are effectively saying, "God, you are not enough, I desire more." This attitude quenches the Holy Spirit and fractures our relationship with the Lord.

Colossians 3:5 states, ***"Therefor put to death your members which are on the earth: fornication, uncleanness, passion, evil desire, and covetousness, which is idolatry. Because of these things the wrath of God is coming upon the sons of disobedience."***

As Colossians 3:5 indicates, covetousness is a form of idolatry. It displaces God from the throne of the heart and replaces Him with material gain, career advancement, or the approval of others. It is subtle and deceitful because it masquerades as happiness, diligence, success, or stewardship. Also, as noted in this scripture, covetousness can place believers under God's wrath which can manifest in many forms.

Covetousness, if unrepented, has eternal ramifications:

- **Ephesians 5:5**: *"No covetous man, who is an idolater, has any inheritance in the kingdom of Christ and of God."*
- **1 Corinthians 6:10**: *"Nor thieves, nor the covetous... will inherit the kingdom of God."*

The Bible is clear: habitual covetousness disqualifies one from God's Kingdom. A professing Christian who lives in covetousness is in spiritual danger of eternal damnation.

When Christians are driven by materialism, status, or comparison, the world sees no difference between the church and its culture. Covetous Christians preach Christ but live for the world. Their witness becomes void, and the gospel they proclaim is overshadowed by their obsession with the same worldly things unbelievers chase.

Biblical Warnings

1. **Exodus 20:17 (The Tenth Commandment)**
   "You shall not covet your neighbor's house; you shall not covet your neighbor's wife... nor anything that is your neighbor's."
   Covetousness is not only a violation of the Tenth Commandment; it is also a gateway to violating others.

2. **Luke 12:15**
   "Take heed and beware of covetousness, for one's life does not consist in the abundance of the things he possesses."
   Jesus warns that covetousness leads to a distorted view of life, making possessions the measure of a person's worth.

3. **Colossians 3:5**
   "Put to death therefore what is earthly in you... covetousness, which is idolatry."
   Here, covetousness is directly equated with **idolatry**—a powerful indictment. Anything we crave more than God has become our god.

4. **1 Timothy 6:9–10**
   "But those who desire to be rich fall into temptation... For the love of money is a root of all kinds of evil..."
   This passage highlights the spiritual danger of covetousness—it opens the door to temptation, destruction, and apostasy.

Examples of Worldly Covetousness Among Christians

1. **Prosperity Gospel Obsession**
   As noted, churches that preach a prosperity gospel and equate faithfulness with financial success are breeding grounds for covetousness. Believers begin seeking God not for who He is, but for what they can get from Him.

2. **Comparison Culture**
   Many Christians constantly compare their lives to others—whether through social media or church circles—leading to jealousy and resentment. Instead of rejoicing in others' blessings, they covet them.

3. **Church Leadership Driven by Prestige**
   Some pastors and ministers are not driven by a burden for souls but by the desire for larger platforms, book deals, and celebrity status.

4. **Luxury Over Stewardship**
   Buying extravagant goods not out of need but to keep up with others is a common modern form of covetousness. This spirit leads to debt, anxiety, and misplaced priorities.

Identifying Covetousness Christians

Covetous people often struggle with **chronic dissatisfaction**. No matter how much they receive or accomplish, it's never enough. This reveals a personality that lacks contentment and peace. They are driven by what they don't have, rather than being thankful for what they do have.

"Godliness with contentment is great gain" (1 Timothy 6:6).

A covetous person may define their **self-worth by possessions, titles, or achievements**. When their identity is tied to what they own or how others perceive them, they are easily threatened by the success of others. This insecurity fosters jealousy, comparison, and resentment.

Covetousness can stem from a **need to outdo others or keep up appearances**. It may reveal a personality prone to **envy**, always measuring their life against others'. This competitiveness breeds strife, not peace.

"Where envy and selfish ambition exist, there is disorder and every evil thing" (James 3:16).

At its core, covetousness is a **form of unbelief**. It reveals a personality that struggles to trust that God's provision is enough. Instead of resting in God's plan, the covetous person believes they must strive to secure what they think they need.

"Your heavenly Father knows that you need all these things" (Matthew 6:32).

Covetousness focuses on **"me, mine, and more."** It reveals a personality that is **absorbed with personal gain**, often at the expense of generosity, humility, and love for others. The covetous heart views people as obstacles or stepping stones to achieve self-focused goals.

When people covet, they often **elevate created things above the Creator**. Their affections are attached more to material objects, success, or people than to God. This reveals a spiritual orientation that leans toward **idolatry**, where something or someone else takes God's rightful place.

Because covetous people are **externally driven**, they're emotionally unstable when they don't get what they desire. They may feel frustrated, anxious, or depressed when they don't get what they desire or others have what they want. This emotional fragility points to a lack of inner peace and spiritual maturity.

Implications of Being a Covetousness Christian

1. Spiritual Drift and Separation from God
Covetousness gradually pulls the heart away from God. It replaces devotion to Christ with devotion to possessions, people, or status. Over time, the believer's **love for God grows cold** because their affections are anchored in worldly things.

"You cannot serve God and mammon" (Matthew 6:24).
"...covetousness, which is idolatry" (Colossians 3:5).

This is not just a weakening of spiritual sensitivity, as noted, it's a form of **idolatry**. The more one feeds covetous desires, the less room there is for God's Spirit to rule.

2. Loss of Peace and Contentment
Covetous people are never truly satisfied. They live in a constant state of **striving, comparison, and anxiety**. Over time, this produces:

- **Restlessness** – an inability to enjoy what they already have.
- **Bitterness** – resentment toward others who appear more blessed.
- **Discontentment** – even God's blessings feel "not enough."

"The eyes of man are never satisfied" (Proverbs 27:20).

3. Damaged Relationships
Covetousness poisons relationships because it turns people into **competitors or tools**. Over time, it may lead to:

- Jealousy and rivalry among friends or family.
- Manipulation or exploitation of others for gain.
- Lack of generosity and selfishness in marriage or parenting.
- Betrayal, dishonesty, and broken trust.

"Where envy and selfish ambition exist, there is disorder and every evil thing" (James 3:16).

4. Moral and Ethical Compromise
A heart driven by covetousness will eventually compromise its values to get what it wants. This may include:

- Financial dishonesty (e.g., stealing, fraud, misrepresentation).
- Compromising integrity at work or in ministry.
- Even **spiritual compromise**, like twisting Scripture to justify greed (common in prosperity teachings).

"Those who desire to be rich fall into temptation and a snare..." (1 Timothy 6:9).

5. Weak or Hypocritical Christian Witness
Covetous Christians look no different than the world. They preach Jesus but pursue the same things unbelievers chase: material possessions, money, fame, comfort, and status. Over time, this inconsistency:

- **Destroys credibility.**
- **Dilutes the message of the gospel.**
- **Repels unbelievers** who are looking for authenticity.

Jesus said we are the **salt of the earth**—but covetousness causes believers to lose their saltiness (Matthew 5:13).

6. Generational Consequences
Covetousness can be passed down to children and younger believers. Parents or leaders who live driven by materialism and discontent often raise the next generation to:

- Measure success by money or appearance.
- Pursue performance over godliness.
- Value "stuff" over spiritual substance.

This creates a culture of **worldly Christians** who are churchgoers in form, but lovers of the world in heart.

7. Eternal Judgment (Repeated for emphasis)
The most sobering implication is eternal. The Bible makes clear that **unrepented covetousness can lead to eternal separation from God.**

"Do you not know that the unrighteous will not inherit the kingdom of God?... nor thieves, nor the covetous... will inherit the kingdom of God."- 1 Corinthians 6:9-10

"No covetous man, who is an idolater, has any inheritance in the kingdom of Christ and God." - Ephesians 5:5

A lifestyle of covetousness is not simply a "bad habit"—it is a **soul-threatening condition** that, if not confronted and repented of, places one outside the kingdom of God.

Deliverance from the Spirit of Covetousness

Deliverance from covetousness is not simply a matter of changing behavior—it is a transformation of the heart. Here are biblical steps to freedom:

1. Cultivate Contentment

Philippians 4:11-13 – *"I have learned in whatever state I am, to be content..."*

Contentment is learned through intimacy with Christ. It is rooted in gratitude and trust that God provides everything we need.

2. Renew the Mind

Romans 12:2 – *"Do not be conformed to this world, but be transformed by the renewing of your mind..."*

Daily meditate on Scripture that reminds you of eternal values, not earthly riches. This renews the heart's desires.

3. Practice Generosity

1 Timothy 6:17-18 – *"Command those who are rich... to be generous and ready to share."*

Giving is a spiritual weapon against greed. When you give freely, you break the hold of materialism on your life.

4. Set Your Mind on Eternal Things

Colossians 3:2 – *"Set your minds on things above, not on earthly things."*

Keep your heart anchored in eternity. Remind yourself daily that this world is not your home.

5. Confess and Repent

1 John 1:9 – *"If we confess our sins, He is faithful and just to forgive us..."*

Ask God to reveal hidden covetousness in your heart and repent sincerely. Ask the Holy Spirit to give you a clean heart.

Closing Challenge: A Heart Check

Covetousness is a deceptive sin. You may not even know it has taken root in your heart until the fruit appears—in discontent, anxiety, envy, or misplaced ambition. But God calls His people to live differently—to be content, generous, and satisfied in Him. Ask yourself:

- Am I seeking something or someone more than I seek God?
- Am I jealous of others' blessings or positions?
- Do I measure success by worldly standards?

If so, the Spirit is calling you to repent, refocus, and return to your first love—Jesus Christ.

We will conclude this chapter with the story of Shirley Edwards.

Shirley Edwards – A Hidden Struggle with Covetousness

Shirley Edwards is well-known and deeply loved within her small Independent church nestled just outside a major city. In many ways, she is a darling within her congregation. She faithfully attends every service, participates in the women's ministry, and regularly volunteers at the local food pantry. Her warm smile and generous spirit have blessed many within the church and the surrounding community. To all who know her, Shirley is the picture of Christian devotion. She is compassionate, prayerful, and committed to the Lord's work.

But behind the scenes, Shirley battles a spiritual issue that few take seriously, including herself: **covetousness**. Her home, though well-kept, is overrun with material possessions—racks of clothing, bins of unopened gadgets, stacks of decorative items she never uses, and an overflowing closet of shoes she hasn't worn in years. Her garage, once meant for her car, is now a storage space for things she bought simply because they were on sale or too pretty to resist.

Shirley doesn't see this as a sin. She often jokes about it to her friends at church, calling it her "little weakness" or "shopping therapy." She rationalizes her habits by pointing to her charitable works—after all, doesn't she give to the poor? Doesn't she help the church financially? Her purchases, she says, are harmless indulgences. She insists that she just has an eye for beauty and a passion for good deals.

However, what Shirley fails to recognize is that her attachment to material things is not just a "hobby," it is **a spiritual stronghold** rooted in **covetousness**, which the Bible plainly identifies as idolatry (Colossians 3:5). Her continual accumulation of possessions, even when unnecessary, reveals a heart not fully surrendered to Christ in this area. Instead of finding her satisfaction and contentment in the Lord, she finds comfort, identity, and even temporary joy in what she owns.

Covetousness, by nature, is a sin of the heart. It operates quietly, often unnoticed or downplayed, but it has serious consequences. Jesus warned that ***"a man's life does not consist in the abundance of the things he possesses"*** (Luke 12:15). Shirley's overflowing house is not just a physical clutter, it is a visible symptom of a spiritual imbalance. She is accumulating more than she needs or could ever use, all while justifying it with a smile and charitable deeds.

In her personal life, Shirley's covetousness has created unnecessary stress. She often feels overwhelmed by the clutter yet is unwilling to let go. Her money, which could be used more wisely, is frequently spent on things that bring only fleeting satisfaction. The joy of giving can easily become overshadowed by the thrill of getting.

More significantly, Shirley's spiritual witness is compromised. Though she shares the gospel and serves faithfully, the example she sets is mixed. Those close to her may question her spiritual priorities. Young believers watching her might confuse godliness with materialism and follow her example. Even unbelievers may struggle to see the difference between Shirley and the consumer-driven world around her.

The Word of God is clear: ***"No covetous person...has any inheritance in the kingdom of Christ and of God"*** (Ephesians 5:5). This does not mean Shirley is eternally lost because she struggles with covetousness, but it does mean her sin is not harmless. If left unchecked, it can harden her heart, distort her values, and hinder her intimacy with God. Persistent unrepentant sin, especially when treated lightly, puts the soul in danger.

What Should Shirley Do?

1. **Acknowledge the Sin**
   Shirley must stop trivializing her behavior and confess it for what it is: a form of idolatry. The first step to freedom is humble repentance. She must ask God to help her see covetousness as He sees it.

2. **Renew Her Mind**
   Through Scripture, she can begin to retrain her thinking. Verses such as Hebrews 13:5 ("Be content with what you have") and Matthew 6:19-21 ("Do not store up for yourselves treasures on earth...") must shape her desires and priorities.

3. **Practice Contentment and Simplicity**
   She should set boundaries on her spending, declutter her home, and learn the joy of simplicity. Contentment is a spiritual discipline that must be cultivated. As she lets go of excess, she makes room for deeper peace and freedom in Christ.

4. **Redirect Her Affections**
   Instead of finding joy in things, Shirley should cultivate a deeper affection for Christ and the eternal riches found in Him. Psalm 73:25 says, "Whom have I in heaven but You? And there is none upon earth that I desire besides You."

5. **Be Accountable**
   A trusted friend or spiritual mentor can walk alongside her in prayer and accountability as she breaks free from materialism.

6. **Bear Fruit Worthy of Repentance**
   Shirley should consider donating the excess to those in need, not as a cover for her sin, but as genuine fruit of a changed heart.

Shirley Edwards is a beloved child of God with a sincere heart for ministry, but like many believers, she has allowed a seemingly harmless habit to grow into a spiritual snare.

Covetousness, no matter how respectable it may appear, is a serious offense to God because it robs Him of the rightful place in our hearts. Until Shirley deals with this hidden flaw, she will remain spiritually hindered, her witness dulled, and her intimacy with God clouded.

But if she repents and yields fully to the Lord in this area, she will not only find freedom and clarity, but her life and witness will shine with even greater purity and power—reflecting the all-satisfying treasure she has in Christ Jesus.

Conclusion: A Window into the Soul

Covetousness is not just a behavioral issue—it's a **window into a soul that is restless, insecure, and easily swayed by the world's values**. It often reveals a deeper need for healing, identity in Christ, and renewal of the mind. A covetous personality is not beyond redemption, but it must be transformed by the Spirit of God through repentance, contentment, and trust in His sufficiency.

Covetousness may appear harmless at first—just a desire for more or better. But left unchecked, it leads to spiritual decay, broken relationships, compromised values, and ultimately, judgment.

The **long-term implications of covetousness** are both profound and devastating—spiritually, relationally, emotionally, and even eternally. Though it often begins subtly, covetousness—when left unchecked—will gradually erode a believer's walk with God, distort their priorities, and ultimately put their soul at risk.

That is why Scripture calls us not just to avoid coveting, but to ***"put it to death"*** (Colossians 3:5), and to live in **contentment, godliness, and trust in Christ.**

"For what will it profit a man if he gains the whole world, and loses his own soul?" - Mark 8:36

Reflection Questions

1. In what ways have you seen covetousness manifest in your life or in the church?
2. How can a believer differentiate between ambition and covetousness?
3. What role does gratitude play in guarding the heart against covetousness?
4. What steps can you begin today to break the grip of materialism or envy in your heart?
5. How might covetousness hinder the effectiveness of a Christian's witness to unbelievers?

Group Study Questions

1. **What is covetousness, and how is it different from healthy ambition or goal-setting?**
   (Read: Exodus 20:17; Luke 12:15)

2. **Why do you think covetousness is often hidden or overlooked in Christian communities?**

   What makes it so easy to justify or ignore?

3. **How does modern society fuel covetousness, and what are some examples of how this affects Christians today?**

   Consider advertising, social media, materialism, or lifestyle pressures.

4. **In what ways can covetousness become a form of idolatry?**
   (Read: Colossians 3:5)
   How does it compete with our devotion to God?

5. **What are the dangers of covetousness to a believer's spiritual life, relationships, and witness?**

6. **Can covetousness exist even in ministry or church settings? If so, how?**
   Consider coveting influence, numbers, recognition, or other churches' success.

7. **What biblical characters struggled with covetousness, and what were the consequences?**
   (Examples: Achan – Joshua 7; Judas Iscariot – Matthew 26:14-16)

8. **How can contentment be cultivated in a culture of covetousness?**
   (Read: Philippians 4:11-13; 1 Timothy 6:6-10)

9. **What practical steps can a believer take to guard their heart against covetousness?**
   How can accountability, gratitude, and stewardship help?

10. **Is there anything you've recently desired that may be rooted in covetousness rather than godly contentment?**
    How can you bring that desire to the Lord in repentance and surrender?

Closing Prayer

Father, search my heart and expose any spirit of covetousness within me. Cleanse me from the desire to have more, to be more, or to appear more for my own glory. Teach me the beauty of contentment, the joy of generosity, and the peace that comes from trusting You fully.

Let my life be a reflection of eternal values, not worldly gain. May I seek first Your kingdom, knowing that all I need will be added according to Your perfect will.

In Jesus' name,

Amen.

"It was with good reason that God commanded through Moses that the vineyard and harvest were not to be gleaned to the last grape or grain; but something to be left for the poor. For covetousness is never satisfied; the more it has, the more it wants. Such insatiable ones injure themselves, and transform God's blessings into evil."

Martin Luther

"Whatever worldly thing we may covet, zealously striving to obtain and then retain never seems to bring an end to our desires. Covetousness, envy, jealousy, and greed always escalate into a vicious spiral, as we seek greater and greater gratification but find less and less contentment. Striving to acquire the things of the world not only does not bring lasting happiness and peace, but it drives us to seek more. When "all we've ever wanted" is grounded in the temporal trappings of this world, it is never enough!"

Brent Top

Chapter 15

Living a Lukewarm and Comfortable Life

One of the most sobering messages in the Bible is found in Revelation 3:15–16. Jesus speaks to the church in Laodicea:

"I know your works, that you are neither cold nor hot. I could wish you were cold or hot. So then, because you are lukewarm, and neither cold nor hot, I will vomit you out of My mouth."

This was not spoken to atheists or pagans. It was spoken to the church, to believers who were active, but indifferent. They were present, but passionless, and religious, but powerless.

Lukewarm Christianity is perhaps the greatest danger facing the modern church. It's not the loud rejection of God, it's the quiet fading away. It's the casual, complacent, half-hearted life that looks spiritual but lacks fire.

The gospel of Jesus Christ is many things. It is good news. It is hope for the broken, and it is the power of God unto salvation. But it is not, and never has been, a message of ease, indulgence, or comfort.

In many churches today, the Gospel has been repackaged, not in the boldness and self-denial of Christ, but in the padded comforts of modern life. We now hear messages filled with motivational speeches, personal success, emotional validation, and promises of worldly ease, all under the banner of Christianity. This message, often referred to as the **"Gospel of Comfort,"** is seductive. It appeals to the flesh, speaks to our fears of suffering, and distorts the mission of the cross of Christ.

But the true Gospel is not one of earthly comfort, it is one of eternal redemption, sanctifying suffering, and resurrection power. It is found in **the crucified Christ**, not the cushioned pew. We must return to the **power of the cross**, where victory over sin, death, and self is won, not by making life easier, but by surrendering our lives entirely to Christ.

Yet in many pulpits today, the gospel has been reshaped into a soft, sanitized version that promises comfort without commitment, blessing without brokenness, and joy without judgment.

This is the gospel of comfort. It is a counterfeit gospel that avoids the cross.

What Is Lukewarmness?

Lukewarmness is spiritual apathy. It's when:

- Prayer is a chore, not a lifeline.
- Worship is routine, not reverent.
- Scripture is optional, not essential.
- Church is habit, not hunger.

The lukewarm believer is content with just enough Jesus to ease the conscience but not enough to transform the life.

Jesus doesn't say He's mildly displeased with lukewarmness. He says it makes Him sick. It's nauseating to a God who gave everything.

Signs of a Lukewarm Life

How can you tell if you're lukewarm? Here are some signs:

- You talk more about God than to God.
- You feel more excitement over entertainment than evangelism.
- You're more concerned with fitting in than standing out.
- You compromise in small areas and justify it with "grace."
- You fear man more than God.

Lukewarmness is not always obvious. It can look like success. It can sound very positive. It can even wear the mask of morality. But underneath, it lacks intimacy with Jesus.

The Danger of Comfort

Lukewarm believers are often successful in the world's eyes. They have jobs, families, reputations, and routines. But their comfort has cost them their conviction.

- They no longer weep over sin.
- They no longer hunger for holiness.
- They no longer tremble at God's Word.

Their lives are safe, but not surrendered, busy, but not burning with the unquenchable fire of God.

Comfort is not the enemy, but when it becomes the goal, it produces spiritual complacency. Jesus didn't call us to comfort. He called us to carry a cross.

Comfort is not inherently wrong. God is a comforter. But when comfort becomes the *goal* of our faith instead of the *fruit* of our obedience, it distorts the gospel.

The comfortable gospel says:

- "God wants you to be happy."
- "Faith will make your life easier."
- "Following Jesus is all about peace and prosperity."

But Jesus said:

"If anyone would come after me, let him deny himself and take up his cross daily and follow me." — Luke 9:23

Ironically, while the Gospel of Comfort offers ease and fails to deliver, the **true Gospel offers a rugged cross**—and delivers eternal comfort:

- **Peace with God** (Romans 5:1)
- **Victory over sin** (Romans 6:6)
- **Joy in suffering** (James 1:2-4)
- **Hope beyond the grave** (1 Corinthians 15:54-57)

This is not comfort that fades with circumstances—it is comfort rooted in **Christ alone**. The true gospel isn't about our comfort. It's about our conformity to the image of Christ. And that conformity often requires discomfort.

The Powerless Church

When the message of the cross is removed from our preaching, we rob the gospel of its weight and wonder.

- Sin becomes a mistake, not rebellion.
- Repentance becomes a suggestion, not a necessity.
- Jesus becomes a life coach, not a Savior.

Soft preaching produces shallow disciples, people who can quote verses but have never been crucified with Christ.

A gospel without a cross has no power to save. The cross is central—not optional. It is where sin was paid for, where love was proven, and where victory was won. But it is also the model for how we are to live.

"I have been crucified with Christ. It is no longer I who live, but Christ who lives in me." — Galatians 2:20

We are not just called to believe in the cross—we are called to carry it.

- That means dying to pride.
- Dying to comfort.
- Dying to sin.

And through that death comes resurrection power.

A lukewarm church has programs but no power. It has crowds but no conviction. It has lights but no light.

The early Church had no buildings, no budgets, no branding—but they had *boldness*. They turned the world upside down. Why? Because they were on fire with the Holy Spirit.

We don't need more polished sermons. We need Pentecost power.

The Power of the Cross of Christ

1. The Cross is the Center of the Gospel

The apostle Paul declared, ***"For I decided to know nothing among you except Jesus Christ and him crucified"*** (1 Corinthians 2:2). The cross is not merely the starting point of faith—it is the **very core of Christianity**. At the cross:

- God's wrath against sin was satisfied (Romans 3:25).
- Satan was defeated (Colossians 2:14-15).
- The way to eternal life was opened (John 14:6).

The Gospel is not about how to make life more comfortable. It's about how to be made right with God through the suffering and sacrifice of Jesus.

2. The Cross Requires Death to Self

Jesus said, *"If anyone would come after me, let him deny himself and take up his cross daily and follow me"* (Luke 9:23). This is not a call to self-improvement, but to self-death. Following Jesus involves:

- Dying to our own will and desires.
- Abandoning our personal kingdoms.
- Embracing suffering for Christ's sake (Philippians 1:29).

The power of the cross is that it transforms the sinner—not through comfort, but through crucifixion of the old life.

4. The Cross Brings True Comfort

Returning to the Power of the Gospel

1. Preach Christ Crucified

The Church must return to preaching the full counsel of God. We cannot skip Calvary and expect resurrection. Every true message of hope must flow from the cross. Preachers and believers alike must proclaim:

- Sin is real and deadly.
- Christ died to save sinners.
- Salvation is by grace, through faith, resulting in holiness.

2. Live a Cross-Centered Life

Believers must reject the Gospel of Comfort by embracing a lifestyle that reflects the cross:

- Suffering with Christ (Romans 8:17)
- Sacrificing for the Gospel (Philippians 3:8)

- Standing for truth even when it costs us (Matthew 5:10-12)

We must let go of ease and embrace eternal purpose.

3. Glory in the Cross

Paul wrote, *"But far be it from me to boast except in the cross of our Lord Jesus Christ..."* (Galatians 6:14). When we understand the power of the cross:

- We stop boasting in ourselves.
- We stop fearing affliction.
- We begin to live with power, humility, and passion for Christ.

Choose the Cross, Not Comfort

The Gospel of Comfort may be popular, but it cannot save. It may fill churches, but it cannot cleanse hearts. It may make life easy, but it leaves the soul in peril.

Only the **Gospel of the Cross** has the power to save, sanctify, and secure. It is a call to die that we may truly live. The power of the cross is not in its ability to remove hardship—but in its power to transform sinners into saints, weak men into warriors, and sufferers into sons of God.

Let us return to the cross. Let us reject the soothing lies of a comfortable gospel. Let us embrace the glorious pain and power of Christ crucified.

The Gospel of Comfort: A Dangerous Deception

1. The Message of Self-Centered Faith

In the Gospel of Comfort, the message revolves around the believer rather than Christ. Sermons become therapeutic sessions, filled with affirmations that God exists to make us feel better, live better, and achieve our dreams. Sin is rarely mentioned, repentance is optional, and holiness is outdated. In this version of the gospel:

- Jesus becomes a life coach, not a crucified Savior.

- The cross becomes a symbol of inspiration, not a call to die.
- God's love is reduced to emotional support rather than holy transformation.

2. Appealing to the Flesh

Paul warned Timothy that *"the time will come when people will not endure sound teaching, but having itching ears they will accumulate for themselves teachers to suit their own passions"* (2 Timothy 4:3). The Gospel of Comfort is just that—a message suited to human passions. It avoids:

- The cost of discipleship (Luke 14:27)
- The offense of the cross (Galatians 5:11)
- The call to crucify the flesh (Galatians 5:24)

3. Comfort Over Conviction

This distorted gospel confuses God's grace with God's permission. It creates a climate where truth is softened so that no one is offended. But the true Gospel is **deeply offensive to the sinful nature**. It tells us:

- We are sinners in need of saving.
- We cannot save ourselves.
- We must die to live (Luke 9:23-24).

The comfort it offers is temporary, but the deception it brings is eternal.

Jesus' Remedy for Lukewarmness

In Revelation 3:18–19, Jesus gives the cure:

"I counsel you to buy from Me gold refined in the fire... as many as I love, I rebuke and chasten. Therefore be zealous and repent."

The cure is not performance—it's repentance. It's not doing more—it's loving more. Jesus calls us to:

- Return to our first love.
- Rekindle the fire of devotion.
- Reject apathy and pursue holiness.

Zeal is not emotional hype—it's spiritual hunger. It's a fire that burns in private before it's seen in public.

Let Him In

Perhaps the most tragic part of Jesus' message to Laodicea is verse 20:

"Behold, I stand at the door and knock."

Jesus was outside His own church. The One who died for her was not welcomed inside. Why? Because they were too full, too busy, too satisfied without Him.

He still knocks today—on the door of the church, on the door of our hearts. Will we let Him in? Not just as a visitor, but as Lord?

The Cost of Discipleship

Jesus never promised a life of ease. He promised persecution, rejection, and trials for those who followed Him. He spoke of narrow roads, self-denial, and spiritual warfare.

- He did not say, "Come and be comfortable."
- He said, "Come and die."

The early church understood this. They embraced suffering for the sake of Christ. They counted it joy to be persecuted. Their lives were marked not by comfort, but by commitment. Yet today, many believers abandon faith when things get hard because they were never taught that hardship is part of the journey.

Conclusion

We must return to the gospel that Jesus preached:

- A gospel that confronts sin.
- A gospel that demands repentance.
- A gospel that calls us to die—so we can truly live.

The gospel is not just about death, it's about resurrection. But resurrection only comes after the cross. Yes, there is joy. Yes, there is comfort. Yes, there is peace. But these are fruits of surrender, not replacements for it.

Jesus went to the cross before He went to the crown. And we must follow in His steps. Let us preach the cross again. Not just as a symbol, but as a lifestyle. Let us stop selling comfort and start offering Christ. Let us prepare believers to suffer well, serve faithfully, and live sacrificially. Because only a crucified life is a resurrected life. And only the true gospel has the power to transform the world.

"For I decided to know nothing among you except Jesus Christ and him crucified." — 1 Corinthians 2:2

Lukewarm Christianity is a counterfeit. It's the enemy's way of numbing believers into spiritual sleep. But Jesus is calling us to wake up, rise up, and burn again. You don't need to stay stuck in complacency. You don't have to live powerless. You can be on fire again.

- Return to prayer.
- Return to fasting.
- Return to the Word.
- Return to worship that costs you something.
- Return to obedience—even when it's hard.

The world doesn't need more comfortable Christians. It needs burning ones, those whose hearts are ablaze with holy fire. Let this be your cry:

"Lord, set me on fire again. Burn away what's lukewarm. I want to burn for You."

He is faithful to answer. He is knocking. Will you open the door?

Reflection Questions

These questions are designed for personal meditation or journaling.

1. **In what ways have I believed or embraced a "Gospel of Comfort"?**
   Have I expected God to prioritize my ease over my holiness?

2. **How often do I think about the cross of Christ in my daily life?**
   What does the cross mean to me personally?
3. **Am I willing to suffer for the name of Christ?**
   If suffering comes for my faith, will I remain faithful or retreat?
4. **How has the modern church shifted from the power of the cross to comfort-driven messages?**
   Have I seen this trend, and how has it affected me?
5. **Do I seek spiritual growth or spiritual ease?**
   What steps can I take to grow deeper in Christ, even if it is uncomfortable?
6. **Is there anything in my life I need to crucify in order to walk in the power of the cross?**
   Are there habits, beliefs, or idols that need to die?
7. **How can I glorify Christ more in suffering or trials rather than escaping them?**
   What does it mean to boast in weakness?

Small Group Study Guide

Use this guide to facilitate a small group discussion centered on the teaching.

Session Title: *"The Gospel of Comfort vs. the Power of the Cross"*

Scripture Readings:

- Luke 9:23-24 – *"Take up your cross daily..."*
- Galatians 6:14 – *"Far be it from me to boast except in the cross..."*
- 2 Timothy 4:3-4 – *"They will not endure sound doctrine..."*
- Romans 6:6 – *"Our old self was crucified with him..."*

Opening Icebreaker:

"What is something you've sacrificed for something more important in life? How did it feel in the moment, and what did it produce later?"

Discussion Questions:

1. **What are some examples of the Gospel of Comfort that we see in the modern church?**
    - How are these messages attractive to people today?
    - Why are they spiritually dangerous?
2. **What does the cross represent in the life of a believer today?**
    - How is it more than a symbol?
3. **Why do you think Paul emphasized 'Christ crucified' instead of comfort, prosperity, or ease?**
4. **How does embracing the cross help us endure suffering, persecution, or loss?**
    - Can you share a testimony where suffering produced spiritual maturity?
5. **What are practical ways we can live "cross-centered" lives in today's world?**

Group Activity: "Comfort vs. Cross"

Supplies Needed: Index cards or sheets of paper.
Instructions:
Ask each group member to write two lists:

- List 1: Comforts I cling to that may be hindering my walk with Christ.
- List 2: Cross-centered practices I want to pursue (i.e., prayer, fasting, witnessing, self-denial, sacrificial giving).

Give time for silent reflection, then invite voluntary sharing and prayer.

Action Challenge:

Each group member chooses one "comfort" to surrender to God this week and one "cross-centered" practice to intentionally embrace. Hold each other accountable in the next session.

<u>Closing Prayer</u>

Lord Jesus, crucified and risen King, I come to You, not seeking ease, but transformation. Forgive me for chasing comfort more than character, and convenience more than the cross.

I lay down my self-will, my pride, my idols, and my fears. Teach me to deny myself, take up my cross, and follow You with boldness and humility.

When I suffer, let me rejoice in sharing in Your suffering. When I'm weak, let me boast in Your strength. May I never trade the power of the cross for the applause of the world.

Purify Your Church. Awaken Your people. And let me be among those who live not for comfort, but for Christ alone. In Your mighty and holy name I pray,

Amen.

Chapter 16

Worldly Success vs. Biblical Success

In a world saturated with ambition, achievement, and applause, the definition of success has become synonymous with wealth, fame, influence, and comfort. However, the Word of God offers a drastically different perspective. The Bible not only redefines success but also warns of the eternal consequences of pursuing worldly success apart from God's will. Understanding the contrast between **worldly success** and **biblical success** is vital for every believer who seeks to honor God with their life.

Defining Worldly Success

Worldly success is often measured by **external accomplishments**. It is a system rooted in materialism, status, and personal fulfillment. Its standards are ever-changing, influenced by culture, media, and societal expectations. Here are some core characteristics of worldly success:

- **Possessions:** Accumulating wealth, luxury items, and financial independence.
- **Power and Prestige:** Climbing the ladder of authority, popularity, or celebrity.
- **Performance:** Achievements in career, education, or social circles.
- **Pleasure:** Pursuing happiness, entertainment, and comfort at any cost.

At its core, worldly success is **self-centered**. It asks, *"What can I gain?"*, *"How can I be recognized?"*, and *"What makes me feel good?"*

What does it mean to succeed? For many, success is defined by status, income, education, possessions, and popularity. From the time we are young, society trains us to chase titles, trophies, and applause. Even within the Church, worldly success is often celebrated as spiritual blessing. But Jesus offers a chilling warning:

"For what will it profit a man if he gains the whole world, and loses his own soul?" — Mark 8:36

This is the tragedy of worldly success. It promises everything and delivers nothing that lasts. It feeds the ego while starving the spirit. It builds up treasure on earth while ignoring eternity.

Worldly success is a mirage. It looks satisfying from a distance, but when you reach it, you're still thirsty. Fame fades. Money runs out. Achievements are forgotten. And yet, many believers spend their lives chasing after these things as if they are eternal. Jesus didn't condemn success, but He redefined it. In the kingdom of God:

- The greatest is the servant.
- The first will be last.
- The rich must give.
- The exalted will be humbled.

Kingdom success is not measured by how high you climb, but by how faithfully you follow.

Signs You're Trapped by Worldly Success

The snare of worldly success can be subtle. Here are some signs:

- Your identity is tied to your achievements.
- You make decisions based on money, not mission.
- You envy others' positions or possessions.
- You compromise integrity to get ahead.
- You measure your worth by how others see you.

If gaining more requires giving up godliness, it's not success—it's seduction.

The Deception of Christianized Ambition

Worldliness in the Church often wears a spiritual disguise. We call our ambition "vision." We call our greed "God's favor." We justify our pride as "confidence." But God sees through it all.

- Building a platform is not the same as building the kingdom.
- A big following is not proof of divine approval.
- Financial blessing is not always a sign of God's pleasure.

God is not impressed by what impresses people. He sees the heart. He weighs the motives. And He rewards what is done in secret.

Defining Biblical Success

True success in God's eyes is simple:

- **Faithfulness**: Did you obey what He asked?
- **Surrender**: Did you yield your will to His?
- **Holiness**: Did you pursue purity of heart?
- **Love**: Did you love Him with all your heart, soul, mind, and strength, and all others more than you love yourself?

At the judgment seat, God won't ask about our resumes, He'll ask about our obedience. He won't be impressed by the size of our ministries, but by the depth of our character.

Biblical success is **God-centered**. It is not about how much we can gain, but how much we can glorify God and serve others. It is rooted in **obedience, faithfulness, humility, and eternal purpose**. Here are the hallmarks of biblical success:

- **Obedience to God's Word:** Living according to Scripture, even when it costs.
- **Faithfulness in Stewardship:** Using all of our time, talent, and treasure to serve God's Kingdom.
- **Character over Credentials:** Valuing integrity, purity, and the fruit of the Spirit.
- **Eternal Focus:** Living for what will last forever, not for fleeting gains.
- **Completing God's will for our lives:** Remaining focused on determining God's perfect will for our lives and its completion.

Joshua 1:8 outlines the foundation of biblical success:

"This Book of the Law shall not depart from your mouth, but you shall meditate in it day and night... For then you will make your way prosperous, and then you will have good success."

Notice the condition: **Success comes through submission to God's Word**, not through ambition or strategy. Therefore, it is important that we make the discipline of Bible study a priority for spiritual success.

The Source of Each Kind of Success

- **Worldly success** often originates from **self-effort, competition, and ambition**. It promotes independence from God and frequently encourages compromise.
- **Biblical success** flows from a life of **surrender, trust, and dependence on God**. It seeks God's will first and delights in pleasing Him above all else.

Proverbs 3:5–6 reminds us:

"Trust in the Lord with all your heart, and lean not on your own understanding; in all your ways acknowledge Him, and He shall direct your paths."

The Fruit of Each Kind of Success

Worldly Success:

- **Temporary satisfaction:** The thrill of achievement quickly fades.
- **Spiritual emptiness:** Despite gaining everything, many remain restless and unsatisfied.
- **Moral compromise:** To maintain worldly success, one may lie, cheat, or trample on others.
- **Eternal loss:** Without Christ, all worldly achievements will perish.

Ecclesiastes 2:11 records Solomon's reflection after acquiring worldly success:

"Then I looked on all the works that my hands had done... and indeed all was vanity and grasping for the wind."

As we reflect upon this final regret of Solomon, be determined to not let this be your final regret.

Biblical Success:

- **Inner peace and joy:** Rooted in a relationship with Christ, not in circumstances.
- **Eternal reward:** God promises crowns and commendation to those who are faithful (2 Timothy 4:7–8).
- **Kingdom impact:** Lives are changed, disciples are made, and God is glorified.
- **Divine approval:** The ultimate goal is to hear, *"Well done, good and faithful servant"* (Matthew 25:21).

The Eternal Implications

The Bible makes it clear: **every earthly crown will one day rust, but heavenly rewards are eternal.** The tragedy is that many people, even believers, are seduced by worldly success and live for things that will not last. Jesus tells the parable of the rich fool in Luke 12:16–21, a man who built bigger barns to store his wealth but died that very night. God called him a fool because he was "not rich toward God."

1 John 2:17 says:

"The world is passing away, and the lust of it; but he who does the will of God abides forever."

Those who live for worldly success without Christ will face **eternal separation from God**, regardless of how celebrated they were on earth. But those who pursue biblical success through Christ will inherit **eternal life, a crown of righteousness, and everlasting joy in God's presence.**

Biblical Success Achieved Through God's Perfect Will

The will of God is God's desired plan or 'blueprint' for His creation to glorify Him. God works through His creation to effect His designed plan and order for spiritual success. Each individual in God's creation is allowed the freedom to accept or reject God's will for their life and their designed input into His kingdom plan.

In effecting His designed kingdom plan, God's will for each individual is a two-fold desire of God. First, his **corporate will** for His church body applies to all believers. Then, there is His (unique) **distinct, personal will** for each believer. Knowledge of both is required to live a Biblically prosperous and spiritually balanced life in the earthly kingdom of God.

The corporate will of God has eternal consequences. Jesus highlighted this eternal truth in a warning to His followers that remains applicable to the twenty-first-century church. In Matthew 7, verses 21-23, He stated,

"Not every one that saith unto me, Lord, Lord, shall enter into the kingdom of heaven; but he that doeth the will of my Father which is in heaven. Many will say to me in that day, Lord, Lord, have we not prophesied in thy name? and in thy name have cast out devils? And in thy name done many wonderful works? And then will I profess unto them, I never knew you: depart from me, ye that work iniquity".

In clarifying God's corporate will, Jesus stated in John 6:40,

"and this is the will of him that sent me, that every one which seeth the Son, and believeth on him, may have everlasting life: and I will raise him up at the last day (ref. 1st John 3:23). *"*

In addressing Matthew 7, verse 21, Matthew Henry stated in his commentary, "Now this is his will, that we believe in Christ, that we repent of sin, that we live a holy life, that we love one another. This is His will, even our sanctification. If we comply not with the will of God, we mock Christ in calling Him Lord, as those did who put on Him a gorgeous robe, and said hail, king of the Jews."[2]

Belief in Christ is not just a belief of the intellect, but a belief of the heart. To believe in Christ is to live for Christ with our whole being, with His sacrificial life before us as our model. There must not be hypocrisy in our confession of faith.

To live God's distinct, personal will for one's life should be viewed as bearing one's cross (Luke 14:27). Biblical success is tied to our association with and living as ambassadors for the cross of Christ, only desiring to glorify Him. Sadly, most professing Christians live their entire lives without ever knowing God's distinct, personal will for their lives. Many twenty-first-century professing Christians live their whole lives committed to a pseudo-Christianity that hinders any revelation of God's distinct, personal will for their lives, their cross to bear.

Far too many churches are committed to a ministry focus that is characterized by worldliness. The informative Spirit of God will not be experienced in this setting. In this setting, more emphasis is placed on living a balanced and wholesome life rather than a sacrificial life determined by God's perfect will. This deceptive strategy of the enemy combines worldliness with a pseudo holiness, which is Biblically unacceptable and must be renounced by all 'true' followers of Christ (ref. James 4:4).

God's distinct, personal will for each believer will have eternal rewards and should be prioritized as an investment in eternal life and God's kingdom here on earth.

Every professing Christian must be mindful that there will be many spiritual challenges in fulfilling God's distinct, personal will. Fulfilling the distinct, personal will of God will be a 'true' test of our faith in God. Not only will it take us out of our comfort zone(s), but it will require that we hold firmly to God's unchanging hand through this adventurous journey of Christianity. As stated, "Living God's distinct, personal will for one's life may be viewed as bearing one's cross."

God's Divine Order mandates that our first decision in life must always be to seek His will for our lives. All other life-altering decisions should follow behind the resolution of this one desire. This priority has always been God's designed order for a prosperous and productive life of spiritual wholeness. Jesus stated in Matthew 6:33,

"But seek ye first the kingdom of God, and his righteousness; and all these things shall be added unto you."

The kingdom of God includes the will of God for our lives. Each distinct, personal will of God has an assigned purpose in His kingdom plan.

A primary reason for many of our regretful and life-altering mistakes in life is that we failed to first seek God's kingdom (His distinct, personal will) and His righteousness before making other major decisions regarding our lives.

A worldly-inspired faith will lead us to make worldly-inspired decisions regarding our lives.

We will often make and commit to life-altering decisions (e.g., educational goals, career paths, property purchases, marriage and family development plans, etc.) without first knowing and understanding God's plan(s) for our lives. Often, later in life, we may genuinely seek God's will for our lives. After receiving His distinct, personal will for our lives, we may, sorrowfully, realize our earlier decisions' incompatibility with God's plan(s).

This is a crucial requirement of God that we commonly neglect.

The results of that neglect will often become obstacles to discipleship development and walking in the perfect will of God for the remainder of our lives.

Before we make any significant decisions and commitments regarding our lives, we are commanded to first seek God's will for our lives. After we receive and honor His will, submit and entrust our lives to His care, God will provide everything else required for lifelong success. All else that He provides will be compatible with His revealed will.

The Role of Godly Parents in Their Children's Success

As Godly parents, it is our duty and must remain our priority to help our children determine God's will for their lives to place them on God's desired pathway for lifelong spiritual success. Our children should gain awareness, as early as possible, of this requirement of God and understand it as their first and foremost priority in life.

They must be taught to view all of their life experiences under the revealing light of this priority. Parents should not instill a priority of worldly financial security but God's kingdom security. It is only in God's kingdom's security that we have lasting and real-life security. Don't train them in the ways of this world but in the ways of God. Parents are commanded to"

"Train up a child in the way he should go, and when he is old, he will not depart from it" (Prov. 22:6).

Real success and security in their life will result from living the perfect will of God. As parents, we should redirect their focus from deciding which career path will provide the most money to the Biblical priority of determining God's planned career path that is designed to glorify His kingdom best.

****

As a **side note**, problem resolution will be a lifelong challenge and requirement for everyone, simply because we live in a fallen society that is influenced by deceptive evilness. We should instruct our children to always use the Bible as their guide for problem resolution in life. The Bible has God's desired answers for all of life's concerns. This lifelong discipline will not just keep their focus on God, but increase their faith in His unlimited ability and reliability, especially as it applies to their life's crises. This also is God's will (ref. Isaiah 26:3).

****

Final Challenge to Believers

The difference between worldly and biblical success is not just in **what you pursue**, but **why and for whom you pursue it**. As believers, we must constantly examine our motives, goals, and priorities. Are we living to make our name great, or to make God's name known? Are we seeking comfort in the temporary, or investing in the eternal?

Paul offers us the proper mindset in Philippians 3:7–8:

"But what things were gain to me, these I have counted loss for Christ... that I may gain Christ."

Let us choose the path of biblical success, obedience over ambition, faithfulness over fame, and Christ above all.

Eternal Loss in the Midst of Earthly Gain

The saddest stories in Scripture are not of those who failed, but of those who succeeded and lost their souls in the process:

- **King Saul** gained a throne but lost God's favor.
- **Judas** gained money but lost his life.
- **Demas** loved the world and abandoned the mission.

How many today are doing the same? Trading eternal treasure for temporary applause? Choosing comfort over calling? Settling for now while forfeiting forever?

Living for What Lasts

Colossians 3:2 exhorts us:

"Set your mind on things above, not on things on the earth."

You were not created to live for applause, promotions, or possessions. You were created for purpose, for eternity, and for glory that cannot be measured by the world.

- Build what won't burn.

- Invest where moth and rust cannot destroy.
- Live for the "well done" of the Master—not the praise of men.

Conclusion: Choose the Better Reward

Worldly success is not inherently evil. But when it becomes your god, it leads to ruin. Jesus doesn't ask us to abandon ambition, He asks us to redeem it.

Let your drive be for His glory. Let your achievements reflect His grace. Let your rewards be stored in heaven.

Success without surrender is empty. Gain without God is loss.
So ask yourself:

Am I climbing a ladder God never asked me to? Am I succeeding in the world while failing in the Spirit? Will what I'm living for matter 100 years from now?

In a world obsessed with gain, choose the path of godliness. For in the end, only what's done for Christ will remain.

May we not just run hard, but run in the right direction. May we not just win the race, but win *His* reward.
For it is far better to hear from Jesus, "Well done," than to hear from the world, "Well liked."

Small Group Discussion Questions

1. **What is your personal definition of success?**
    - How has that definition been shaped by culture, family, or media?
2. **According to Scripture, what does it mean to be successful in God's eyes?**
    - Read Joshua 1:8 and Matthew 25:21 together.
3. **Have you ever felt torn between pursuing worldly success and living faithfully for God?**
    - What pressures influence that conflict?
4. **Why do you think worldly success is so appealing—even for believers?**

5. **What are some examples of people in the Bible who were successful by God's standards but not by the world's?**
    - (e.g., Joseph, John the Baptist, Paul, Ruth)
6. **What does Jesus mean when He says, "What does it profit a man to gain the whole world and lose his soul?" (Mark 8:36)**
    - What are some modern examples of this principle?
7. **How can we pursue excellence in life, career, or ministry without falling into the trap of worldly ambition?**
8. **What does it mean to pursue God's "corporate will" and His "distinct, personal will" for one's life? Can we explain why they are both necessary for spiritual success?**
9. **What does "eternal reward" mean to you personally?**
    - How does the idea of eternity influence your daily decisions?

Key Reflection Points

- **Success is not about accumulation, but obedience.**
  Biblical success is measured by faithfulness to God's Word and will.
- **Worldly success ends at the grave; eternal success begins there.**
  What we invest in now will echo in eternity—either for reward or loss.
- **A faithful life may not always look impressive to others.**
  Some of the most successful people in God's eyes live humble, quiet lives of devotion and service.
- **Your identity must be rooted in Christ, not in achievements.**
  The world says *"You are what you do,"* but God says *"You are Mine."*
- **Eternal perspective fuels daily purpose.**
  When we fix our eyes on eternity, we begin to make different choices today.

<u>Closing Prayer</u>

Heavenly Father,

Thank You for reminding us that true success is not measured by what we accumulate or achieve, but by how closely we walk with You. Forgive us for the times we have chased worldly applause more than Your approval. Help us to hunger for Your Word, obey Your voice, and live for what matters most.

Teach us to number our days and invest them wisely for Your Kingdom. Let our lives bring You glory, not just for a season, but for eternity. Strengthen us to resist the fleeting pleasures of this world and to run the race with endurance, keeping our eyes on Jesus—the Author and Finisher of our faith.

May we one day stand before You and hear, "Well done, good and faithful servant."

In Jesus' name we pray,
Amen.

Chapter 17

Christians Trapped in Idolatry

When we think of idolatry, our minds often wander to golden calves and pagan temples. But idolatry in the modern Church is much more subtle, and far more dangerous. It hides behind the façade of good intentions. It wears religious clothing. It sits comfortably in pews. It sings worship songs while secretly serving self.

"You shall have no other gods before me." — Exodus 20:3

Modern idolatry isn't always about statues. It's about anything that takes the place of God in our hearts.

What Is Idolatry?

An "**idol**" is anything loved more than God, wanted more than God, enjoyed more than God, or treasured more than God. An idol can be something such as a statue or other object that we worship as a god. It can also be a person or thing that we love, admire, want, or treasure more than God. **"Idolatry" is the worship of any other thing or person other than God.**

Idolatry is when anything or anyone becomes more important to us than God. It can be:

- A relationship
- A career
- A dream
- A pastor or spiritual leader
- Our comfort, reputation, or even ministry

An idol doesn't have to be evil, it just has to be enthroned. And the modern Church is filled with idols.

As believers in Christ, we reverence and serve the one and only true God who will not allow worship of any other gods. God said in Exodus 20:5, *"I the LORD thy God am a jealous God."*

All other gods are false gods. They are made and created in our own minds and hearts. Anything that we can create in our minds and hearts is not a real God, and we should not honor it, worship it, or have anything to do with it. God commanded us to have no other gods, which is the first commandment from God.

****

Note: When we are referencing our heavenly Father as God, we use the capital letter "G." When we are referencing all other gods (false gods), we use the lower case "g."

****

Other gods (false gods) can come in many different forms. Anything in this world can become a god when we cherish it and begin to worship it. **Worship** is the expression of ultimate devotion, honor, respect, and adoration.

Idolatry is Satan's roadblock to realizing God's 'Great Commandment.' It is his centerpiece, crown jewel, and primary strategy behind worldliness.

As we have already said, God commanded in the Bible that we shall have no other gods before Him. Our Bible tells us in 1st Corinthians 10:14, *"So dear friends, carefully avoid idol worship of every kind."* Also, it tells us in 1st John 5:21, *"Dear children, keep away from anything that might take God's place in your hearts."* The Bible reminds us that it is a sin to worship anything else in this world. We must only worship God. If we own anything in this world that we love or desire more than God, that thing has become an idol to us, and we should get rid of it and ask God to forgive us of that sin. We should ask God to help us not love or desire anything in this world more than we love or desire Him. We should also ask God to show us anything in our possession or this world that we have allowed to become an idol. Once God reveals it to us, we must remove it or remove ourselves from it.

Shadrach, Meshach, and Abednego

There is a story in the Bible (Dan. 3) about a king whose name was Nebuchadnezzar. He made a golden statue that was ninety feet high and nine feet wide. King Nebuchadnezzar loved this statue, and to him, it was his god. So he called everyone in his kingdom to come together to show them this great statue that he had made. He had it announced that every time the band would start to play music, everyone had to fall flat on the ground to worship his statue.

When the band started to play, everyone but three men fell to the ground and worshiped the statue as the king commanded. King Nebuchadnezzar was informed that these three men did not do as he commanded. The names of these three men were Shadrach, Meshach, and Abednego. These three men loved God more than anything else. Our love for God is shown in our obedience to Him. Because they loved God and were obedient to God, they would not worship anything else or anybody but God. Because they had learned about God, they knew the commands that God had given. They knew that God had commanded in Exodus 34:17, *"You must have nothing to do with idols."* Also, God had commanded in Leviticus 26:1, *"You must have no idols; carved images, obelisks, or shaped stones, for I am the Lord your God."* So they refused to fall and worship the statue that King Nebuchadnezzar had made.

King Nebuchadnezzar became very angry with these three men. **People will often become angry with you when you refuse to worship their idols.** He gave them one more chance to worship his golden statue. He told them that if they refused again to worship his statue, he would throw them into a flaming furnace.

Shadrach, Meshach, and Abednego said to king Nebuchadnezzar, *"O Nebuchadnezzar, we are not worried about what will happen to us. If we are thrown into the flaming furnace, our God is able to deliver us; and he will deliver us out of your hand. We will never under any circumstance serve your gods or worship the golden statue you have erected"* (Daniel 3:16-18).

Like these men, we also must have total faith (trust) in God.

****

"Faith" in God is complete trust and confidence in God based on a true understanding of who He is. We show our faith in God when we trust Him to do what he says in the Bible that He will do. We show our faith in God by believing everything that He says. We must study the Bible to know what to expect and what not to expect from God. Sometimes, we expect God to do things for us that He has not promised in the Bible that He will do. **We**

are expected to do the things that we can do, and trust God to do what we cannot do. So we must pray to Him in accordance with what the Bible reveals about Him.

****

After the three men said this to the king, he became even more furious. He was so angry that he had the furnace heated up seven times hotter than usual. He had the three men bound with ropes and threw them into the flaming furnace. The flames were so hot that they killed the soldiers as they threw them into the furnace. Amazingly, Shadrach, Meshach, and Abednego did not die in the flames as the king had hoped. They did not even get burned in the fire because an angel of God entered into the furnace with them and protected them from the flames.

****

When we trust and obey God like these three men, He will assign His angels to help us in life. They will often protect us when we are in trouble. **"Angels"** are beings that God has created to serve Him and help us when needed. They have greater power and ability than we do. Because we don't often see them does not mean that they are not with us.

****

When these three men emerged from the furnace, they did not even smell like smoke. When king Nebuchadnezzar saw them, he said, ***"Blessed be the God of Shadrach, Meshach, and Abednego, for he sent his angel to deliver his trusting servants when they defied the king's commandment, and were willing to die rather than serve or worship any god except their own"*** (Daniel 3:28).

God protected these three men because they loved Him more than anything else and trusted Him completely. They refused to worship anything besides Him. As servants of God, we must be like Shadrach, Meshach, and Abednego and, at all cost, refuse to allow any idols into our lives, and God will bless us.

The Deception of Idolatry

Idolatry is often misunderstood as a problem of the ancient world—statues, altars, and golden calves. But idolatry is not confined to the past; it is alive and thriving in the modern world, just wearing special clothes that we cherish can lead to them becoming idols. The deception of idolatry today is not that it no longer exists, but that it is harder to detect. It hides behind ambition, entertainment, relationships, careers, comfort, and even religious activity. It masks itself as harmless passion, personal freedom, or self-expression. Yet beneath the surface lies the same root issue: a heart that puts something, or someone, above God.

Idolatry is not just about worshipping something with your hands; it's about surrendering your heart to something other than the one true God.

"Dear children, keep yourselves from idols." - 1 John 5:21

Many believers unknowingly live in idolatry. It happens when our hearts cling to anything more tightly than they cling to God. The deception is subtle but deadly.

What are some things in our lives that can become an idol?

1. Items of clothing or footwear that we love more than God.
2. Cars, vehicles, and houses can become idols when we love them more than we love God. Our yards and plants can become idols. Even our hobbies and pets can become idols.
3. Electronics or games that we spend more time with than we spend with God.
4. A person that we admire more than we admire God, such as a rock star, a movie star, an athlete, or any other individual.
5. Sports and sports franchises can become idols when we love them more than we love God (e.g., football or soccer team).
6. Money, jewelry, and precious stones can become idols when we begin to love them.
7. Cell phones, iPads, iPhones, and social media can become idols when we love spending more time with them than with God (Social media can be asset for Christianity when it is used to glorify God. Christians must avoid the worldliness of social media).
8. Televisions can become idols when we love watching them and spend more time watching them than with God (Christians must also avoid the worldliness of televisions).

9. Our jobs can become idols when we love them more than we love God.
10. Even church buildings, religious leaders, and religious activities can become idols when we love them more than we love God.
11. Family members can become idols. We can become our own idols when we love ourselves more than we love God.

These are just a few examples of modern day idols. Again, idols can come in many different forms, so we must be careful not to have any idols in our lives.

Cultural Idols in Today's Church

1. **Celebrity Preachers** – When our allegiance is more to personalities than to Christ, we're in danger. We follow names instead of truth.
2. **Buildings and Branding** – Churches compete for attention, building massive sanctuaries and sophisticated programs, yet sometimes neglect prayer, holiness, and the Word. The Bible does not instruct us to build cathedrals and monuments to God. Far too many of them have resulted from the deadly sin of pride.
3. **Entertainment** – Worship becomes a performance. Preaching becomes motivational speech. The fear of offending replaces the fear of God.
4. **Money and Prosperity** – The prosperity gospel has turned God into a vending machine. We worship Him for what He gives, not for who He is.
5. **Comfort and Convenience** – We design faith around our schedules, rather than orchestrating our schedules around our faith. Far too many professing Christians follow Jesus only when it's easy or beneficial.

These idols are often cloaked in spiritual language, which makes them harder to detect.

Personal Idols

Beyond the corporate idols, many believers harbor hidden idols in their hearts:

- **Control** – We refuse to trust God unless we can understand everything.

- **Pride** – We care more about our image than our character.
- **Entertainment** – Hours spent scrolling and binge-watching worldly entertainment, but little time with God.
- **Relationships** – We prioritize romantic or social connections over obedience to Christ.

Jesus asked Peter three times, "Do you love Me more than these?" That is the question He asks us today: ***Do you love Me more than your comforts, your platforms, your dreams?***

The Danger of Hidden Idols

Idolatry leads to:

- Compromised faith
- Shallow worship
- Powerless prayer
- Broken intimacy with God

God will not share His throne. He is a jealous God, not because He is insecure, but because He knows that anything less than Him will ultimately destroy us.

"Little children, keep yourselves from idols." — 1 John 5:21

Tearing Down Modern Idols

Just like Gideon tore down his father's altar to Baal (Judges 6:25), modern believers must identify and destroy the idols in their lives. This requires courage, honesty, and repentance.

- **Examine your heart**: What do you think about most? What are you most afraid to lose?
- **Confess and repent**: Acknowledge where you have allowed idols to take God's place.
- **Reorder your priorities**: Make God, not your job, not your phone, not your desires, first.
- **Fill your life with truth**: Replace worldly noise and distractions with God's Word and prayer.
- **Worship God alone**: Worship is war. It re-centers your heart on the only One worthy of it.

"Flee from idolatry."- 1 Corinthians 10:14

Why Idolatry Is So Dangerous

Idolatry is not just wrong—it is **spiritually deadly**. Every idol promises what only God can give: peace, purpose, identity, security, and love. But every idol also lies. It demands your time, energy, loyalty, and affection, and gives nothing eternal in return.

"Those who make them will be like them, and so will all who trust in them."— Psalm 115:8

When you worship an idol, you eventually become like it: hollow, blind, deaf to the truth, and spiritually numb. The longer you serve a false god, the more it shapes your heart and distorts your soul.

Idolatry also **robs God of the glory He alone deserves**. As stated, He is a jealous God, not in petty insecurity, but in holy righteousness. He knows that placing our trust in anything other than Him will destroy us.

"You shall not make for yourself an image... You shall not bow down to them or worship them; for I, the Lord your God, am a jealous God."— Exodus 20:4–5

The Subtle Drift Toward Idolatry

Idolatry usually doesn't start with open rebellion. It begins with slow compromise. A Christian may slowly replace time in God's Word with hours on social media. Prayer becomes optional. Church becomes a routine. Conviction is dulled. Eventually, the idol no longer feels like an idol. It feels normal.

The danger lies in the **deception**: You can still sing worship songs while serving an idol. You can still attend church while your heart bows to another master.

"No one can serve two masters. Either you will hate the one and love the other... You cannot serve both God and money."
— Matthew 6:24

Conclusion: A Heart That Belongs to God

In a world full of digital altars and cultural golden calves, God is still calling His people to wholehearted devotion and true worship. He is not interested in part-time praise or shared loyalty. He desires our **complete trust**, our **undivided worship**, and our **surrendered hearts**.

"Love the Lord your God with all your heart and with all your soul and with all your strength." - Deuteronomy 6:5

Modern idolatry may wear a suit or carry a smartphone, but it's no less deadly than the altars of Baal. Let us not be deceived. **Let us tear down every high place in our hearts and give God the throne He alone deserves.**

Idolatry must be exposed, confessed, and removed. We don't need another golden calf. We need a blazing altar.

Let every other throne be overturned. Let every idol be crushed. Let Jesus take His rightful place.

"Those who cling to worthless idols turn away from God's love for them." — Jonah 2:8

Let us not turn away but turn back to the One who is worthy, to the One who is holy, to the One who alone deserves our worship.

Old Testament Verses on Idolatry

1. **Exodus 20:3-5 (ESV)**
   "You shall have no other gods before me. You shall not make for yourself a carved image... You shall not bow down to them or serve them, for I the Lord your God am a jealous God..."
   God's first commandment shows how seriously He views idolatry.
2. **Deuteronomy 6:14-15 (NIV)**
   "Do not follow other gods, the gods of the peoples around you; for the Lord your God, who is among you, is a jealous God and his anger will burn against you..."
   Even subtle forms of idolatry provoke God's discipline.

3. **1 Samuel 15:23 (NIV)**
   "For rebellion is like the sin of divination, and arrogance like the evil of idolatry..."
   Idolatry isn't always external. It often starts with pride and rebellion in the heart.
4. **Isaiah 44:9 (NLT)**
   "How foolish are those who manufacture idols. These prized objects are really worthless. The people who worship them don't know this, so they are all put to shame."
   Idolatry deceives and ultimately leads to shame.

New Testament Verses on Idolatry

5. **Matthew 6:24 (NIV)**
   "No one can serve two masters... You cannot serve both God and money."
   Jesus teaches that divided loyalty is impossible in the kingdom of God.
6. **Romans 1:25 (NIV)**
   "They exchanged the truth about God for a lie, and worshiped and served created things rather than the Creator..."
   Idolatry is the result of rejecting God's truth and glorifying the temporary.
7. **1 Corinthians 10:14 (ESV)**
   "Therefore, my beloved, flee from idolatry."
   Paul urges believers not just to avoid idolatry, but to actively flee from it.
8. **Colossians 3:5 (NIV)**
   "Put to death, therefore, whatever belongs to your earthly nature... greed, which is idolatry."
   Even internal desires like greed are a form of idolatry.
9. **1 John 5:21 (NIV)**
   "Dear children, keep yourselves from idols."
   A short but strong warning to maintain spiritual vigilance.

Personal Reflection Questions

1. **What does idolatry look like in my life today?**
   Are there things, such as success, money, relationships, or personal image, what I prioritize over my relationship with God?
2. **Do I turn to anything more quickly than I turn to God for comfort, identity, or direction?**
   What does that reveal about where my heart is anchored?
3. **Have I allowed cultural values or personal desires to take God's rightful place in my life?**
   How can I reclaim God's supremacy in those areas?
4. **What habits or patterns in my daily life suggest that I am serving something or someone other than God?**
   Am I willing to surrender those idols and trust God fully?
5. **How does idolatry affect my witness as a Christian?**
   In what ways might others see more of my idols than my Savior?
6. **Have I grown numb to the convicting voice of the Holy Spirit concerning idolatry?**
   How can I restore sensitivity to God's leading?

Group Discussion Questions

1. **What are some examples of modern idols that Christians commonly struggle with today?**
   (See: 1 John 5:21, Exodus 20:3-5)
2. **Why is idolatry considered spiritual adultery in Scripture? What does it say about our relationship with God?**
   (See: Ezekiel 6:9, James 4:4)
3. **How can believers detect hidden idols in their lives? What are some practical steps for tearing them down?**
   (See: Psalm 139:23–24, Judges 6:25)
4. **Why do you think idolatry is so deceptive in the modern world, even among faithful churchgoers?**
   (See: Romans 1:21–25, Matthew 6:24)
5. **In what ways can we guard our hearts against drifting into idolatry in today's culture?**
   (See: Proverbs 4:23, 1 Corinthians 10:14)
6. **What are some indicators that a person or church has allowed idolatry to take root in place of true worship?**
   (See: Revelation 2:4–5, Isaiah 44:9–20)

Closing Prayer

Father God,

You alone are worthy of all my worship, love, and devotion. Yet I confess that I have often placed other things before You, things that promised satisfaction but left me empty.

Lord, forgive me for the idols I have built in my heart, whether in secret or in plain view. Tear them down and cleanse me with Your truth.

Create in me a heart that hungers for You above all else. Teach me to love You with all my heart, soul, mind, and strength. Help me to recognize the subtle ways idolatry creeps into my life, and give me the courage to renounce anything that competes with Your Lordship.

Let my life be marked by loyalty to You alone. Restore my focus, renew my mind, and reign in my heart. May I live to please You and reflect Your holiness in a world full of distractions and false gods.

In Jesus' powerful name I pray,
Amen.

"It is as impossible for a man to live without having an object of worship as it is for a bird to fly if it is taken out of the air. The very composition of human life, the mystery of man's being, demands a center of worship as a necessity of existence. <u>All life is worship.</u> There may be a false god at the center of the life, but every activity of being, all the energy of life, the devotion of powers - these things are all worship. The question is whether the life and powers of man are devoted to the worship of the true God or to that of a false one."

G. Campbell Morgan

Chapter 18

The Narrow Road to Spiritual Wholeness

"Enter by the narrow gate: for wide is the gate and broad is the way that leads to destruction, and there are many who go in by it. Because narrow is the gate and difficult is the way which leads to life, and there are few who find it." (Matthew 17:13-14)

As we come to the close of this journey of revelation for spiritual correction and restoration, we are faced with the realization that the intricately designed strategies of worldliness will be a complex fix in our own strength and wisdom. However, we know that God is more than **"able to do exceedingly abundantly above all that we ask or think, according to the power that works in us"** (Ephesians 3:2).

Spiritual restoration must first begin with our unyielding determination to find God. God has promised that **"You will seek Me and find Me, when you search for Me with all your heart."** (Jeremiah 29:13. This is now a whole-hearted moment.
These strategies were not instituted instantly, but over many centuries from deceptive and erroneous teachings and unscriptural lifestyle allowances within the body of Christ. These strategies remain deeply rooted in the culture of God's professing church and require intervention by the Holy Spirit for immediate and permanent correction.

From the creation of this world, God has desired for his people to reflect His character in obedience and faith. However, spiritual compromise was seen from the beginning with the disobedience of Adam and Eve in the Garden of Eden. They have persisted until today.

In a time when the lines between right and wrong are blurred and spiritual compromise is common, the call for spiritual purity is not only urgent—it is essential. Spiritual purity is not about external perfection but about an undivided heart. It is about being clean before God, sincere in our motives, and faithful in our devotion.

"Blessed are the pure in heart, for they shall see God." — Matthew 5:8

The path to spiritual purity is not complicated, but it is costly. It demands humility, repentance, and a hunger for God.

Understanding Spiritual Purity

Spiritual purity is wholehearted devotion that stems from loving God with all of our heart, soul, mind, and strength as required in God's "Great Commandment" of love. We must desire to do the Biblically correct things for the right reason of giving glory to God. We must no longer seek glory for ourselves, the way of the world. We must have a desire to live a life of integrity before God and humanity, a life that is free from sin. We must receive the truth of the Holy Bible with a determined effort of conforming our lives to its mandates. Purity is not about looking religious—it's about living real before God.

With a renewed passion for obedience, we will honor God's command to *"Come out from among them* (the world)*, and be ye separate"* (2 Corinthians 6:17). This is not a call to isolation, but a divine summons to consecration — a charge to be in the world, but not of it. We must seek to live a consecrated life, free of worldly attachments and distractions.

"Who may ascend the mountain of the Lord? Who may stand in His holy place? The one who has clean hands and a pure heart." — Psalm 24:3-4

If revival is to come, it must begin with purified hearts.

The Church doesn't need more entertainment—it needs more repentance. We don't need better programs—we need sacred altars.

God is calling His people back to spiritual purity, back to holiness, back to Him, because only the pure in heart shall see God. And that is worth everything. That is worth committing our all and laying everything upon His altar of sacrifice and living as a bona fide and holy people, committed to His service. Let us answer that call with boldness and sincerity. Let us cleanse our hearts and purify our minds.

Let us be a people prepared for His presence.

Steps Toward Spiritual Purity

1. Recognize the Need for Cleansing

We must first admit our need. Spiritual impurity thrives in denial. Ask the Holy Spirit to search your heart and reveal anything that grieves Him.

2. Confess and Repent

True repentance is more than saying *"I am sorry."* It's a turning away from sin and completely turning to God. Confess hidden sins. Renounce compromise. Ask God to break any stronghold of impurity.

"If we confess our sins, He is faithful and just to forgive us our sins and to cleanse us from all unrighteousness." — 1 John 1:9

3. Cleanse Your Life of Contaminants

Evaluate your influences—music, movies, friendships, habits, organizations of affiliation. What is shaping your spirit? Remove what dulls your hunger for God.

4. Rebuild Spiritual Disciplines

Purity is sustained through spiritual habits:
- Daily time in the Word
- Consistent prayer
- Worship in spirit and truth
- Accountability and fellowship

5. Guard Your Heart

Stay vigilant. The world is constantly pushing impurity. Guard your heart, for it is the wellspring of life (Proverbs 4:23)

Spiritual purity leads to:

- **Clarity** – You hear God more clearly.
- **Power** – You walk in greater spiritual authority.
- **Joy** – Sin steals joy; purity restores it.
- **Witness** – The pure in heart reflect Christ to the world.

Holiness is not a burden—it is freedom. Purity is not restrictive—it is liberating.

We are to be a people who remain set apart. From the very beginning, God's desire has been to have a people who reflect His holiness, who walk in His truth, and who bear His light in the midst of a dark and perverse society. Yet too many believers settled for compromise, choosing convenience over conviction and comfort over the cross. The deception of worldliness is not always loud and obvious; more often, it is subtle, seductive, and slow-moving — like a current that gradually carries the drifting soul far from shore.

But we are not without hope. Christ has overcome the world (John 16:33), and in Him, we too can overcome. The same grace that saved us is the grace that sanctifies us, teaching us to deny ungodliness and worldly lusts, and to live soberly, righteously, and godly in this present age (Titus 2:11-12).

Now is the time for self-examination. Not just of what we do on the outside, but what we love on the inside.

We traded spiritual power for popularity? We replaced truth with trends? We have been more concerned with appearing righteous than with being holy?

Worldliness is not merely what we possess, but what possesses us. It is not simply about external behaviors, but about internal loyalties. Where is your heart?

"For where your treasure is, there will your heart be also" (Matthew 6:21).

Our heart-felt cry to God must be for Him to *"Create in me a clean heart, O God, and renew a right spirit within me."* — Psalm 51:10

God is able, and just as important, He is willing.

For those who recognize they have been entangled, whether in entertainment-driven churches, secret societies, covetousness, materialism, lust, racism, pride, honoring pagan initiated holidays and celebrations, or seeking the praise of men, there is a way back. It begins with repentance: true, godly sorrow that leads to change. It continues with separation: the courageous decision to break ties with what defiles. And it leads to restoration: the beautiful journey to One Who should have been our first love, Jesus Christ.

God is not calling us to legalism or lifeless religion, but to a life of vibrant, Spirit-filled holiness that glorifies Him in every area. He is raising up a remnant who will not bow to the gods of this age, who will shine as lights in the world, and who will walk in power.

We were never meant to be trapped by this world. We were created for something greater, to become an ambassador of Christ and a temple of the Holy Spirit and ultimately a citizen of heaven. This world is not our home. Its systems will fade, its pleasures will perish, and its values will be exposed for what they are. But the one who does the will of God abides forever (1 John 2:17).

So come out.

Come out from compromise.
Come out from spiritual apathy.
Come out from deception.
Come out from the bondage of worldliness.

Begin your journey on the narrow road to a new life in Christ. Seek the Lord while He may be found. Set your affections on things above. Live for eternity. Let your life be a testimony that, though you were once trapped by the world, you have been set free by the power of the cross. **There is power in the cross!**

Let the words of Christ ring in your heart today:

"If any man will come after me, let him deny himself, and take up his cross daily, and follow me." - Luke 9:23

Reflection Questions

1. **In what areas of your life have you sensed the pull of worldliness the most?**
   - How have those influences affected your relationship with God?
2. **Have you ever justified compromise in your walk with Christ for the sake of acceptance, comfort, or convenience?**
   - What has the Holy Spirit revealed to you about those choices?
3. **What does "coming out from among them" look like in your daily life?**
   - Are there specific environments, relationships, or habits that you need to separate from?
4. **How has your love for God grown or diminished over time?**
   - What steps can you take today to return to your first love?
5. **Are there areas where you have been more influenced by culture than by Scripture?**
   - What would repentance and renewal look like in those areas?
6. **What is one practical decision you can make this week to pursue spiritual purity and resist worldliness?**
   - Who can walk with you for accountability and encouragement?

Closing Prayer

A Prayer of Surrender and Separation

Heavenly Father,

I come before You with a humble heart. I now recognize how easily I have been entangled by the things of this world. Forgive me for the times I have chosen compromise over conviction, entertainment over edification, self over surrender, and religious contentment over sanctification.

Lord, I no longer want to be trapped by worldliness. I want to be transformed by Your Spirit. Cleanse my heart, renew my mind, and give me a burning passion for You. Teach me to love You with all my heart, all my soul, all my mind, and all my strength and to love my neighbor as I love myself. Give me the strength to separate from anything that draws me away from Your presence.

Teach me to love what You love and to hate what You hate. Help me to walk the narrow road that leads to life with boldness, holiness, and joy. Let my life be a light in this dark world, not blending in, but standing out and set apart for Your glory.

I choose today to come out from among them. I choose Christ. I choose the cross. I choose eternity with You.

In Jesus' name,

Amen.

Group Study Questions

1. Defining Spiritual Purity

- What does "spiritual purity" mean to you personally?
- How does the Bible define purity? (Read Matthew 5:8, Psalm 24:3-4)
- Why do you think God places such a high value on purity of heart?

2. God's Standard for Purity

- Read 1 Peter 1:14-16. What does it mean to be "holy as God is holy"?
- In what areas of your life do you feel you're compromising God's standard?
- What does purity look like in daily choices (e.g., relationships, speech, habits)?

3. The Battle Within

- Read Galatians 5:16-17. How does the conflict between the flesh and the Spirit affect your pursuit of purity?
- What does it mean to "walk in the Spirit" in the context of purity?
- Can a Christian live a pure life without God's help? Why or why not?

4. The Role of the Word and Prayer

- Read Psalm 119:9-11. What role does Scripture play in remaining pure?
- How can prayer help guard your heart and mind?
- Do you have a regular spiritual discipline (Bible reading, prayer, fasting)? How does it help?

5. Practical Steps Toward Purity

- What are some habits or influences you may need to remove from your life?
- Who are godly people you can be accountable to in your walk toward purity?
- What does it look like to "flee youthful lusts" (2 Timothy 2:22) in a digital world?

6. Forgiveness and Restoration
- Have you ever struggled with guilt or shame over impurity? How did you deal with it?
- Read 1 John 1:9. How does God respond when we confess our sins?
- What steps can you take to restore spiritual purity after failure?

7. Living Pure in an Impure World
- What pressures make it hard to stay pure in our culture today?
- How can your life be a witness to others through purity?
- What encouragement would you give to someone struggling to live purely?

8. Jesus: Our Model of Purity
- How did Jesus demonstrate purity in His thoughts, words, and actions?
- Read Hebrews 4:15. Why is Jesus uniquely qualified to help us with our struggles?
- How does staying close to Jesus help us remain pure?

9. Commitment and Prayer
- What area of your life do you need to surrender to God for the sake of purity?
- How can the group support one another in living a pure and holy life?
- Take time to pray for each other, asking God to create clean hearts (Psalm 51:10).

(Appendix 1)

Christian Consecration

(ref. 2nd Tim. 2:21)

I, this day, consecrate my entire life to glorify my Heavenly Father by my obedience to the principles of Jesus Christ through the power of the Holy Spirit. *I endeavor to love the Lord my God with all my heart, soul, mind, and strength. I endeavor to love all humanity as Jesus loved me, regardless of race, color, creed, gender, sexual orientation, financial or social status, or spiritual condition. In so doing, I will consider the needs of all others before my own.* All my effort from now on will be directed to demonstrate the righteousness of God in whatsoever I may be engaged. *(Mk. 12:30, Jn. 13:34)*

I sever all attachments to worldliness (carnality). I purge my home, my place of employment, my vehicle(s), and my life of all ungodliness. I now realize that an association with Freemasonry, Eastern Star, Greek fraternities & sororities, and all ungodly organizations is incompatible with God's holy word, and now sever my membership(s) and renounce my vows. (ref. Appendix 2)

****

I, _____, this day _____, ____ sever my membership in _____ and renounce all vows related to this membership. Father, forgive me for all other unholy vows in my life and forgive me for any ungodly influence I may have been on others. I denounce all things of the cult and the occult found in Freemasonry, the Eastern Star, Greek fraternities and sororities, and all other ungodly organizations or associations veiled in secrecy or yoked with unbelievers. I ask for Your forgiveness for every evil, unrighteous act that I have committed as a member. I realize that there is only one association in the kingdom of God, the universal body (brotherhood and sisterhood) of Christ, united under His precious blood, to which I now commit my life. (1st Cor. 6:17, Rom. 12:1-2, 2nd Tim. 2:20-21)

****

Principle 1

All the earthly things that I possess shall not be considered my own, but belonging to my Heavenly Father, and shall be held in trust by me to be used as directed by the wisdom of the Spirit of God, as the *love of Christ may dictate. I will follow the mandate of God for distribution during and after my service.* If at any time in my life I should be engaged in any earthly business and should employ *others* to aid me in conducting it, I shall reward them justly and equally, comparing their energy expended with my own after adding a sufficient amount to my own to cover all risk that may be involved in the operation of my business. I shall consider my employees *as my equal* with rights to the blessings of nature and life equal to my own. I shall not strive to elevate myself to a position of comfort above the rest of my employees and shall direct all my efforts to bring all *humanity* to an equal plane, where all enjoy the comforts of life and fellowship together. *(1st Cor. 10:24)*

Principle 2

I shall not cease to *implore God* to deliver *humanity* from the effects of sin *as* long as sin lasts, *and* shall cooperate with God in the redemption of *humanity*. I will have seasons of prayer and fasting on behalf of *humanity*, bewailing their lost condition, and imploring God to grant them repentance unto life as the Spirit of God may lead me. *(1st Tim. 2:1)*

Principle 3

I shall live my life in meekness, never defending my personal rights, but shall leave all judgment to God, Who judges righteously and rewards all according to their works. I shall not render evil for evil or railing for railing, but shall bless all and do good to my enemies in return for evil. By God's grace, I shall keep all hardness and harshness out of my life and actions, but shall be gentle and unassuming, not professing above what God has imparted to me, nor lifting myself above *others*. *(Matt. 5:5, 11:29)*

Principle 4

I shall consider righteous acts as more necessary to life and happiness than food and drink, and not *allow* myself to be bribed or coerced into any unrighteous action for any earthly consideration. *I shall do all within my power to elevate the poor and alleviate all hunger, pain, and suffering among the 'least' in God's kingdom whenever possible.* (1st Tim. 6:11; 2nd Tim. 2:22)

Principle 5

By God's grace, I will always be merciful, forgiving those who have transgressed against me and endeavoring to correct the ills of humanity instead of merely punishing them for their sins. *(Mk. 11:25,26; Eph. 4:32)*

Principle 6

I shall not harbor any impure thoughts in my mind but shall endeavor to make my every act uplifting. I shall regard my procreative organs as sacred and holy and never use them for any purpose other than that which God created them for. I shall regard the home as sacred and always guard my actions in the presence of the opposite sex, so as not to cause a man or his wife to break their vows to one another *or cause an unmarried person to commit fornication.* I shall be chaste with *those of* the opposite sex, *other than my spouse*, considering them as sisters *or brothers.* I shall be careful not to cause them undue pain by playing on their affections. *Because life begins at conception and is sacred to God, I will stand against abortion and the taking of innocent life at every opportunity. Because God made woman for man, I will stand against homosexuality at every opportunity but honor the God-given rights of everyone.* (Lev 18:22, 20:13, Deut. 5:17, 1st Cor. 6:9-10, 18, 1st Thess. 4:3-5, 1st Tim. 1:10, Rom. 1:26-27)

Principle 7

I will always strive to be a peacemaker. First, by being peaceful myself and avoiding all unfruitful contentions. *Secondly, by* treating *everyone justly*, regarding their rights and their free agency, never trying to force any to my point of view.

If I should *knowingly* offend anyone, I shall immediately apologize. I will not scatter evil reports about any person and so try to defame their character, or repeat things that I am not certain of being true. I will strive to remove the curse of strife among *all others* by acting as a peacemaker. *I will stand for justice and stand against injustice for all of God's creation.* (Matt. 5:9; Rom. 12:18)

Principle 8

I shall not become discouraged when I am persecuted on account of the righteousness mentioned above nor murmur on account of any suffering I undergo. *I shall gladly give my life rather than depart from this high standard of life, rejoicing because I know that* I have a great reward in Heaven. I shall strive to make the above principles the ideal of *the entire* world and give my life and energy to see *humanity receive* the power from God to practice the same. *(John. 15:20)*
– John G. Lake

Sign:_____

Date:_____

(To realize this new life commitment of holiness, as an exercise of faith, we need and must pray for the Holy Spirit's empowerment to work in us "to will and to do.") (Phil. 2:13)

(Words in *italics* were added to the original)

(Appendix 2)
Consecration Considerations
(1 Peter 1:13-16)

1. Purging ourselves before God
   - Past sins must be resolved (Isa. 59:2)
   - Repentance (Luke 13:3), Confession (James 5:16), Restitution (Luke 19:8, Numbers 5:5-10)

2. Controlling the tongue [The power of words – the tongue has great power (James 3:5)]
   - We will eat what we speak (Prov. 18:20-21). Speak only the truth, never lie. (Prov. 6:16-19)
   - All idle (careless) words will be accounted for. Justification and condemnation. (Matt. 12:35-37)
   - An unbridled tongue equates to a worthless religion. (James 1:26)
   - Speak faith and hope in all situations. (Phil. 4:13) Everything (except man and living creatures) that God created was done by words, and His creation responds to words. (Mk. 11:12-14, 21-23). Jesus did not use vain or idle words. Some words and phrases should be excluded from Christian conversation. [(e.g., lucky, magic, self-made, self-sufficient, words and actions of superstition (e.g., knock on wood, cross your fingers, don't walk under a ladder, black cat crossing your path, broken mirror, Friday the 13th, no umbrellas inside, etc.), words and phrases of profanity (1 Tim. 6:20)]

We should only speak words of faith that glorify God.

3. We must prioritize spiritual disciplines, including daily prayer (1st Thess. 5:17-19), regularly partaking of Holy Communion (1st Cor. 11:26), and anointing ourselves with oil (Matt. 6:17). Most theologians believe that the first-century believers, our Biblical models, had daily prayer and regular Holy Communion (the Lord's Supper) in their homes. Today, many will attest to the spiritual and physical benefits of daily communion. By and

large, the twenty-first-century institutional church does not reflect this same spiritual priority. Most churches of today only partake of Holy Communion once per month or per quarter. We must not forsake or marginalize this life-altering requirement of God by restricting ourselves to the infrequency of the institutional church. This remembrance is vital in our walk with God. As Jesus' disciples, we should return to the disciplines of our first-century church model. An excellent resource for spiritual disciplines is "Celebration of Discipline" by Richard J. Foster.

4. Purging our environments (homes, offices, cars, etc.) of all ungodliness.#

- Anything related to Halloween, Mardi Gras, Valentine's Day, Easter, Christmas (Ref. @ eternalcog.org, radiomissions.org, fwa@faithfulword.com, and TomorrowsWorld.org)
- Paraphernalia associated with ungodly associations & Oaths* [i.e., ungodly clubs and organizations (2nd Cor. 6:14 -18) (e.g., Freemasonry, Eastern Star, Greek fraternities and sororities, Mardi Gras organizations, social and pleasure clubs, hate groups, etc.)] (Reference @ Bibliog., Chap. 2$^{/3}$).
- Excesses that reflect covetousness, which is idolatry (Colossians 3:5, Matt. 6:19, 1st Cor. 6:10)
- Many African artifacts (Many are related to false religions).
- Items associated with New Age cults, false religions, Greek gods, and goddesses (Common in Mardi Gras paraphernalia).
- Items related to astrology and fortune-telling.
- Ungodly videos (e.g., Wizard of Oz, The Wiz, etc.), music, books (e.g., Harry Potter, books glorifying demons, witches, and warlocks, etc.), games (e.g., Ouija Board, video games of violence or sexual overtones, etc.), ungodly pictures, etc.

\# The above list is not all-inclusive but is provided to serve as a guide. You should seek the guidance of the Holy Spirit in purging your environments. Ask Him to reveal any ungodliness that you may not have an awareness of or readily recognize.

As a general rule, our character, environment, and possessions must glorify God (1 Cor. 10:31).

After thoroughly purging our environments of all ungodliness, they should be anointed and dedicated to the glory of God.

*Repentance is a three-step process: the renunciation of all vows, the end of all practices, and the destruction of all associated artifacts. The retention of cursed artifacts will remain a curse to those who keep them in their possession.

(Appendix 3)

Prayers for Freedom and Restoration

In a world filled with deception, temptation, and spiritual compromise, many believers find themselves **trapped by influences they never expected to embrace**. Whether it is the pull of worldliness, entanglement with secret societies, or the subtle drift away from truth, these snares are real, often hidden and are often fatal.

This book was written to expose those traps and call God's people back to holiness, sincerity, and full devotion to Christ. But exposure alone is not enough. **True transformation comes through repentance, deliverance, and a life surrendered to the power of God.**

That is why this appendix includes four prayers:

- A **Prayer of Deliverance**, for breaking spiritual chains and ungodly alliances.
- A **Prayer of Repentance**, for turning back to God with a clean heart.
- A **Prayer for Spiritual Warfare**, for standing against the attacks of the enemy.
- A **Prayer of Restoration**, for those who feel broken and long to be renewed.

These prayers are not magical formulas. They are guides to help you pray with sincerity and faith, using God's Word as your foundation. **Pray them slowly. Pray them often. Let them be a doorway into deeper healing, freedom, and intimacy with Jesus Christ.**

"Draw near to God, and He will draw near to you." – James 4:8

If you are ready to be free, ready to be clean, and ready to walk in the light—then begin here, in prayer.

Prayer of Deliverance

For freedom from spiritual bondage, compromise, and hidden alliances.

Heavenly Father,

I come to You in the name of Jesus Christ, my Lord and Savior. I acknowledge that You alone are holy, sovereign, and worthy of my complete devotion. I confess my sins and shortcomings before You, and I repent for every way I have turned from Your truth.

Lord, I ask for Your mercy and cleansing. Wash me by the blood of Jesus. Purify my heart and renew a right spirit within me.

Today, I renounce every form of worldliness that has entangled my life. I break agreement with every unholy alliance, every secret society, every vow, and every ritual that opposes Your Word. I renounce every hidden work of darkness, and I cancel the power of any oath, ritual, or covenant that I made outside of Your will.

In the name of Jesus:

- I break every spiritual chain.
- I command every spirit of bondage, deception, pride, and compromise to leave my life.
- I silence the voice of the enemy and reject every lie I have believed.

I declare that Jesus Christ is Lord over my life: spirit, soul, and body. I surrender every area of my life to His authority. I receive the forgiveness, freedom, and deliverance that only He can give.

Holy Spirit, fill every part of me. Guide me in truth, empower me to walk in obedience, and give me boldness to live a life set apart. Let every ungodly influence be broken, and every door to the enemy be shut.

"Therefore if the Son makes you free, you shall be free indeed." – John 8:36

Thank You, Lord, for hearing my prayer. I receive Your freedom by faith. I am no longer a slave to sin, to fear, or to deception. I belong to You and You alone.

In the mighty name of Jesus Christ,
Amen.

Prayer of Repentance

For those ready to turn fully from sin and return to God with a clean heart.

Heavenly Father,

I come before You with a broken and contrite heart. I confess that I have sinned against You in thought, word, and deed. I have chased after the things of this world, allowed pride to blind me, and tolerated compromise in my life.

Lord, I repent for every way I have rebelled against Your Word and grieved Your Spirit. Forgive me for placing other desires, people, and priorities before You. Cleanse me with the blood of Jesus, and create in me a clean heart, O God.

I renounce every form of ungodliness and come to You with my whole heart. Teach me to walk in humility, righteousness, and obedience. Let my life be a testimony of Your mercy and grace.

"If we confess our sins, He is faithful and just to forgive us and to cleanse us from all unrighteousness." – 1 John 1:9

Thank You, Lord, for not casting me away. I receive Your forgiveness, and I choose this day to follow You in spirit and in truth.

In Jesus' name,
Amen.

Prayer for Spiritual Warfare

For resisting the enemy and walking in spiritual victory and authority.

Lord God Almighty,

I thank You that in Christ Jesus, I have victory over every scheme, trap, and lie of the enemy. I put on the full armor of God today, the belt of truth, the breastplate of righteousness, the shoes of the gospel of peace, the shield of faith, the helmet of salvation, and the sword of the Spirit, which is Your Word.

In the name of Jesus, I bind every power of darkness assigned against my life, my mind, my family, and my destiny. I cancel every curse, hex, spell, or word curse spoken over me, and I declare that **no weapon formed against me shall prosper** (Isaiah 54:17).

I take authority over every spirit of fear, confusion, temptation, and oppression. Satan, you are defeated by the blood of the Lamb and the word of my testimony.

I declare that I am more than a conqueror through Christ who loves me. I submit to God and resist the devil, and he must flee.

Strengthen me, Lord, to stand firm in the evil day. Surround me with angels of protection, fill me with the fire of the Holy Spirit, and let Your Word be my weapon and shield.

In the powerful name of Jesus,
Amen.

Prayer of Restoration

For those needing healing, renewal, and a fresh beginning with God.

Father God,

I come to You weary and broken, but full of hope in Your promises. You are the God who restores, revives, and makes all things new. I ask You now to restore everything the enemy has stolen: my peace, my joy, my purpose, my purity, and my closeness with You.

Lord, heal every wound in my heart. Mend what is broken, revive what has died, and breathe life into my spirit again. Restore my passion for prayer, for Your Word, and for holiness.

Your Word says,
"I will restore to you the years that the locust has eaten..."
- Joel 2:25

Let that promise be fulfilled in my life. Renew my mind, renew my strength, and restore the joy of my salvation. Let my testimony be one of redemption, healing, and renewal.

I trust You, Lord, to finish the good work You began in me. I surrender all to You and ask You to make me whole: spirit, soul, and body.

In Jesus' mighty name,
Amen.

Bibliography

Chapter 3

1. MacArthur, John. *Worldliness: Resisting the Seduction of a Fallen World*. Wheaton, IL: Crossway, 2008.
2. Nee, Watchman. *Love Not the World*. New York: Christian Fellowship Publishers, 1968.
3. Tozer, A. W. *The Pursuit of God*. Harrisburg, PA: Christian Publications, 1948.
4. Wilkins, Michael J. *Following the Master: Discipleship in the Steps of Jesus*. Grand Rapids: Zondervan, 1992.

Chapter 4

1. Lewis, C.S. *The Weight of Glory*. New York: HarperOne, 2001.
2. Tozer, A.W. *The World: Playground or Battleground?* Camp Hill, PA: Christian Publications, 1990.

Chapter 5

1. Tozer, A.W. *God Tells the Man Who Cares*. Harrisburg, PA: Christian Publications, 1970.
2. Greear, J.D. *Not God Enough: Why Your Small God Leads to Big Problems*. Grand Rapids, MI: Zondervan, 2018.
3. MacArthur, John. *The Gospel According to Jesus*. Grand Rapids, MI: Zondervan, 2008.

Chapter 6

1. Bridges, Jerry. *Trusting God: Even When Life Hurts*. Colorado Springs: Nav Press, 2008.
2. Piper, John. *Future Grace: The Purifying Power of the Promises of God*. Colorado Springs: Multnomah, 2012.
3. Packer, J. I. *Knowing God*. Downers Grove, IL: InterVarsity Press, 1993.
4. Yancey, Philip. *Disappointment with God: Three Questions No One Asks Aloud*. Grand Rapids: Zondervan, 1988.

Chapter 7

1. Bridges, Jerry. *The Pursuit of Holiness*. Colorado Springs: NavPress, 2006.
2. Evans, Tony. *No More Excuses: Be the Man God Made You to Be*. Colorado Springs: Focus on the Family, 1995.
3. Tada, Joni Eareckson. *Holiness in Hidden Places*. Grand Rapids: Zondervan, 2005.

Chapter 8

1. Tozer, A.W. *Entertainment Is the Devil's Substitute for Joy*. Camp Hill, PA: Christian Publications, n.d.
2. MacArthur, John. *Ashamed of the Gospel: When the Church Becomes Like the World*. Wheaton, IL: Crossway, 2010.
3. Chan, Francis. *Letters to the Church*. Colorado Springs, CO: David C. Cook, 2018.
4. Postman, Neil. *Amusing Ourselves to Death: Public Discourse in the Age of Show Business*. New York: Penguin Books, 1985.

Chapter 10

1. Emerson, Michael O., and Christian Smith. *Divided by Faith: Evangelical Religion and the Problem of Race in America*. Oxford University Press, 2000.
2. Moore, Russell. *Onward: Engaging the Culture without Losing the Gospel*. B&H Publishing, 2015.
3. Tisby, Jemar. *The Color of Compromise: The Truth about the American Church's Complicity in Racism*. Zondervan, 2019.

Chapter 9

(References are listed at the end of Chapter 9)

Chapter 11

(Reference are listed at the end of Chapter 10)

Chapter 12

1. Hanegraaff, Hank. *Christianity in Crisis: 21st Century*. Nashville, TN: Thomas Nelson, 2009.

2. Challies, Tim. *The Discipline of Spiritual Discernment.* Wheaton, IL: Crossway, 2007.
3. Stott, John. *Between Two Worlds: The Art of Preaching in the Twentieth Century.* Grand Rapids, MI: Eerdmans, 1982.
4. **MacArthur, John.** *Charismatic Chaos.* Grand Rapids: Zondervan, 1992.
5. **Hanegraaff, Hank.** *Counterfeit Revival.* Nashville: Thomas Nelson, 1997.
6. **Storms, Sam.** *Understanding Spiritual Gifts: A Comprehensive Guide.* Grand Rapids: Zondervan, 2020.

Chapter 13

1. Bowler, Kate. *Blessed: A History of the American Prosperity Gospel.* New York: Oxford University Press, 2013.
2. Jones, David W. and Russell S. Woodbridge. *Health, Wealth, and Happiness: Has the Prosperity Gospel Overshadowed the Gospel of Christ?* Grand Rapids: Kregel Publications, 2011.
3. Piper, John. "Ten Aspects of the Prosperity Gospel That Pervert the Gospel of Christ." *Desiring God.* Accessed July 2025. https://www.desiringgod.org/articles/ten-aspects-of-the-prosperity-gospel
4. McConnell, D. R. *A Different Gospel: A Bold and Revealing Look at the Biblical and Historical Basis of the Word of Faith Movement.* Peabody, MA: Hendrickson Publishers, 1988.
5. Fee, Gordon D. *The Disease of the Health and Wealth Gospels.* Vancouver: Regent College Publishing, 2006.

Chapter 14

1. Piper, John. *Desiring God: Meditations of a Christian Hedonist.*
Multnomah Books, 2003.
2. Bonhoeffer, Dietrich. *The Cost of Discipleship.*
SCM Press, 1959.
3. Challies, Tim. *The Next Story: Faith, Friends, Family, and the Digital World.* Zondervan, 2011.

Chapter 15

1. Augustine. *Confessions.* Trans. Henry Chadwick. Oxford University Press, 2008.
2. Lewis, C.S. *The Screwtape Letters.* HarperOne, 2001.
3. Tozer, A.W. *The Root of the Righteous.* Moody Publishers, 1955.

Chapter 16

1. Keller, Timothy. *Center Church: Doing Balanced, Gospel-Centered Ministry in Your City.* Zondervan, 2012.
2. Carson, D.A. *Christ and Culture Revisited.* Eerdmans, 2008.
3. *"The Fanaticism of Christian Discipleship,"* Walter B. Pennington; 2020
4. Driscoll, Mark. *A Call to Resurgence.* Tyndale, 2013.

Chapter 17

1. Exodus 20:3 – "You shall have no other gods before me." *The original commandment against idolatry.*
2. 1 John 5:21 – "Dear children, keep yourselves from idols." *A New Testament warning.*
3. Matthew 6:21 – "Where your treasure is, there your heart will be also." *Reveals the location of our loyalty.*
4. Tim Keller, *Counterfeit Gods* – Defines modern idolatry as good things turned ultimate

Chapter 18

1. Willard, Dallas. *The Spirit of the Disciplines.* HarperOne, 1991.
2. Bridges, Jerry. *The Pursuit of Holiness.* NavPress, 2006.
3. Whitney, Donald. *Spiritual Disciplines for the Christian Life.* NavPress, 2014.

Notes

Made in United States
Orlando, FL
02 August 2025